THE ROUTLEDGE ATLAS OF BRITISH HISTORY

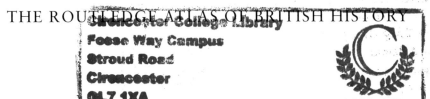

The changing story of the British Isles forms the central theme of this fascinating and compelling atlas, which covers England, Ireland, Scotland and Wales – and the expansion and gradual disintegration of Britain's overseas empire. This new edition includes:

- Politics – from the Saxon kingdoms and the collapse of Britain's French Empire to Jacobites, Parliamentary Reform, the Commonwealth and Europe
- War and Conflict – from Viking attacks and the Norman Invasion to the Armada, World War and the revolt against empire
- Trade and Industry – from the post-Norman economy and Tudor trade to industrial unrest and the opening of international trade routes
- Religion – from the Saxon Church to the Reformation
- Society and Economics – from civilian life in Roman Britain to the Industrial and Agricultural revolutions, the Great Strike and the growth of universities.

Sir Martin Gilbert is one of the most prolific historians of his generation. An Honorary Fellow of Merton College, Oxford, he is Churchill's official biographer as well as the author of the three-volume *The History of the Twentieth Century* (HarperCollins, 1998–9).

BOOKS BY MARTIN GILBERT

The Routledge Atlas of American History
The Routledge Atlas of the Arab–Israeli Conflict
The Routledge Atlas of British History
The Routledge Atlas of the First World War
The Routledge Atlas of the Holocaust
The Routledge Atlas of Jewish History
The Routledge Atlas of Russian History

Recent History Atlas, 1860–1960
Jerusalem Illustrated History Atlas
Children's Illustrated Bible Atlas
The Appeasers (*with Richard Gott*)
The European Powers, 1900–1945
The Roots of Appeasement
Sir Horace Rumbold, Portrait of a Diplomat
Churchill, A Photographic Portrait
Jerusalem, Rebirth of a City
Exile and Return, The Struggle for Jewish
    Statehood
Auschwitz and the Allies
Shcharansky, Hero of our Time

The Jews of Hope, The Plight of Soviet
    Jewry Today
The Holocaust, The Jewish Tragedy
First World War
Second World War
In Search of Churchill
History of the Twentieth Century (in three
    volumes)
From the Ends of the Earth: The Jews in the
    Twentieth Century
Letters to Auntie Fori: The 5000-Year History of
    the Jewish People and Their Faith
The Righteous: The Unsung Heroes of the
    Holocaust

THE CHURCHILL BIOGRAPHY IS COMPLETE IN EIGHT VOLUMES:

Volume I. Youth, 1874–1900 *by Randolph S. Churchill*
    Volume I. Companion (in two parts)
Volume II. Young Statesman, 1900–1914 *by Randolph S. Churchill*
    Volume II. Companion (in three parts)
Volume III. 1914–1916 *by Martin Gilbert*
    Volume III. Companion (in two parts)
Volume IV. 1917–1922 *by Martin Gilbert*
    Volume IV. Companion (in three parts)
Volume V. 1922–1939 *by Martin Gilbert*
    Volume V. Companion 'The Exchequer Years' 1922–1929
    Volume V. Companion 'The Wilderness Years' 1929–1935
    Volume V. Companion 'The Coming of War' 1936–1939
Volume VI. 1939–1941, 'Finest Hour' *by Martin Gilbert*
    The Churchill War Papers: Volume I 'At the Admiralty'
    The Churchill War Papers: Volume II 'New Surrender', May–December
    The Churchill War Papers: Volume III '1941, The Ever-Widening War'
Volume VII. 1941–1945, 'Road to Victory' *by Martin Gilbert*
Volume VIII. 1945–1965, 'Never Despair' *by Martin Gilbert*

Churchill – A Life *by Martin Gilbert*

Editions of documents
Britain and Germany Between the Wars
Plough My Own Furrow, The Life of Lord Allen of Hurtwood
Servant of India, Diaries of the Viceroy's Private Secretary, 1905–1910

THE ROUTLEDGE ATLAS OF
BRITISH HISTORY

3rd edition

Martin Gilbert

Routledge
Taylor & Francis Group

LONDON AND NEW YORK

First published 1968 as *The Dent Atlas of British History*
by J. M. Dent Ltd
Second edition published 1993

Third edition first published 2003
by Routledge
11 New Fetter Lane, London EC4P 4EE

Simultaneously published in the USA and Canada
by Routledge
29 West 35th Street, New York, NY 10001

Routledge is an imprint of the Taylor & Francis Group

Printed and bound in Great Britain by
Bell & Bain Ltd, Glasgow

British Library Cataloguing in Publication Data
A catalogue record for this book is available from the British Library

Library of Congress Cataloging in Publication Data
A catalog record for this book has been requested

ISBN 0–415–28147–4 (Hbk)
ISBN 0–415–28148–2 (Pbk)

Preface

The maps in this atlas are intended to provide a visual introduction to British history. I have used the word 'British' in its widest sense, including when relevant England, Scotland, Ireland and Wales, the changing overseas empire, the wars and treaties in which Britain engaged, the alliances in time of peace, the growth of industry and trade, and, on five of the maps, famine and plague.

The story of the British Isles forms the central theme. I have included maps to illustrate economic, social and political problems as well as territorial and military ones. I hope this atlas will help to show that there is more to British history than Hastings and Crécy, Blenheim and Waterloo, Passchendaele and Dunkirk, all of which moments of glory I have tried to put in their wider, and no less important, contexts.

For the maps covering the period before the Norman Conquest the sources are often conflicting on specific details. I have therefore drawn these maps on the basis of probability. In many instances precise knowledge of early frontiers is lacking. I have tried nevertheless to give a clear if also, of necessity, an approximate picture.

As British history advances from wattle huts to timber mansions, and thence on to steel and concrete, so too do the number and variety of facts available to the historian. This is reflected in the maps themselves. I have tried to avoid too complex or too cluttered a page; but a map cannot always satisfy all the demands made upon it, and only the reader can judge where clarity of design and sufficiency of information have been successfully combined.

I am under an obligation of gratitude to those historians and colleagues who kindly scrutinised my draft maps at an early stage, and who made many suggestions for their scope and improvement; in particular Dr J. M. Wallace-Hadrill, Dr Roger Highfield, Mr Ralph Davis, Mr T. F. R. G. Braun, Dr C. C. Davies and Miss Barbara Malament. When the maps were more completed, they were checked by Mr Adrian Scheps, Mr Edmund Ranallo, Mrs Elizabeth Goold, Mr Tony Lawdham and Mrs Jean Kelly, to all of whom my thanks are due.

Twenty-five years have passed since the first edition of this atlas. Within a year of its publication, violence in Northern Ireland re-emerged at the centre of the political stage: I have drawn three new maps to reflect this. The evolution of the European Community has led to growing British participation in Europe, culminating in the Maastricht Treaty of February 1992 and the Edinburgh Summit of December 1992, both of which are a part of the new maps. The Falkland Islands and Persian Gulf wars are included, as are the natural and man-made disasters of the past forty years. Also mapped are many of the problems and challenges of the 1990s, among them asylum, charity, homelessness, unemployment, trade, education, religious diversity, and ethnic minorities. Britain's oil and gas resources are a new feature, as is the most recent phase of the reduction of British overseas possessions, her dwindling military and naval commitments world wide, and her new overseas responsibilities.

The first 118 maps were produced for this atlas by Arthur Banks and his team of cartographers, including Terry Bicknell. The new maps in this edition were produced by Tim Aspden and Robert Bradbrook; I have been helped considerably in the task of compiling them by Abe Eisenstat and Kay Thomson. For their help in providing material for this volume, I would also like to thank the Information Officer, Private Secretary's Office, Buckingham Palace; the Board of Deputies of British Jews, Central Information Desk; the Building Societies Association Press Office; the Lesotho High Commission; the Race Relations Commission; the Refugee Arrivals Project, London Airport; and the Royal Ulster Constabulary Press Office, Belfast.

24 June 1993

MARTIN GILBERT
Merton College, Oxford

Note to the Third Edition

For this third edition, I have prepared twelve new maps, which bring British history into the twenty-first century. As with the second edition, this could not have been done without the cartographic expertise of Tim Aspden. I am also grateful to Her Majesty's Stationery Office for access to their considerable reference holdings.

12 July 2002

MARTIN GILBERT
Merton College, Oxford

Maps

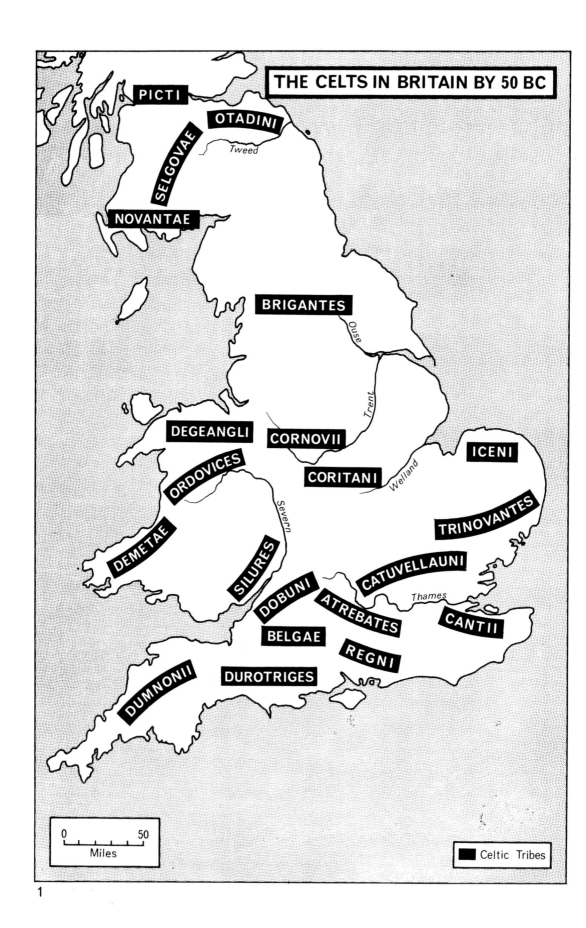

THE CELTS IN BRITAIN BY 50 BC

PICTI

OTADINI

Tweed

SELGOVAE

NOVANTAE

BRIGANTES

Ouse

Trent

DEGEANGLI

CORNOVII

ICENI

CORITANI

Welland

ORDOVICES

Severn

TRINOVANTES

DEMETAE

SILURES

CATUVELLAUNI

DOBUNI

ATREBATES

Thames

BELGAE

CANTII

REGNI

DUMNONII

DUROTRIGES

0   50
Miles

■ Celtic Tribes

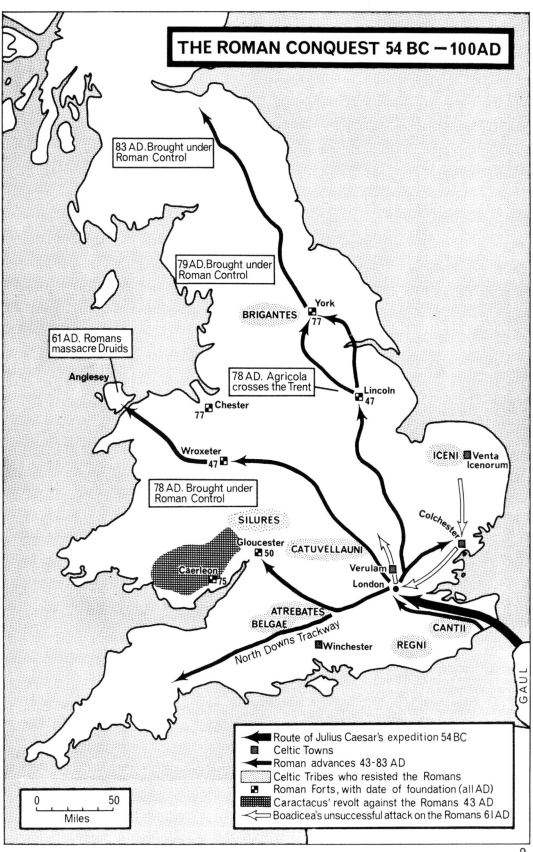

THE ROMAN CONQUEST 54 BC – 100 AD

83 AD. Brought under Roman Control

79 AD. Brought under Roman Control

61 AD. Romans massacre Druids

78 AD. Agricola crosses the Trent

78 AD. Brought under Roman Control

BRIGANTES

York 77

Anglesey

Chester 77

Lincoln 47

Wroxeter 47

ICENI ■ Venta Icenorum

SILURES

Gloucester ■ 50

Caerleon ■ 75

CATUVELLAUNI

Colchester

Verulam

London

ATREBATES

BELGAE

North Downs Trackway

■ Winchester

REGNI

CANTII

GAUL

Route of Julius Caesar's expedition 54 BC
Celtic Towns
Roman advances 43-83 AD
Celtic Tribes who resisted the Romans
Roman Forts, with date of foundation (all AD)
Caractacus' revolt against the Romans 43 AD
Boadicea's unsuccessful attack on the Romans 61 AD

0   50
Miles

2

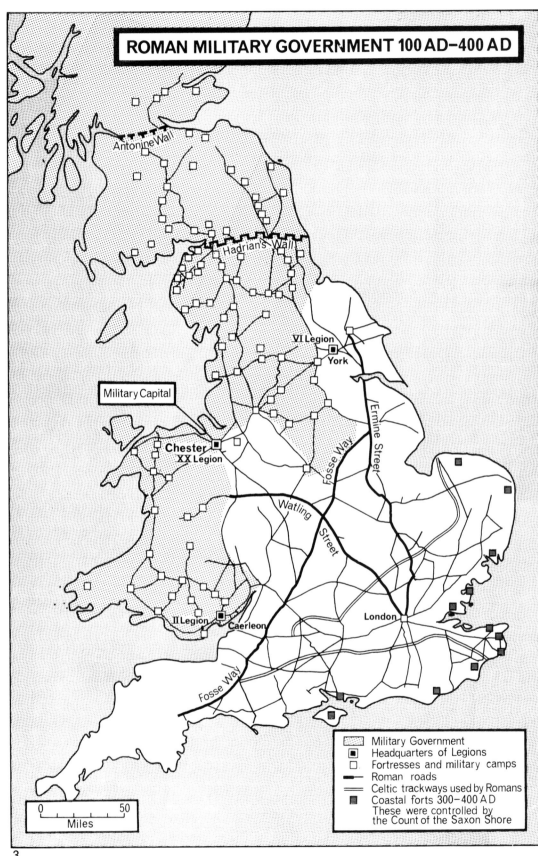

ROMAN MILITARY GOVERNMENT 100 AD–400 AD

Antonine Wall

Hadrian's Wall

VI Legion
York

Military Capital

Chester
XX Legion

Fosse Way

Ermine Street

Watling Street

II Legion
Caerleon

London

Fosse Way

Military Government
■ Headquarters of Legions
□ Fortresses and military camps
━ Roman roads
═ Celtic trackways used by Romans
▥ Coastal forts 300–400 AD
These were controlled by
the Count of the Saxon Shore

0   50
Miles

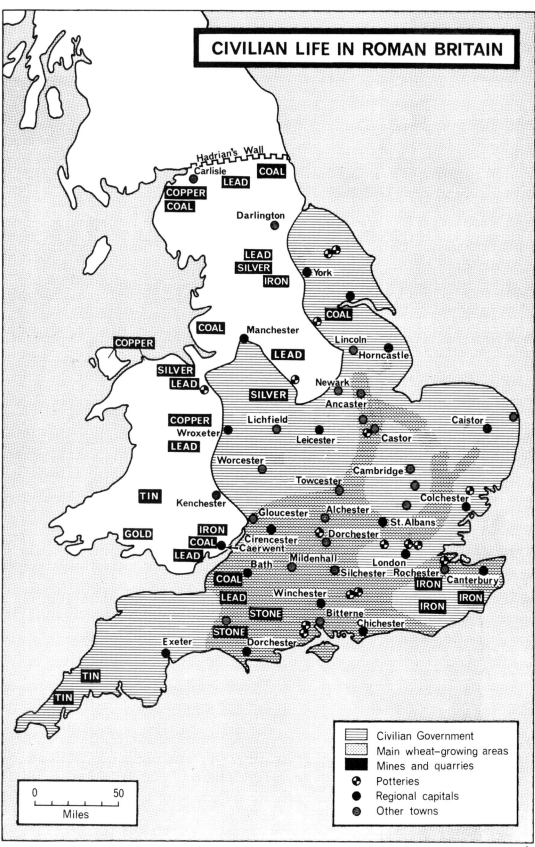

CIVILIAN LIFE IN ROMAN BRITAIN

Hadrian's Wall
Carlisle
COAL
LEAD
COPPER
COAL
Darlington
LEAD
SILVER
IRON
York
COAL
COAL
Manchester
Lincoln
COPPER
Horncastle
SILVER
LEAD
LEAD
Newark
SILVER
Ancaster
COPPER
Lichfield
Caistor
Wroxeter
LEAD
Leicester
Castor
Worcester
Cambridge
TIN
Towcester
Kenchester
Colchester
GOLD
Gloucester
Alchester
IRON
St. Albans
COAL
Cirencester
Dorchester
LEAD
Caerwent
Mildenhall
London
COAL
Bath
Silchester
Rochester
LEAD
Winchester
Canterbury
IRON
STONE
Bitterne
IRON
IRON
STONE
Chichester
Exeter
Dorchester
TIN
TIN

	Civilian Government
	Main wheat-growing areas
■	Mines and quarries
◓	Potteries
●	Regional capitals
◉	Other towns

0   50
Miles

4

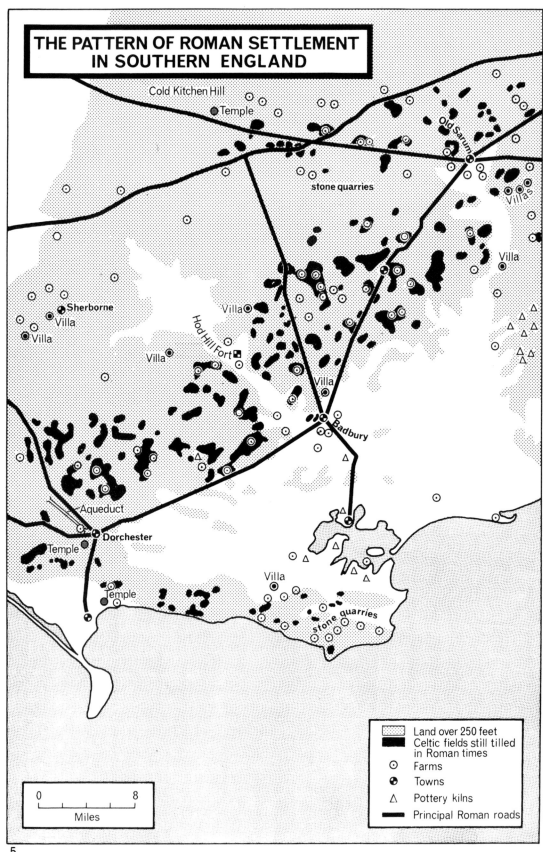

THE PATTERN OF ROMAN SETTLEMENT IN SOUTHERN ENGLAND

Cold Kitchen Hill

Temple

Old Sarum

stone quarries

Villas

Villa

Sherborne
Villa
Villa
Villa

Hod Hill Fort

Villa

Villa

Villa

Badbury

Aqueduct

Dorchester

Temple

Villa

Temple

stone quarries

	Land over 250 feet
	Celtic fields still tilled in Roman times
⊙	Farms
◉	Towns
△	Pottery kilns
▬	Principal Roman roads

0   8
Miles

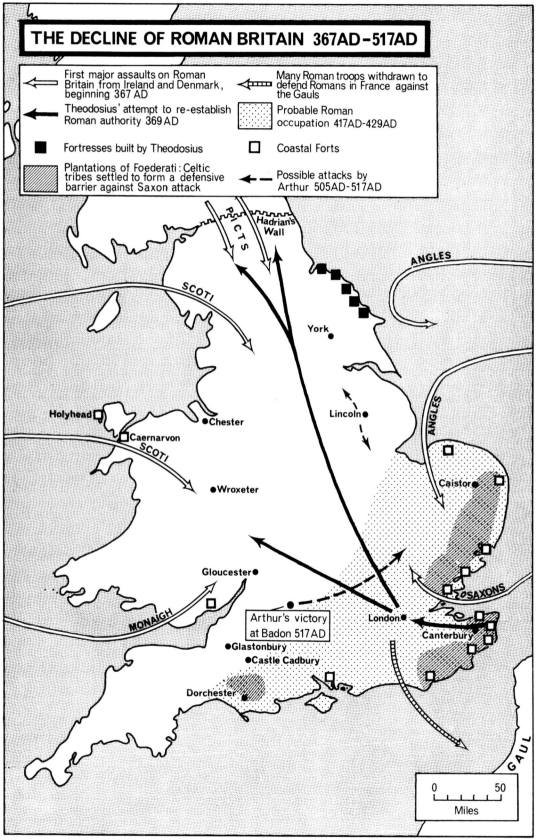

THE DECLINE OF ROMAN BRITAIN 367AD–517AD

First major assaults on Roman Britain from Ireland and Denmark, beginning 367 AD

Theodosius' attempt to re-establish Roman authority 369 AD

Fortresses built by Theodosius

Plantations of Foederati: Celtic tribes settled to form a defensive barrier against Saxon attack

Many Roman troops withdrawn to defend Romans in France against the Gauls

Probable Roman occupation 417AD–429AD

Coastal Forts

Possible attacks by Arthur 505AD–517AD

PICTS

Hadrian's Wall

ANGLES

SCOTI

York

ANGLES

Holyhead

Chester

Caernarvon

SCOTI

Lincoln

Caistor

Wroxeter

Gloucester

SAXONS

MONAIGH

London

Arthur's victory at Badon 517AD

Canterbury

Glastonbury

Castle Cadbury

Dorchester

GAUL

0   50
Miles

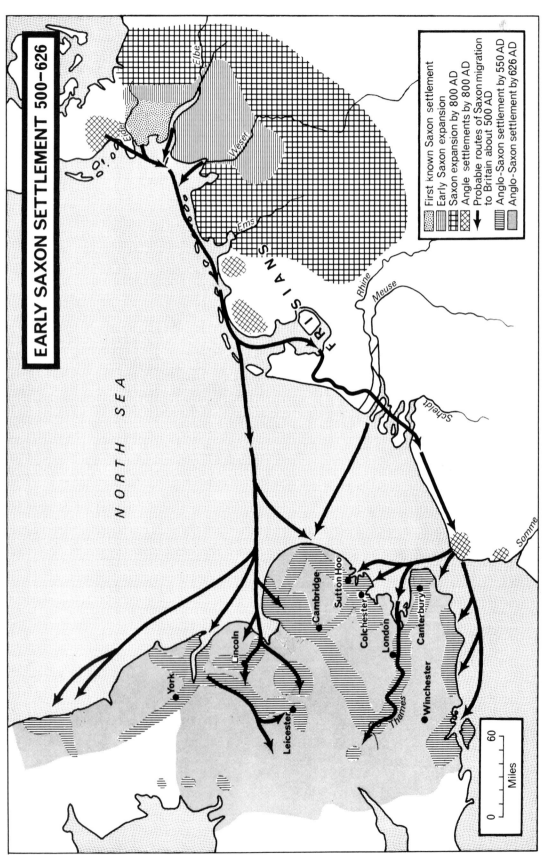

EARLY SAXON SETTLEMENT 500–626

Legend:
- First known Saxon settlement
- Early Saxon expansion
- Saxon expansion by 800 AD
- Angle settlements by 800 AD
- Probable routes of Saxon migration to Britain about 500 AD
- Anglo-Saxon settlement by 550 AD
- Anglo-Saxon settlement by 626 AD

NORTH SEA

FRISIANS

Elbe
Weser
Ems
Eider
Rhine
Meuse
Scheldt
Somme

York
Lincoln
Leicester
Cambridge
Sutton Hoo
Colchester
London
Canterbury
Winchester
Thames

0   60
Miles

7

SAXON KINGDOMS AND BRETWALDASHIPS 630-829

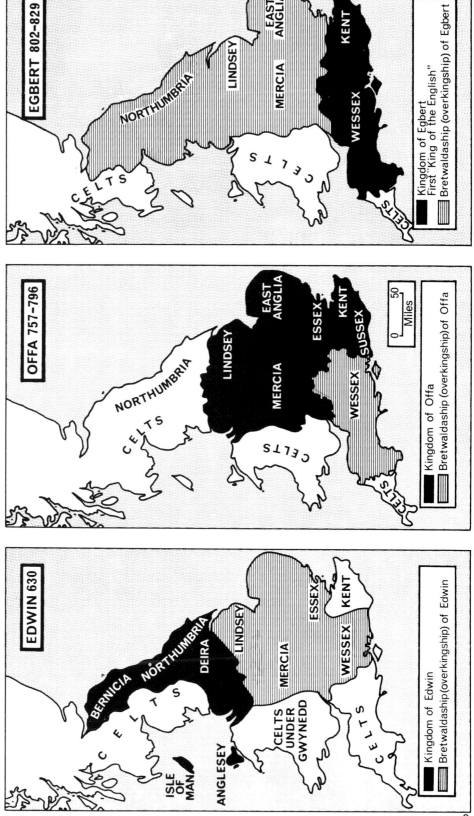

THE CHURCH 700–850

† Abercorn
Coldingham ⊕
Lindisfarne
† Melrose

LINDISFARNE

⋔ Coquet Island

WHITHORN

† Tynemouth
Hexham † † Jarrow
⋔ Monkwearmouth
HEXHAM
† Whithorn
⊕ Hartlepool
† Gainford
Gilling † Sockburn ⊕ Whitby
Lastingham † †
Hackness †
† Ripon
Y O R K
† York

† Barrow
Syddensis Civitas
(site not known)
LINDSEY

LICHFIELD
Repton ⊕ † Breedon
Lichfield
Peterborough †
Leicester † Oundle
Elmham
E L M H A M
† Brixworth
LEICESTER
Ely ⊕
Dunwich †
† Bury St.
Edmunds
DUNWICH

HEREFORD
Worcester
Hereford
WORCESTER
DORCHESTER
† Malmesbury
Abingdon † Dorchester
LONDON
⊕ Barking
London
† Reculver
ROCH-
ESTER Minster
CANTER-
BURY Canterbury Dover
Folkestone
Lyminge
WINCHESTER † Woking
Glastonbury † Winchester
Sherborne † Tisbury
SELSEY
SHERBORNE Nursling †
Exeter † Wimborne † Selsey

†	Religious houses founded by 850
⊕	Double houses where monks and nuns lived under the rule of an abbess
—	Approximate diocesan boundaries
●	Diocesan seats
▨	Archbishoprics

0   50
Miles

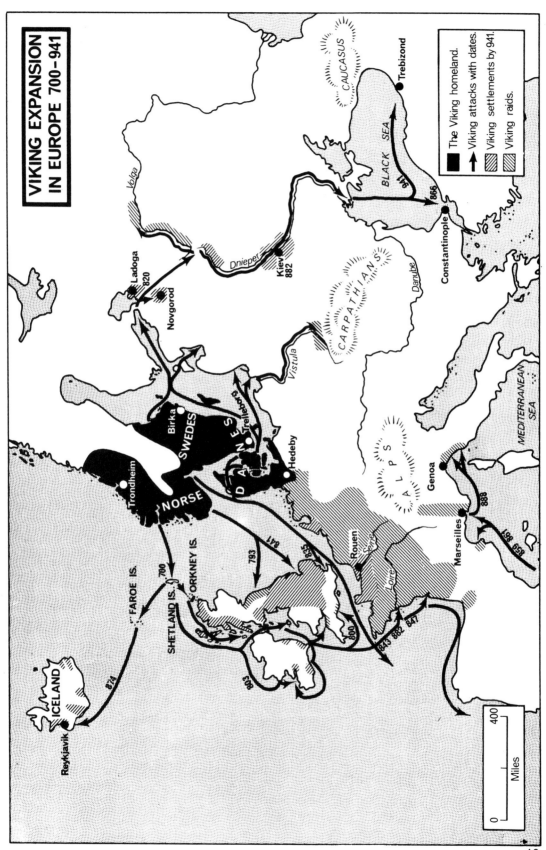

VIKING EXPANSION IN EUROPE 700–941

The Viking homeland.

Viking attacks with dates.

Viking settlements by 941.

Viking raids.

CAUCASUS

Trebizond

BLACK SEA

941

866

Constantinople

CARPATHIANS

Danube

Volga

Dnieper

Kiev
882

Ladoga
820

Novgorod

Vistula

MEDITERRANEAN SEA

ALPS

Genoa

Marseilles
838

859 860

Rouen

Seine

Loire

Birka

SWEDES

Gotland

D A N E S

Hedeby

NORSE

Trondheim

FAROE IS.

700

SHETLAND IS.

ORKNEY IS.

793

841

857

843 882
847

860

866

ICELAND

874

Reykjavik

Miles

0   400

10

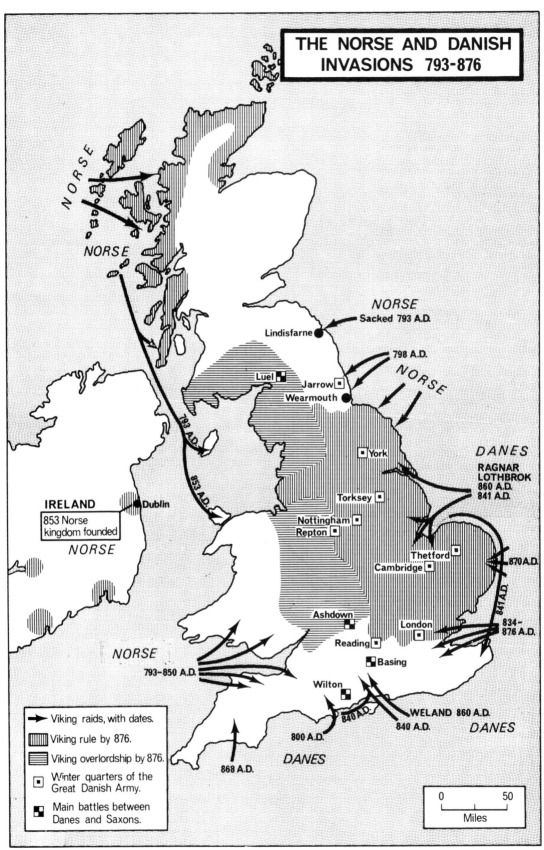

THE NORSE AND DANISH INVASIONS 793-876

NORSE

NORSE

NORSE

NORSE
Sacked 793 A.D.
Lindisfarne

798 A.D.

NORSE

Luel

Jarrow

Wearmouth

York

DANES

RAGNAR
LOTHBROK
860 A.D.
841 A.D.

Torksey

IRELAND
Dublin

853 Norse
kingdom founded

NORSE

Nottingham
Repton

Thetford

Cambridge

870 A.D.

Ashdown

London

834-
876 A.D.

Reading

Basing

NORSE

793-850 A.D.

Wilton

WELAND 860 A.D.
840 A.D.

840 A.D.

DANES

800 A.D.

868 A.D.

DANES

Viking raids, with dates.

Viking rule by 876.

Viking overlordship by 876.

Winter quarters of the Great Danish Army.

Main battles between Danes and Saxons.

0   50
Miles

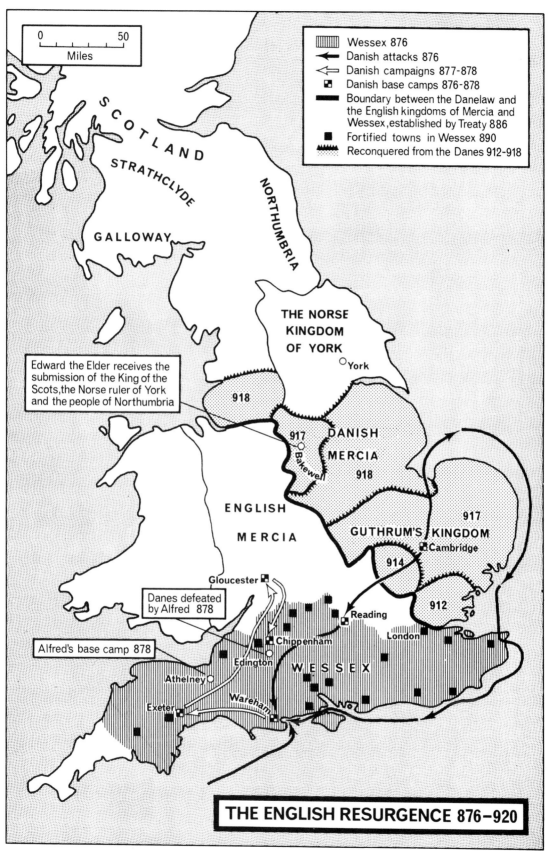

THE ENGLISH RESURGENCE 876–920

Legend:

|||||||	Wessex 876
←	Danish attacks 876
⇐	Danish campaigns 877-878
▣	Danish base camps 876-878
▬	Boundary between the Danelaw and the English kingdoms of Mercia and Wessex, established by Treaty 886
■	Fortified towns in Wessex 890
∿	Reconquered from the Danes 912-918

Scale: 0 — 50 Miles

SCOTLAND

STRATHCLYDE

GALLOWAY

NORTHUMBRIA

THE NORSE KINGDOM OF YORK

○ York

Edward the Elder receives the submission of the King of the Scots, the Norse ruler of York and the people of Northumbria

918

917 ○ Bakewell

DANISH MERCIA

918

ENGLISH MERCIA

GUTHRUM'S KINGDOM

917

▣ Cambridge

914

912

Gloucester ▣

Danes defeated by Alfred 878

Alfred's base camp 878

■ Chippenham

Reading ▣

London

Edington

WESSEX

Athelney ○

Exeter ▣

Wareham

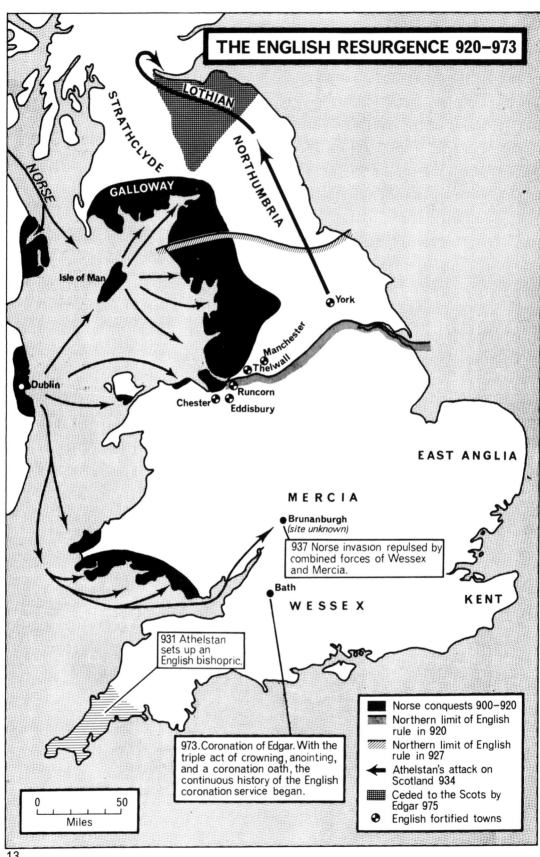

THE ENGLISH RESURGENCE 920–973

STRATHCLYDE

NORSE

LOTHIAN

NORTHUMBRIA

GALLOWAY

Isle of Man

Dublin

Manchester

Thelwall

Runcorn

Chester

Eddisbury

York

EAST ANGLIA

MERCIA

●Brunanburgh
(site unknown)

937 Norse invasion repulsed by
combined forces of Wessex
and Mercia.

Bath

WESSEX

KENT

931 Athelstan
sets up an
English bishopric.

973. Coronation of Edgar. With the
triple act of crowning, anointing,
and a coronation oath, the
continuous history of the English
coronation service began.

0   50
Miles

Norse conquests 900–920
Northern limit of English
rule in 920
Northern limit of English
rule in 927
Athelstan's attack on
Scotland 934
Ceded to the Scots by
Edgar 975
English fortified towns

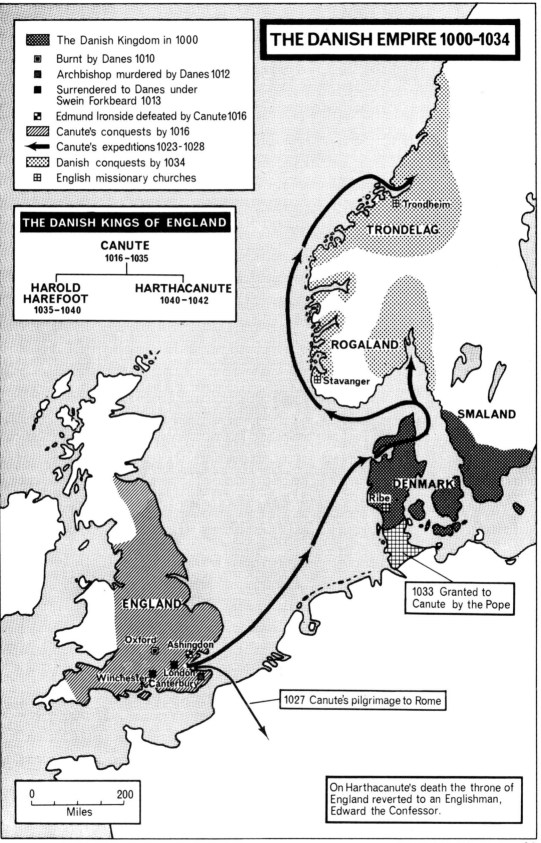

THE DANISH EMPIRE 1000-1034

Legend:
- The Danish Kingdom in 1000
- Burnt by Danes 1010
- Archbishop murdered by Danes 1012
- Surrendered to Danes under Swein Forkbeard 1013
- Edmund Ironside defeated by Canute 1016
- Canute's conquests by 1016
- Canute's expeditions 1023-1028
- Danish conquests by 1034
- English missionary churches

THE DANISH KINGS OF ENGLAND

CANUTE
1016-1035

HAROLD HAREFOOT
1035-1040

HARTHACANUTE
1040-1042

Trondheim

TRØNDELAG

ROGALAND

Stavanger

SMALAND

DENMARK

Ribe

1033 Granted to Canute by the Pope

ENGLAND

Oxford   Ashingdon

Winchester   London
Canterbury

1027 Canute's pilgrimage to Rome

0 — 200
Miles

On Harthacanute's death the throne of England reverted to an Englishman, Edward the Confessor.

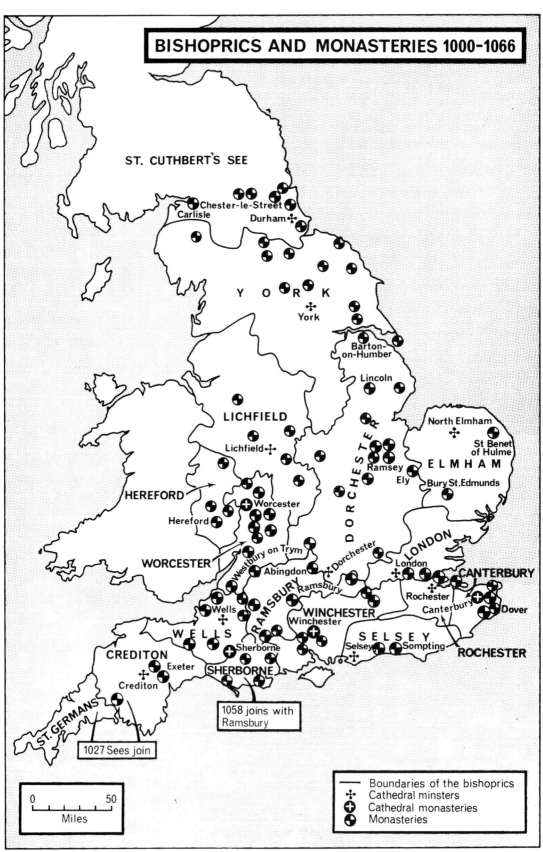

BISHOPRICS AND MONASTERIES 1000-1066

ST. CUTHBERT'S SEE

Chester-le-Street
Carlisle
Durham ✢

Y O R K

York ✢

Barton-on-Humber

Lincoln

LICHFIELD

Lichfield ✢

North Elmham ✢
St Benet of Hulme

E L M H A M

Ramsey
Ely
Bury St.Edmunds

HEREFORD

Worcester ✢

Hereford

WORCESTER

Westbury on Trym
Abingdon
Dorchester ✢
London ✢

D O R C H E S T E R

LONDON

Ramsbury
Rochester ✢

CANTERBURY

WELLS

Wells ✢

R A M S B U R Y

WINCHESTER

Winchester ✢

Canterbury ✢
Dover

Sherborne

S E L S E Y

Selsey ✢
Sompting

ROCHESTER

CREDITON

Exeter
Crediton ✢

SHERBORNE

ST. GERMANS

1058 joins with Ramsbury

1027 Sees join

0 ____ 50
Miles

— Boundaries of the bishoprics
✢ Cathedral minsters
✪ Cathedral monasteries
● Monasteries

15

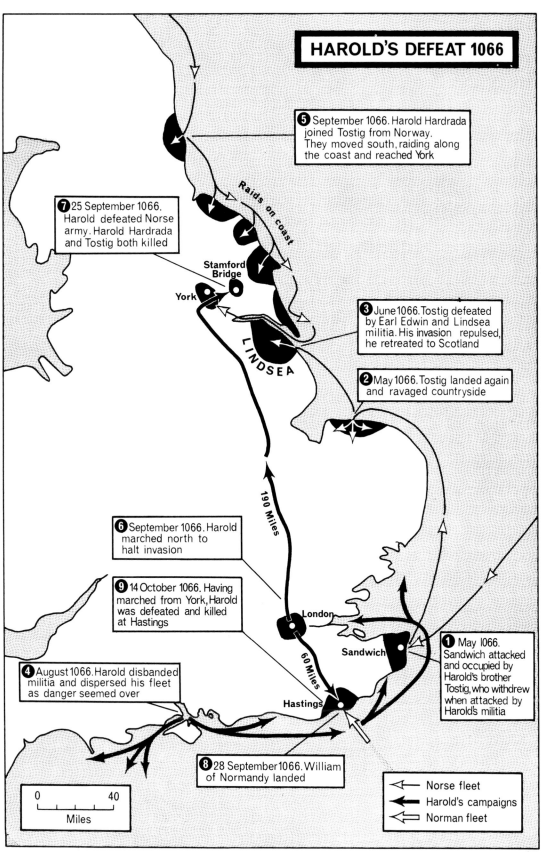

HAROLD'S DEFEAT 1066

5 September 1066. Harold Hardrada joined Tostig from Norway. They moved south, raiding along the coast and reached York

7 25 September 1066. Harold defeated Norse army. Harold Hardrada and Tostig both killed

Raids on coast

Stamford Bridge

York

LINDSEA

3 June 1066. Tostig defeated by Earl Edwin and Lindsea militia. His invasion repulsed, he retreated to Scotland

2 May 1066. Tostig landed again and ravaged countryside

190 Miles

6 September 1066. Harold marched north to halt invasion

9 14 October 1066. Having marched from York, Harold was defeated and killed at Hastings

London

60 Miles

Sandwich

1 May 1066. Sandwich attacked and occupied by Harold's brother Tostig, who withdrew when attacked by Harold's militia

4 August 1066. Harold disbanded militia and dispersed his fleet as danger seemed over

Hastings

8 28 September 1066. William of Normandy landed

0   40
Miles

◁── Norse fleet
◀━━ Harold's campaigns
⇦── Norman fleet

16

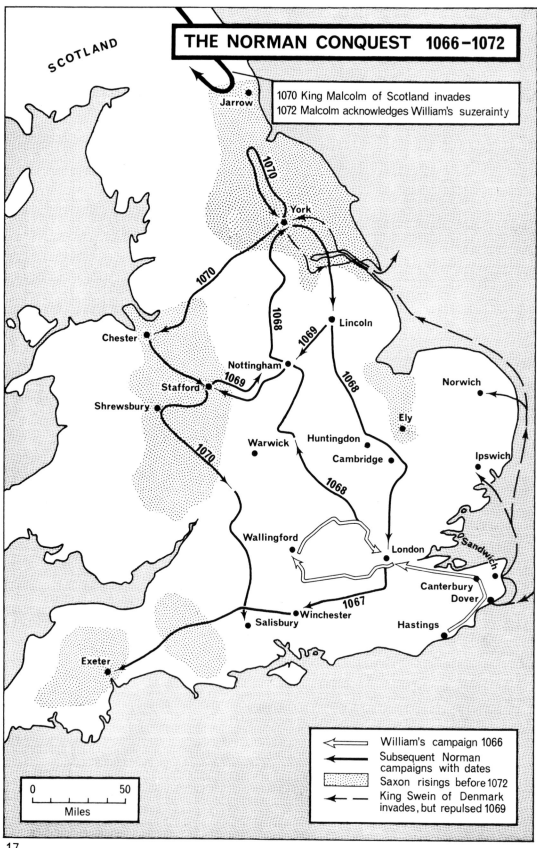

THE NORMAN CONQUEST 1066-1072

1070 King Malcolm of Scotland invades
1072 Malcolm acknowledges William's suzerainty

SCOTLAND

Jarrow

York

Chester

Nottingham

Stafford

Shrewsbury

Lincoln

Norwich

Ely

Warwick

Huntingdon

Cambridge

Ipswich

Wallingford

London

Sandwich

Canterbury
Dover

Salisbury

Winchester

Hastings

Exeter

1070

1068

1069

1070

1069

1070

1068

1068

1068

1067

William's campaign 1066
Subsequent Norman
campaigns with dates
Saxon risings before 1072
King Swein of Denmark
invades, but repulsed 1069

0   50
Miles

17

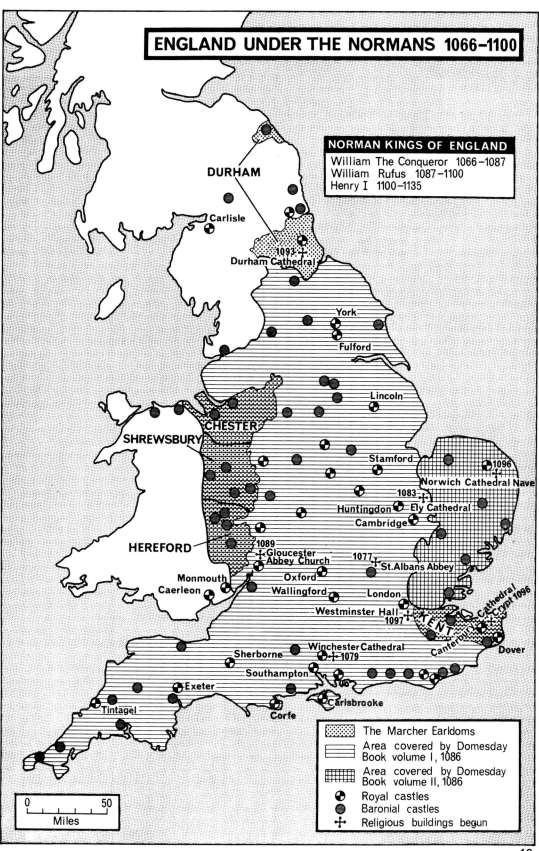

ENGLAND UNDER THE NORMANS 1066–1100

NORMAN KINGS OF ENGLAND
William The Conqueror 1066–1087
William Rufus 1087–1100
Henry I 1100–1135

DURHAM

Carlisle

1093 Durham Cathedral

York

Fulford

Lincoln

CHESTER

SHREWSBURY

Stamford

1096 Norwich Cathedral Nave

1083 Ely Cathedral
Huntingdon
Cambridge

HEREFORD

1089 Gloucester Abbey Church

1077 St.Albans Abbey

Monmouth
Caerleon

Oxford
Wallingford
London

Westminster Hall 1097

KENT

Canterbury Cathedral Crypt 1096

Winchester Cathedral
Sherborne 1079

Dover

Southampton

Exeter

Carisbrooke

Tintagel

Corfe

The Marcher Earldoms
Area covered by Domesday Book volume I, 1086
Area covered by Domesday Book volume II, 1086
⊕ Royal castles
◉ Baronial castles
✝ Religious buildings begun

0 — 50
Miles

18

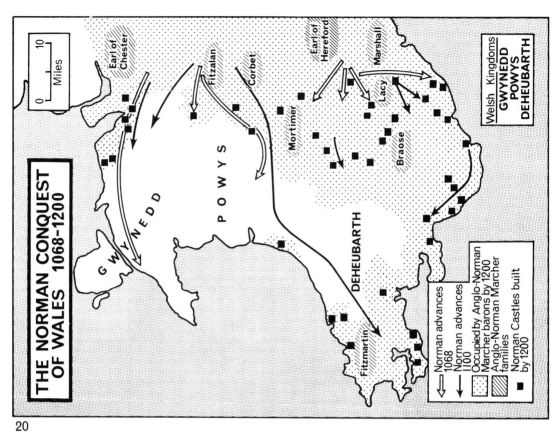

THE NORMAN CONQUEST OF WALES 1068–1200

Welsh Kingdoms
GWYNEDD
POWYS
DEHEUBARTH

Earl of Chester

Fitzalan

Corbet

Earl of Hereford

Marshall

Lacy

Mortimer

Braose

G W Y N E D D

P O W Y S

DEHEUBARTH

Fitzmartin

0 10 Miles

Norman advances 1068
Norman advances 1100
Occupied by Anglo-Norman Marcher barons by 1200
Anglo-Norman Marcher families
Norman Castles built by 1200

20

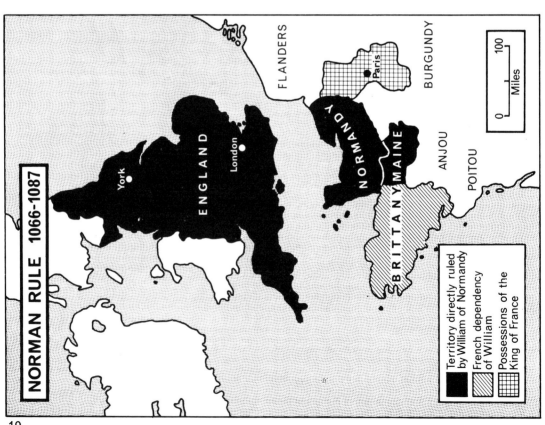

NORMAN RULE 1066–1087

FLANDERS

BURGUNDY

ENGLAND

York

London

NORMANDY

Paris

MAINE

BRITTANY

ANJOU

POITOU

0 100 Miles

Territory directly ruled by William of Normandy
French dependency of William
Possessions of the King of France

19

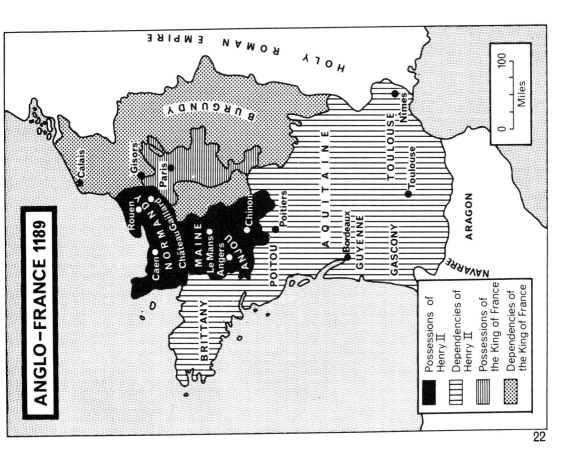

ANGLO–FRANCE 1189

HOLY ROMAN EMPIRE

BURGUNDY

Calais

Gisors
Rouen
Château Gaillard
Paris
NORMANDY
Caen
MAINE
Le Mans
Angers
ANJOU
Chinon
Poitiers
BRITTANY
POITOU
Bordeaux
GUYENNE
AQUITAINE
GASCONY
TOULOUSE
Toulouse
Nîmes
ARAGON
NAVARRE

0   100
Miles

Possessions of Henry II

Dependencies of Henry II

Possessions of the King of France

Dependencies of the King of France

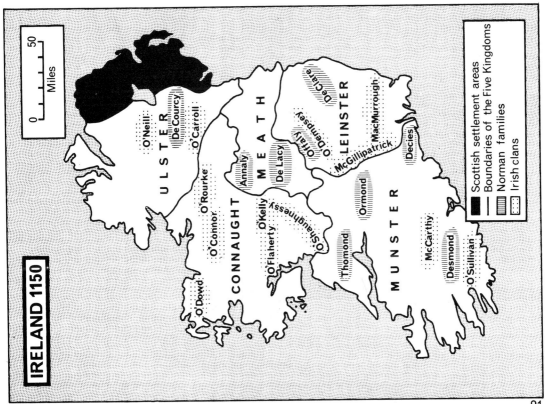

IRELAND 1150

0   50
Miles

ULSTER
O'Neill
De Courcy
O'Carroll
O'Rourke
O'Dowd
O'Connor
CONNAUGHT
O'Flaherty
O'Shaughnessy
O'Kelly
Annaly
MEATH
De Lacy
Offaly
O'Dempsey
O'Dempsey
Decies
LEINSTER
MacMurrough
McGillipatrick
Decies
Thomond
Ormond
MUNSTER
McCarthy
Desmond
O'Sullivan

Scottish settlement areas

Boundaries of the Five Kingdoms

Norman families

Irish clans

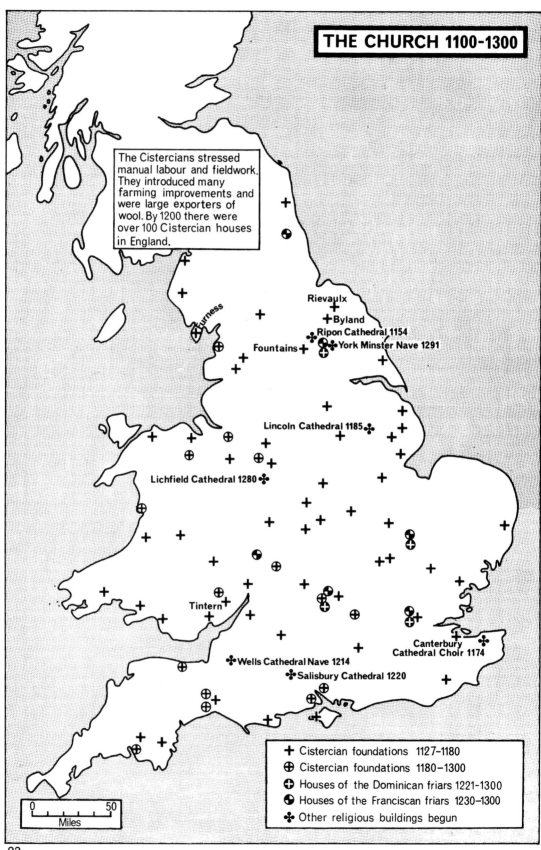

THE CHURCH 1100-1300

The Cistercians stressed manual labour and fieldwork. They introduced many farming improvements and were large exporters of wool. By 1200 there were over 100 Cistercian houses in England.

Furness

Rievaulx
Byland
Ripon Cathedral 1154
Fountains York Minster Nave 1291

Lincoln Cathedral 1185

Lichfield Cathedral 1280

Tintern

Canterbury
Cathedral Choir 1174

Wells Cathedral Nave 1214
Salisbury Cathedral 1220

+ Cistercian foundations 1127-1180
⊕ Cistercian foundations 1180-1300
✪ Houses of the Dominican friars 1221-1300
✪ Houses of the Franciscan friars 1230-1300
✤ Other religious buildings begun

0   50
Miles

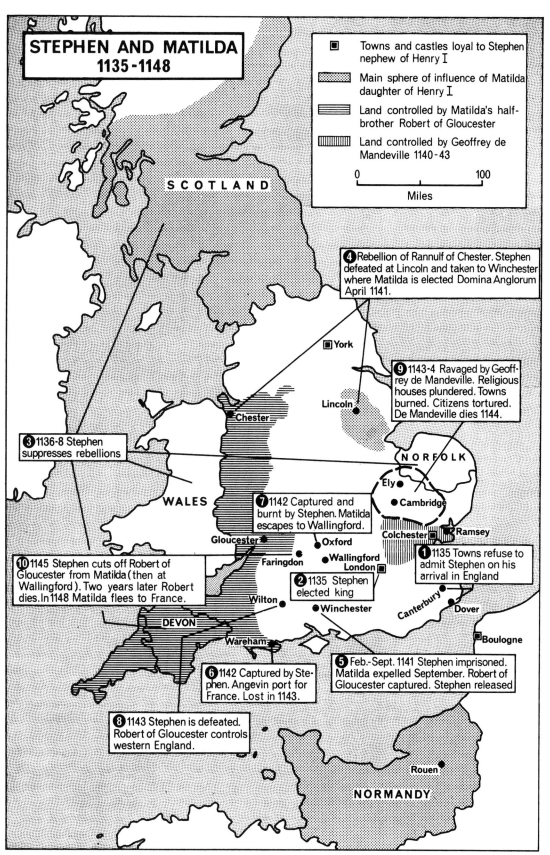

STEPHEN AND MATILDA 1135-1148

Legend:
- ■ Towns and castles loyal to Stephen nephew of Henry I
- ▦ Main sphere of influence of Matilda daughter of Henry I
- ▤ Land controlled by Matilda's half-brother Robert of Gloucester
- ▥ Land controlled by Geoffrey de Mandeville 1140-43

0 _____ 100
Miles

SCOTLAND

4 Rebellion of Rannulf of Chester. Stephen defeated at Lincoln and taken to Winchester where Matilda is elected Domina Anglorum April 1141.

■ York

9 1143-4 Ravaged by Geoffrey de Mandeville. Religious houses plundered. Towns burned. Citizens tortured. De Mandeville dies 1144.

Lincoln •

■ Chester

3 1136-8 Stephen suppresses rebellions

NORFOLK

Ely •

WALES

• Cambridge

7 1142 Captured and burnt by Stephen. Matilda escapes to Wallingford.

Colchester ■ ■ Ramsey

Gloucester •

• Oxford

10 1145 Stephen cuts off Robert of Gloucester from Matilda (then at Wallingford). Two years later Robert dies. In 1148 Matilda flees to France.

Faringdon • • Wallingford
London ■

1 1135 Towns refuse to admit Stephen on his arrival in England

2 1135 Stephen elected king

Wilton •

Canterbury

• Dover

DEVON

• Winchester

5 Feb.-Sept. 1141 Stephen imprisoned. Matilda expelled September. Robert of Gloucester captured. Stephen released

Wareham •

■ Boulogne

6 1142 Captured by Stephen. Angevin port for France. Lost in 1143.

8 1143 Stephen is defeated. Robert of Gloucester controls western England.

Rouen •

NORMANDY

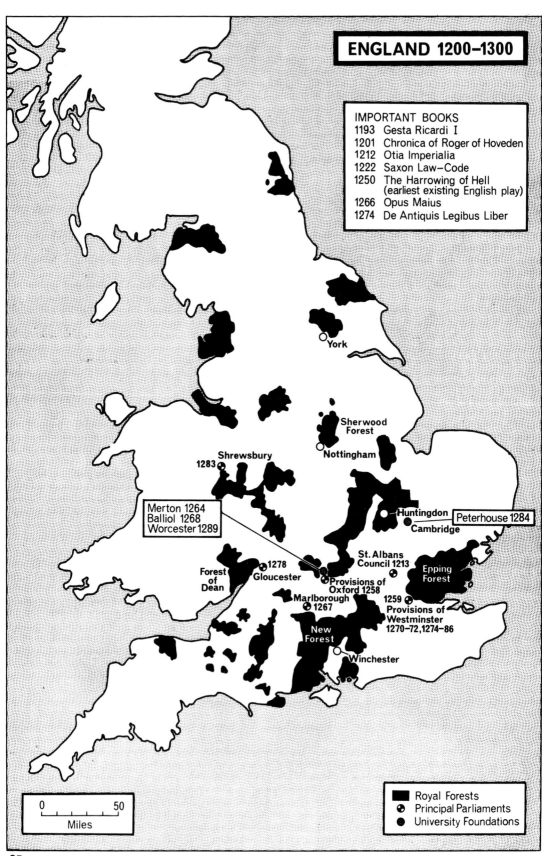

ENGLAND 1200–1300

IMPORTANT BOOKS
1193 Gesta Ricardi I
1201 Chronica of Roger of Hoveden
1212 Otia Imperialia
1222 Saxon Law–Code
1250 The Harrowing of Hell
     (earliest existing English play)
1266 Opus Maius
1274 De Antiquis Legibus Liber

York

Sherwood
Forest

Shrewsbury
1283

Nottingham

Merton 1264
Balliol 1268
Worcester 1289

Huntingdon
Cambridge

Peterhouse 1284

St. Albans
Council 1213

1278
Gloucester

Forest
of
Dean

Epping
Forest

Provisions of
Oxford 1258

Marlborough
1267

1259
Provisions of
Westminster
1270–72,1274–86

New
Forest

Winchester

0   50
Miles

■ Royal Forests
◐ Principal Parliaments
● University Foundations

THE ECONOMY 1200–1300

1245 Papal money-raiser expelled from England by king, clergy and barons
1274 Anglo-Flanders Commercial Treaty
1275 King to receive duty on wool
1280 German merchants in England form a Hansa
1290 Expulsion of the Jews from England
1299 Act to repress bad coinage passed

York
blues
Beverley

Lincoln scarlets
Lincoln

Nottingham

Stamfords

Norwich

Leicester
Stamford

Coventry
Huntingdon
Somersham
Ramsey

Northampton
Bury St. Edmunds

Worcester
Warwick
Cambridge
Ipswich

Bedford
Sudbury

Gloucester
russets
russets
Colchester

Oxford

Chepstow
Wallingford
russets

Bristol
London

Marlborough

Devizes
Canterbury
Sandwich

russets
Hythe
Romney
Dover

Wilton
Winchester
Rye

Salisbury
Winchelsea
Hastings

Cloth producing areas with names of cloth
Towns with weavers guilds by 1200
The Cinque Ports : special liberties granted 1278
The liberties of Chepstow, Ramsey and Somersham
Towns with Jewish settlements where Jewish loans were recorded 1190 – 1290

0   50
Miles

26

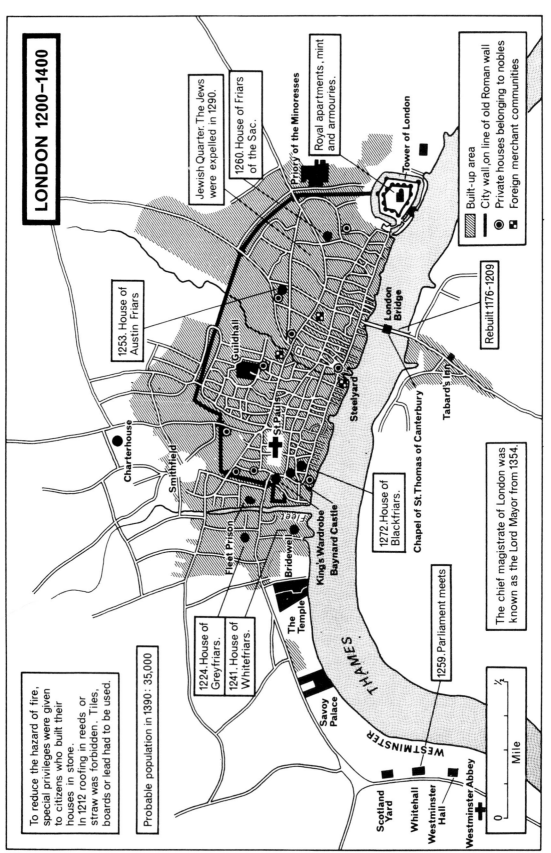

LONDON 1200–1400

Jewish Quarter. The Jews were expelled in 1290.

1260. House of Friars of the Sac.

Priory of the Minoresses

Royal apartments, mint and armouries.

Tower of London

1253. House of Austin Friars

Guildhall

St. Paul's

Steelyard

London Bridge

Rebuilt 1176-1209

Chapel of St.Thomas of Canterbury

Tabard's Inn

1272. House of Blackfriars.

The chief magistrate of London was known as the Lord Mayor from 1354.

Charterhouse

Smithfield

Fleet

Fleet Prison

Bridewell

King's Wardrobe
Baynard Castle

1259. Parliament meets

The Temple

1224. House of Greyfriars.

1241. House of Whitefriars.

Savoy Palace

THAMES

WESTMINSTER

Scotland Yard

Whitehall

Westminster Hall

Westminster Abbey

To reduce the hazard of fire, special privileges were given to citizens who built their houses in stone.
In 1212 roofing in reeds or straw was forbidden. Tiles, boards or lead had to be used.

Probable population in 1390 : 35,000

Built-up area

City wall, on line of old Roman wall

⊙ Private houses belonging to nobles

▪ Foreign merchant communities

0 ½ Mile

27

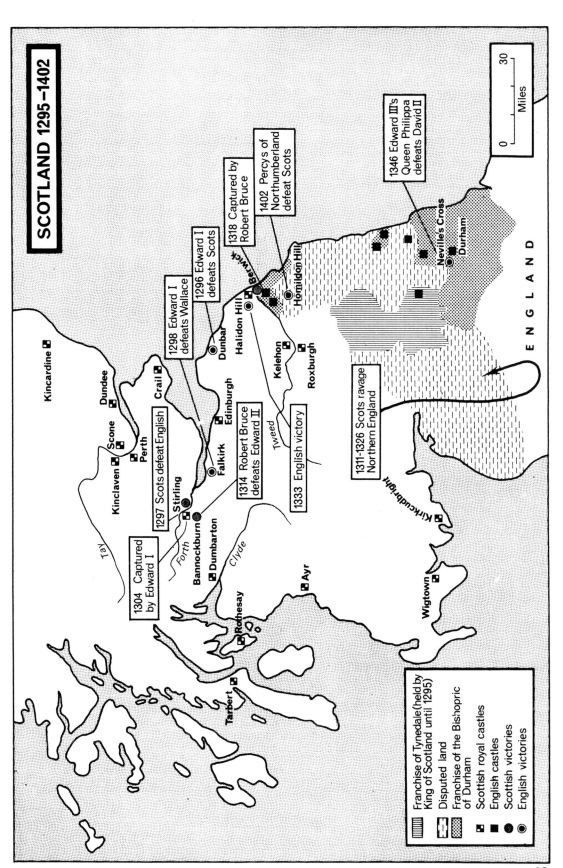

SCOTLAND 1295–1402

Kincardine

Dundee

Scone

Perth

Crail

Kinclaven

Falkirk

1297 Scots defeat English

Stirling

Edinburgh

1298 Edward I defeats Wallace

1296 Edward I defeats Scots

Dunbar

Halidon Hill

Berwick

1318 Captured by Robert Bruce

1402 Percys of Northumberland defeat Scots

Homildon Hill

Kelehon

Roxburgh

1333 English victory

1314 Robert Bruce defeats Edward II

1304 Captured by Edward I

Bannockburn

Dumbarton

Rothesay

Ayr

Tweed

Forth

Clyde

Tay

Kirkcudbright

1311-1326 Scots ravage Northern England

1346 Edward III's Queen Philippa defeats David II

Neville's Cross

Durham

ENGLAND

Wigtown

Tarbert

0   30
Miles

Franchise of Tynedale (held by King of Scotland until 1295)

Disputed land

Franchise of the Bishopric of Durham

Scottish royal castles

English castles

Scottish victories

English victories

28

THE HUNDRED YEARS' WAR
1259-1368

Calais
Etaples
Crécy
Abbeville

Barfleur
Rouen
Caen

NORMANDY

Paris

Bretigny

F
R
A
N
C
E

ANJOU
Tours

Bourges

Poitiers
POITOU

AQUITAINE
Bordeaux
GUYENNE

QUERCY
ROUERGUE

GASCONY
Bayonne

Toulouse

Narbonne

Vitoria
Pass of Roncesvalles
To Burgos
Pamplona
NAVARRE

ARAGON

HOLY

ROMAN

EMPIRE

DAUPHINÉ

0   100
Miles

Possessions of Henry III, 1259
Possessions of the King of France, 1259
English gains 1275
English gains at the Treaty of Bretigny, 1368

Edward III's campaign 1346-1349
the three campaigns of Edward the Black Prince:
to Narbonne 1355
to Poitiers 1356
to Burgos 1367

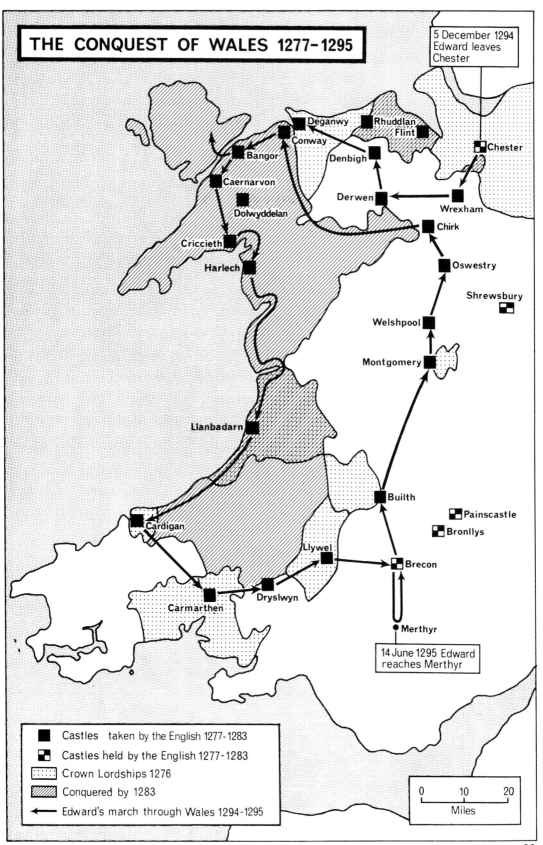

THE CONQUEST OF WALES 1277–1295

5 December 1294
Edward leaves
Chester

Deganwy
Rhuddlan
Flint
Conway
Chester
Bangor
Denbigh
Caernarvon
Derwen
Wrexham
Dolwyddelan
Criccieth
Chirk
Harlech
Oswestry
Shrewsbury
Welshpool
Montgomery
Llanbadarn
Builth
Painscastle
Bronllys
Cardigan
Llywel
Brecon
Carmarthen
Dryslwyn
Merthyr

14 June 1295 Edward
reaches Merthyr

■ Castles taken by the English 1277–1283
▣ Castles held by the English 1277–1283
⋯⋯ Crown Lordships 1276
▨ Conquered by 1283
← Edward's march through Wales 1294–1295

0   10   20
Miles

30

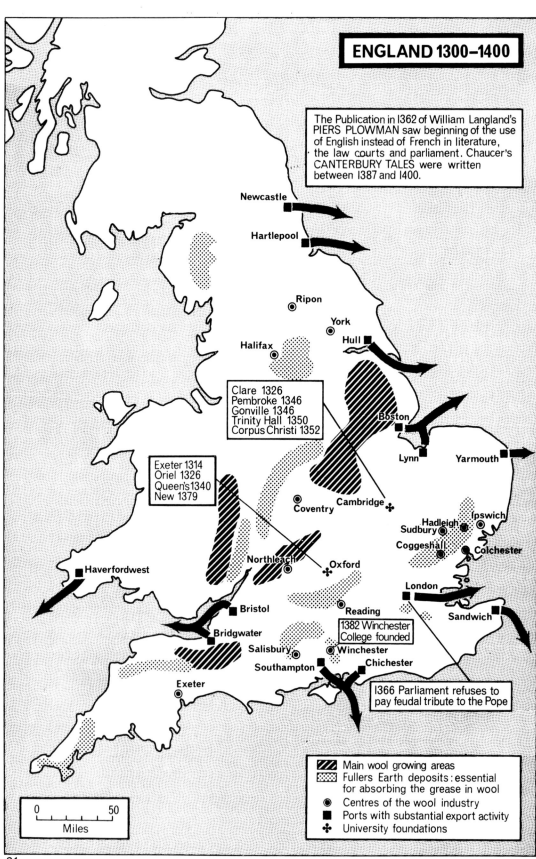

ENGLAND 1300–1400

The Publication in 1362 of William Langland's PIERS PLOWMAN saw beginning of the use of English instead of French in literature, the law courts and parliament. Chaucer's CANTERBURY TALES were written between 1387 and 1400.

Newcastle

Hartlepool

Ripon

York

Hull

Halifax

Clare 1326
Pembroke 1346
Gonville 1346
Trinity Hall 1350
Corpus Christi 1352

Boston

Lynn

Yarmouth

Exeter 1314
Oriel 1326
Queen's 1340
New 1379

Coventry

Cambridge

Ipswich
Hadleigh
Sudbury
Coggeshall
Colchester

Northleach

Oxford

London

Haverfordwest

Bristol

Reading

Sandwich

Bridgwater

1382 Winchester
College founded

Salisbury

Winchester

Chichester

Southampton

Exeter

1366 Parliament refuses to
pay feudal tribute to the Pope

/// Main wool growing areas
::: Fullers Earth deposits: essential
     for absorbing the grease in wool
◎   Centres of the wool industry
■   Ports with substantial export activity
✣   University foundations

0   50
Miles

31

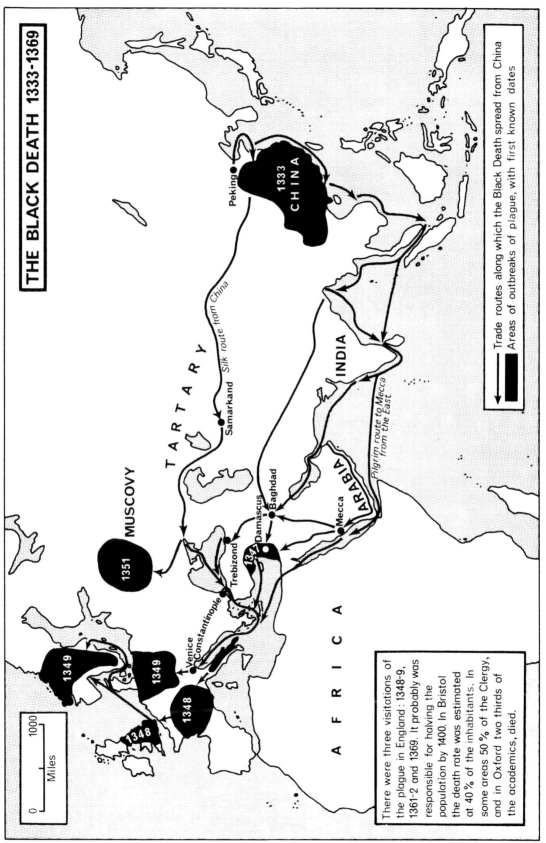

THE BLACK DEATH 1333-1369

CHINA 1333

Peking

Silk route from China

T A R T A R Y

Samarkand

MUSCOVY 1351

Baghdad

Trebizond

Damascus

1347

Constantinople

Venice 1349

1349

1348

1348

Mecca

ARABIA

Pilgrim route to Mecca from the East

INDIA

A F R I C A

0 — 1000
Miles

→ Trade routes along which the Black Death spread from China

■ Areas of outbreaks of plague, with first known dates

There were three visitations of the plague in England : 1348-9, 1361-2 and 1369. It probably was responsible for halving the population by 1400. In Bristol the death rate was estimated at 40% of the inhabitants. In some areas 50% of the Clergy, and in Oxford two thirds of the academics, died.

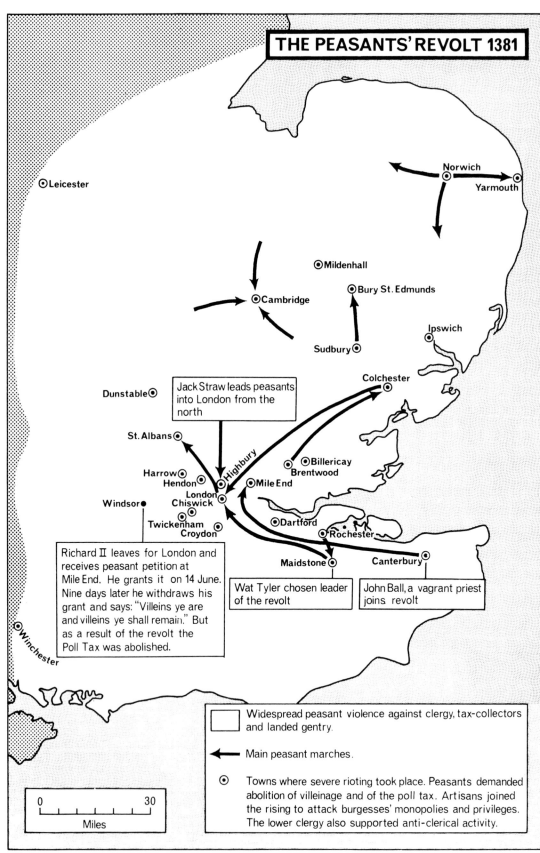

THE PEASANTS' REVOLT 1381

Leicester

Norwich

Yarmouth

Mildenhall

Bury St. Edmunds

Ipswich

Cambridge

Sudbury

Colchester

Dunstable

Jack Straw leads peasants into London from the north

St. Albans

Highbury

Billericay

Brentwood

Harrow
Hendon

Mile End

London
Chiswick

Windsor

Dartford

Twickenham
Croydon

Rochester

Richard II leaves for London and receives peasant petition at Mile End. He grants it on 14 June. Nine days later he withdraws his grant and says: "Villeins ye are and villeins ye shall remain." But as a result of the revolt the Poll Tax was abolished.

Maidstone

Canterbury

Wat Tyler chosen leader of the revolt

John Ball, a vagrant priest joins revolt

Winchester

Widespread peasant violence against clergy, tax-collectors and landed gentry.

Main peasant marches.

Towns where severe rioting took place. Peasants demanded abolition of villeinage and of the poll tax. Artisans joined the rising to attack burgesses' monopolies and privileges. The lower clergy also supported anti-clerical activity.

0   30

Miles

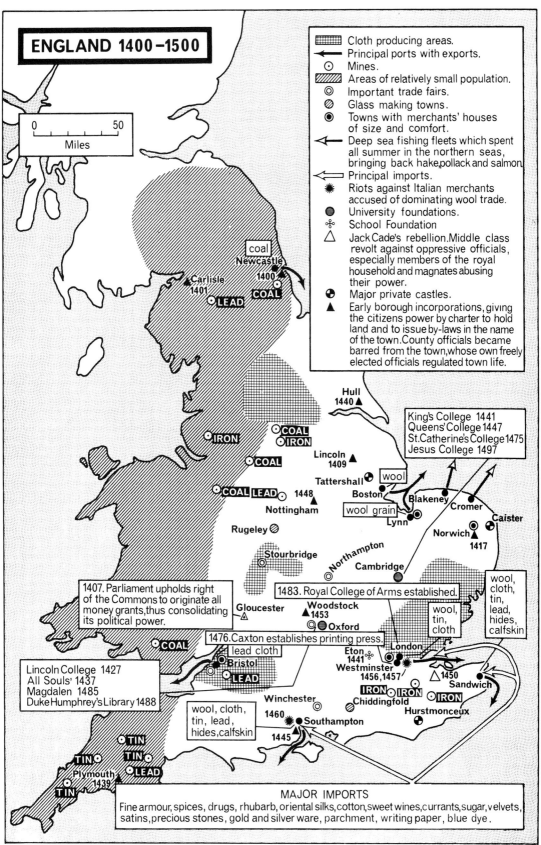

ENGLAND 1400–1500

0   50
Miles

Cloth producing areas.
Principal ports with exports.
⊙ Mines.
Areas of relatively small population.
◎ Important trade fairs.
⊘ Glass making towns.
◉ Towns with merchants' houses of size and comfort.
⇐ Deep sea fishing fleets which spent all summer in the northern seas, bringing back hake, pollack and salmon.
⇐ Principal imports.
✳ Riots against Italian merchants accused of dominating wool trade.
⬤ University foundations.
⚜ School Foundation
△ Jack Cade's rebellion. Middle class revolt against oppressive officials, especially members of the royal household and magnates abusing their power.
⬤ Major private castles.
▲ Early borough incorporations, giving the citizens power by charter to hold land and to issue by-laws in the name of the town. County officials became barred from the town, whose own freely elected officials regulated town life.

coal
Newcastle 1400
COAL

Carlisle 1401
LEAD

Hull 1440 ▲

King's College 1441
Queens' College 1447
St. Catherine's College 1475
Jesus College 1497

IRON
COAL
IRON

COAL

Lincoln 1409 ▲

Tattershall ● wool
COAL LEAD ⊙ 1448 ▲
Nottingham

Boston
Blakeney **Cromer**
wool grain
Lynn
Caister

Rugeley ⊘

Stourbridge

Northampton

Norwich ◎ ▲ 1417

Cambridge

wool, cloth, tin, lead, hides, calfskin

1407. Parliament upholds right of the Commons to originate all money grants, thus consolidating its political power.

Gloucester △

Woodstock ▲ 1453
◎⬤ **Oxford**

1483. Royal College of Arms established.

wool, tin, cloth

COAL
1476. Caxton establishes printing press.
lead cloth
Eton ⚜ 1441
Bristol
LEAD
Westminster 1456,1457

London

△ 1450
Sandwich

Lincoln College 1427
All Souls' 1437
Magdalen 1485
Duke Humphrey's Library 1488

IRON ⊙ **IRON** ⊙ **IRON**
Chiddingfold
Hurstmonceux

Winchester ◎ 1460

wool, cloth, tin, lead, hides, calfskin

Southampton
1445 ▲

TIN
TIN
TIN
LEAD
Plymouth 1439
TIN

MAJOR IMPORTS
Fine armour, spices, drugs, rhubarb, oriental silks, cotton, sweet wines, currants, sugar, velvets, satins, precious stones, gold and silver ware, parchment, writing paper, blue dye.

THE DEFEAT OF OWEN GLENDOWER 1405-1412

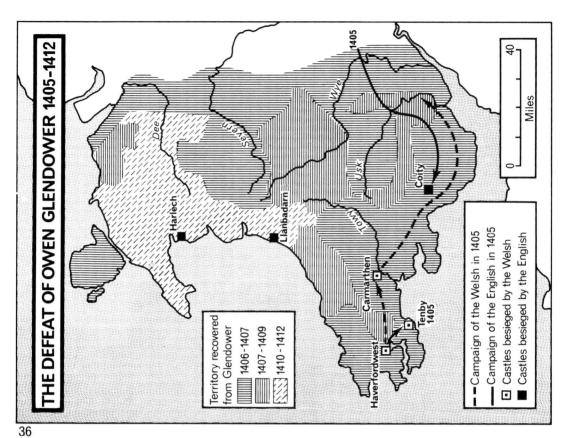

Territory recovered from Glendower

- 1406-1407
- 1407-1409
- 1410-1412

- – – – Campaign of the Welsh in 1405
- ——— Campaign of the English in 1405
- ☐ Castles besieged by the Welsh
- ■ Castles besieged by the English

Harlech
Llanbadarn
Coity
Carmarthen
Haverfordwest
Tenby 1405
1405

Dee
Severn
Wye
Usk
Towy

Miles 0   40

OWEN GLENDOWER'S REVOLT 1400 – 1405

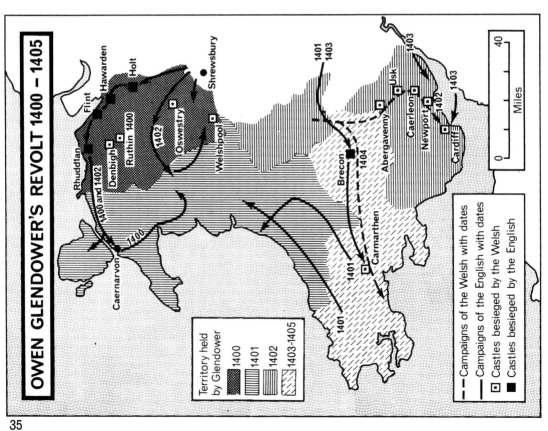

Territory held by Glendower

- 1400
- 1401
- 1402
- 1403-1405

- – – – Campaigns of the Welsh with dates
- ——— Campaigns of the English with dates
- ☐ Castles besieged by the Welsh
- ■ Castles besieged by the English

Hawarden
Flint
Holt
Rhuddlan
Denbigh
Ruthin 1400
Oswestry
Welshpool
Shrewsbury
Caernarvon
1400 and 1402
1400
1402
1401
1403
Brecon
1404
Abergavenny
Usk
Caerleon
Newport
1402
Cardiff
1403
Carmarthen
1401
1401
1403

Miles 0   40

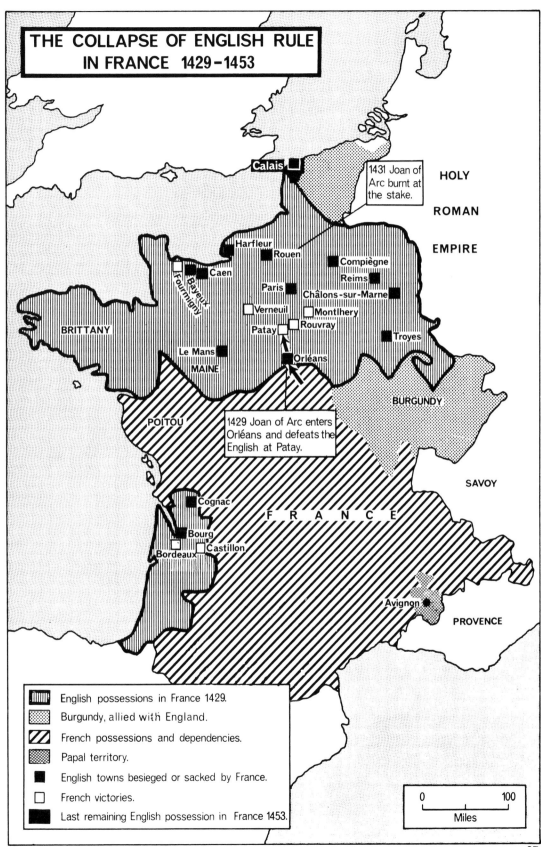

THE COLLAPSE OF ENGLISH RULE IN FRANCE 1429–1453

1431 Joan of Arc burnt at the stake.

HOLY

ROMAN

EMPIRE

Calais

Harfleur

Rouen

Compiègne

Caen

Bayeux

Fourmigny

Reims

Paris

Châlons-sur-Marne

Verneuil

Montlhery

BRITTANY

Patay

Rouvray

Troyes

Le Mans

Orléans

MAINE

BURGUNDY

POITOU

1429 Joan of Arc enters Orléans and defeats the English at Patay.

SAVOY

Cognac

F R A N C E

Bourg

Bordeaux

Castillon

Avignon

PROVENCE

English possessions in France 1429.

Burgundy, allied with England.

French possessions and dependencies.

Papal territory.

■ English towns besieged or sacked by France.

☐ French victories.

■ Last remaining English possession in France 1453.

0   100

Miles

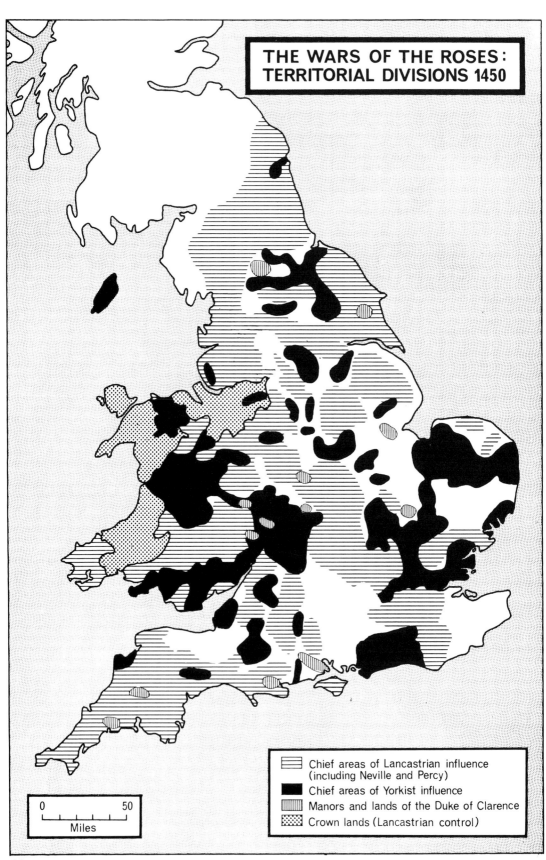

**THE WARS OF THE ROSES:
TERRITORIAL DIVISIONS 1450**

Chief areas of Lancastrian influence
(including Neville and Percy)

Chief areas of Yorkist influence

Manors and lands of the Duke of Clarence

Crown lands (Lancastrian control)

0   50
Miles

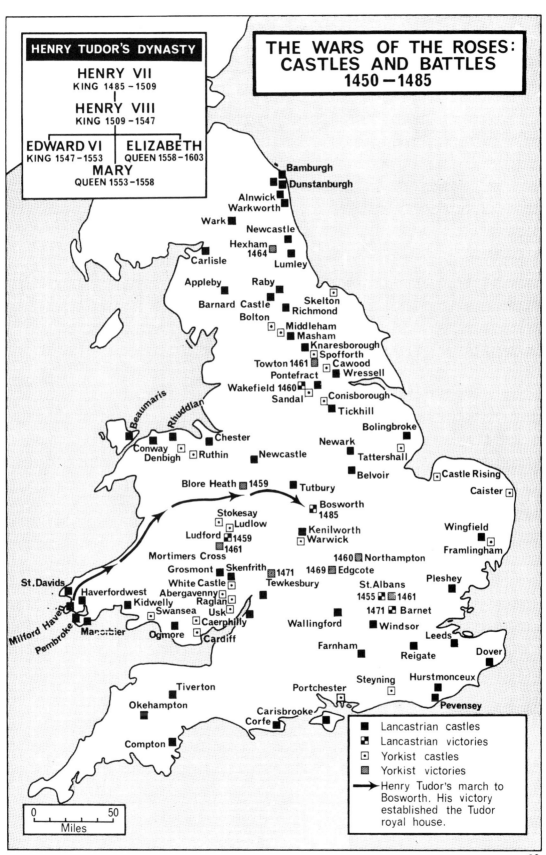

THE WARS OF THE ROSES: CASTLES AND BATTLES 1450 – 1485

HENRY TUDOR'S DYNASTY

HENRY VII
KING 1485 – 1509

HENRY VIII
KING 1509 – 1547

EDWARD VI
KING 1547 – 1553

ELIZABETH
QUEEN 1558 – 1603

MARY
QUEEN 1553 – 1558

Bamburgh
Dunstanburgh
Alnwick
Warkworth
Wark
Newcastle
Hexham 1464
Carlisle
Lumley
Appleby
Raby
Barnard Castle
Skelton
Richmond
Bolton
Middleham
Masham
Knaresborough
Spofforth
Towton 1461
Cawood
Pontefract
Wressell
Wakefield 1460
Sandal
Conisborough
Tickhill
Bolingbroke
Chester
Newark
Beaumaris
Rhuddlan
Conway
Denbigh
Ruthin
Newcastle
Tattershall
Belvoir
Castle Rising
Caister
Blore Heath 1459
Tutbury
Bosworth 1485
Stokesay
Ludlow
Kenilworth
Warwick
Wingfield
Ludford 1459 1461
Mortimers Cross
Framlingham
Grosmont
Skenfrith
1471
1460 Northampton
1469 Edgcote
Pleshey
White Castle
Tewkesbury
Abergavenny
Raglan
St.Albans
1455 1461
St.Davids
Haverfordwest
Usk
1471 Barnet
Kidwelly
Swansea
Caerphilly
Wallingford
Windsor
Leeds
Ogmore
Cardiff
Milford Haven
Pembroke
Manorbier
Farnham
Reigate
Dover
Steyning
Hurstmonceux
Tiverton
Portchester
Pevensey
Okehampton
Carisbrooke
Corfe
Compton

■ Lancastrian castles
▣ Lancastrian victories
☐ Yorkist castles
▨ Yorkist victories
→ Henry Tudor's march to Bosworth. His victory established the Tudor royal house.

0 50 Miles

39

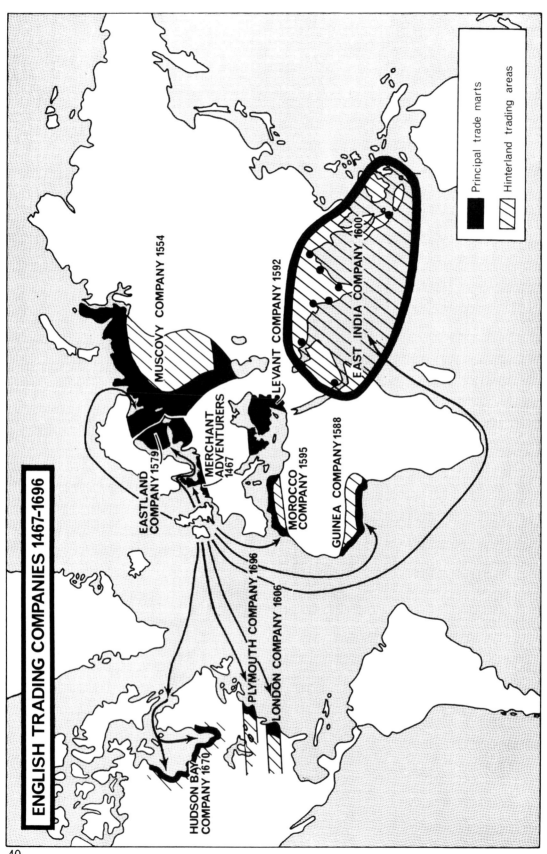

ENGLISH TRADING COMPANIES 1467-1696

Principal trade marts
Hinterland trading areas

MUSCOVY COMPANY 1554

LEVANT COMPANY 1592

EAST INDIA COMPANY 1600

EASTLAND COMPANY 1579

MERCHANT ADVENTURERS 1467

MOROCCO COMPANY 1595

GUINEA COMPANY 1588

PLYMOUTH COMPANY 1696

LONDON COMPANY 1696

HUDSON BAY COMPANY 1670

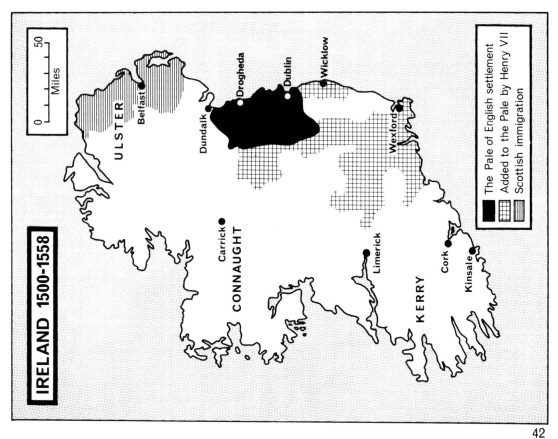

IRELAND 1500-1558

0 _____ 50
Miles

ULSTER

Belfast •
Dundalk •
Drogheda ○
Dublin ○
Wicklow •
Wexford •

Carrick •
CONNAUGHT

Limerick •

KERRY

Cork •
Kinsale •

The Pale of English settlement
Added to the Pale by Henry VII
Scottish immigration

42

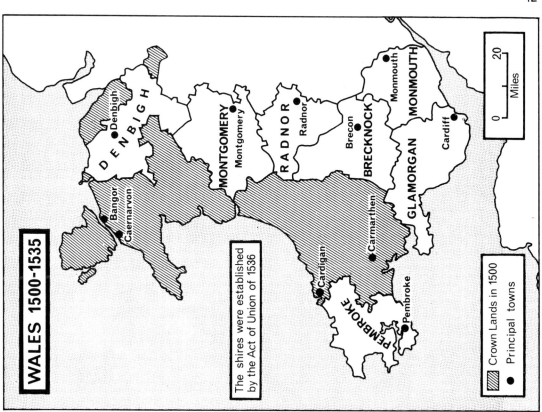

WALES 1500-1535

Bangor •
Caernarvon

DENBIGH
Denbigh •

MONTGOMERY
Montgomery •

RADNOR
Radnor •

BRECKNOCK
Brecon •

MONMOUTH
Monmouth •

GLAMORGAN
Cardiff •

Carmarthen •

Cardigan •

PEMBROKE
Pembroke •

The shires were established
by the Act of Union of 1536

0 _____ 20
Miles

Crown Lands in 1500
• Principal towns

41

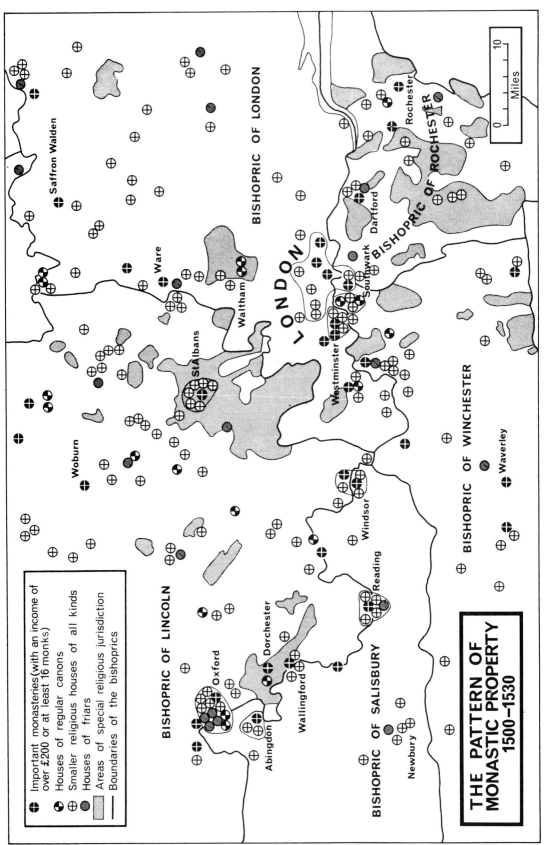

THE PATTERN OF
MONASTIC PROPERTY
1500–1530

Legend:
- Important monasteries (with an income of over £200 or at least 16 monks)
- Houses of regular canons
- Smaller religious houses of all kinds
- Houses of friars
- Areas of special religious jurisdiction
- Boundaries of the bishoprics

BISHOPRIC OF LONDON

BISHOPRIC OF ROCHESTER

BISHOPRIC OF WINCHESTER

BISHOPRIC OF LINCOLN

BISHOPRIC OF SALISBURY

LONDON

Saffron Walden

Ware

Waltham

St Albans

Woburn

Westminster

Southwark

Dartford

Rochester

Waverley

Windsor

Reading

Oxford

Dorchester

Wallingford

Abingdon

Newbury

Miles
0   10

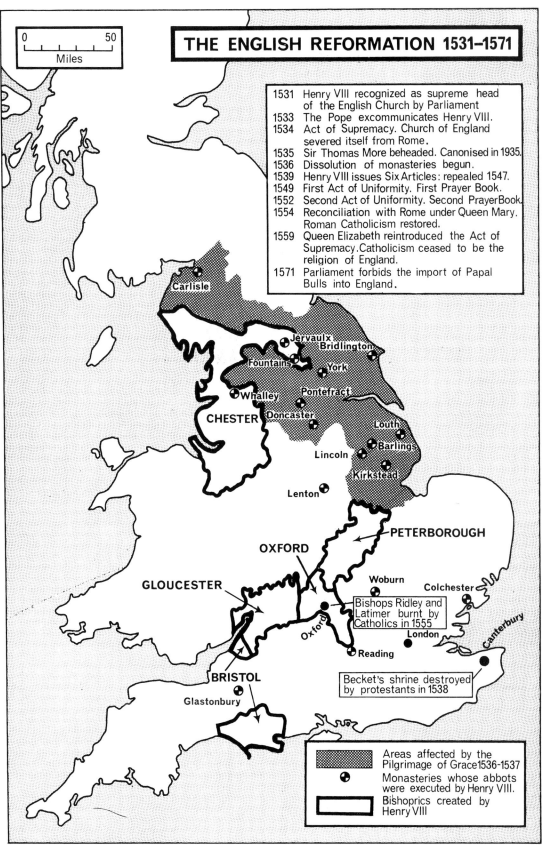

THE ENGLISH REFORMATION 1531–1571

0 — 50 Miles

1531 Henry VIII recognized as supreme head of the English Church by Parliament
1533 The Pope excommunicates Henry VIII.
1534 Act of Supremacy. Church of England severed itself from Rome.
1535 Sir Thomas More beheaded. Canonised in 1935.
1536 Dissolution of monasteries begun.
1539 Henry VIII issues Six Articles: repealed 1547.
1549 First Act of Uniformity. First Prayer Book.
1552 Second Act of Uniformity. Second Prayer Book.
1554 Reconciliation with Rome under Queen Mary. Roman Catholicism restored.
1559 Queen Elizabeth reintroduced the Act of Supremacy. Catholicism ceased to be the religion of England.
1571 Parliament forbids the import of Papal Bulls into England.

Carlisle

Jervaulx
Bridlington
Fountains
York
Whalley
Pontefract
CHESTER
Doncaster
Louth
Barlings
Lincoln
Kirkstead
Lenton

PETERBOROUGH

OXFORD

GLOUCESTER

Woburn
Colchester

Bishops Ridley and Latimer burnt by Catholics in 1555

Oxford
London
Canterbury

Reading

BRISTOL

Glastonbury

Becket's shrine destroyed by protestants in 1538

Areas affected by the Pilgrimage of Grace 1536-1537
Monasteries whose abbots were executed by Henry VIII.
Bishoprics created by Henry VIII

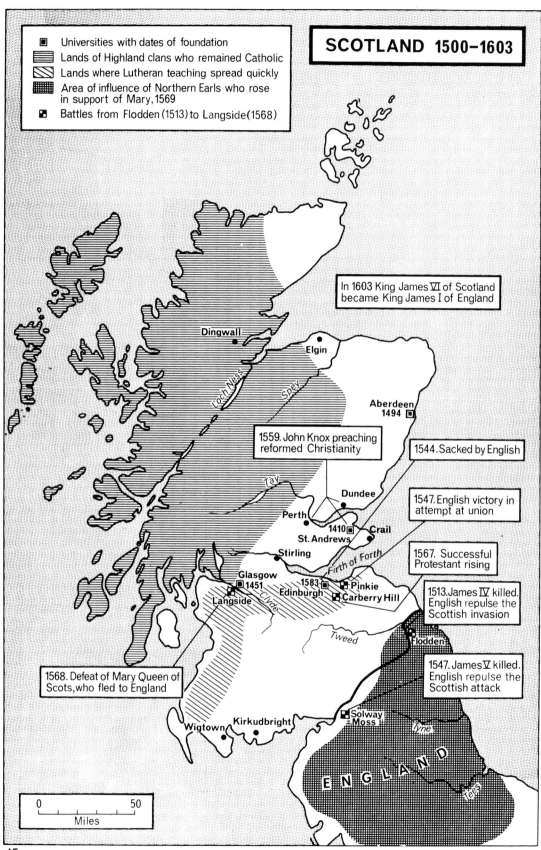

SCOTLAND 1500–1603

Universities with dates of foundation

Lands of Highland clans who remained Catholic

Lands where Lutheran teaching spread quickly

Area of influence of Northern Earls who rose in support of Mary, 1569

Battles from Flodden (1513) to Langside (1568)

In 1603 King James VI of Scotland became King James I of England

Dingwall

Elgin

Loch Ness

Spey

Aberdeen 1494

1559. John Knox preaching reformed Christianity

1544. Sacked by English

Tay

Dundee

1547. English victory in attempt at union

Perth

1410 Crail

St. Andrews

1567. Successful Protestant rising

Stirling

Firth of Forth

Glasgow

1451

1583 Pinkie

Edinburgh

Carberry Hill

1513. James IV killed. English repulse the Scottish invasion

Langside

Clyde

Tweed

Flodden

1547. James V killed. English repulse the Scottish attack

1568. Defeat of Mary Queen of Scots, who fled to England

Wigtown

Kirkudbright

Solway Moss

Tyne

ENGLAND

Tees

0   50

Miles

45

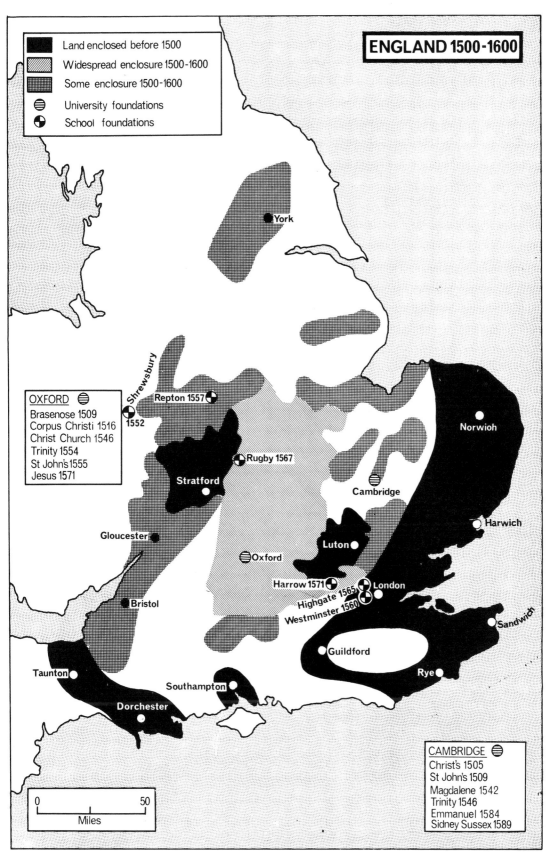

ENGLAND 1500-1600

Land enclosed before 1500
Widespread enclosure 1500-1600
Some enclosure 1500-1600
University foundations
School foundations

OXFORD
Brasenose 1509
Corpus Christi 1516
Christ Church 1546
Trinity 1554
St John's 1555
Jesus 1571

CAMBRIDGE
Christ's 1505
St John's 1509
Magdalene 1542
Trinity 1546
Emmanuel 1584
Sidney Sussex 1589

York
Shrewsbury
Repton 1557
1552
Norwioh
Rugby 1567
Stratford
Cambridge
Harwich
Gloucester
Luton
Oxford
Harrow 1571
Highgate 1565
London
Westminster 1560
Sandwich
Bristol
Guildford
Rye
Taunton
Southampton
Dorchester

0   50
Miles

46

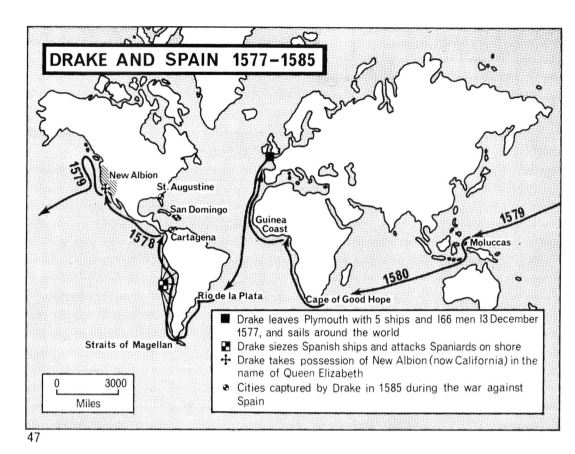

DRAKE AND SPAIN 1577–1585

1579

New Albion

St. Augustine

San Domingo

Guinea Coast

Cartagena

1578

Rio de la Plata

Cape of Good Hope

Straits of Magellan

Moluccas

1579

1580

■ Drake leaves Plymouth with 5 ships and 166 men 13 December 1577, and sails around the world

▣ Drake siezes Spanish ships and attacks Spaniards on shore

✝ Drake takes possession of New Albion (now California) in the name of Queen Elizabeth

◉ Cities captured by Drake in 1585 during the war against Spain

0   3000
Miles

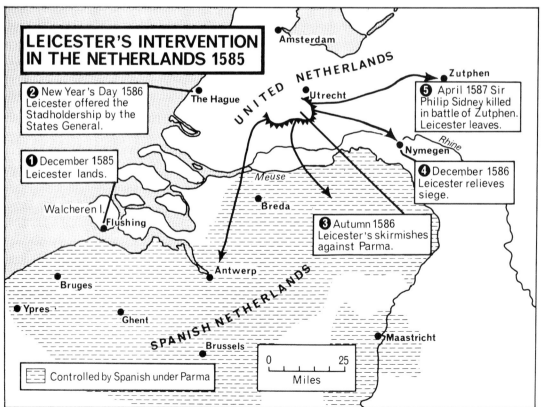

LEICESTER'S INTERVENTION IN THE NETHERLANDS 1585

Amsterdam

UNITED NETHERLANDS

Zutphen

The Hague

Utrecht

❷ New Year's Day 1586 Leicester offered the Stadholdership by the States General.

❺ April 1587 Sir Philip Sidney killed in battle of Zutphen. Leicester leaves.

Rhine

Nymegen

❶ December 1585 Leicester lands.

Meuse

❹ December 1586 Leicester relieves siege.

Walcheren I.

Flushing

Breda

❸ Autumn 1586 Leicester's skirmishes against Parma.

Antwerp

Bruges

SPANISH NETHERLANDS

Ypres

Ghent

Maastricht

Brussels

0   25
Miles

▨ Controlled by Spanish under Parma

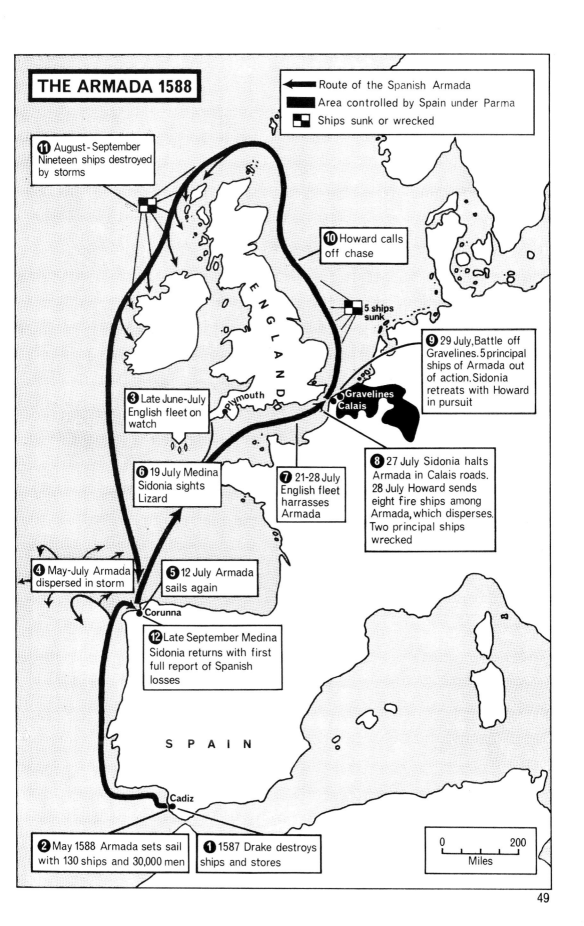

THE ARMADA 1588

Route of the Spanish Armada
Area controlled by Spain under Parma
Ships sunk or wrecked

11 August-September Nineteen ships destroyed by storms

10 Howard calls off chase

5 ships sunk

9 29 July, Battle off Gravelines. 5 principal ships of Armada out of action. Sidonia retreats with Howard in pursuit

3 Late June-July English fleet on watch

E N G L A N D

Plymouth

Gravelines
Calais

8 27 July Sidonia halts Armada in Calais roads. 28 July Howard sends eight fire ships among Armada, which disperses. Two principal ships wrecked

6 19 July Medina Sidonia sights Lizard

7 21-28 July English fleet harrasses Armada

4 May-July Armada dispersed in storm

5 12 July Armada sails again

Corunna

12 Late September Medina Sidonia returns with first full report of Spanish losses

S P A I N

Cadiz

2 May 1588 Armada sets sail with 130 ships and 30,000 men

1 1587 Drake destroys ships and stores

0   200
Miles

49

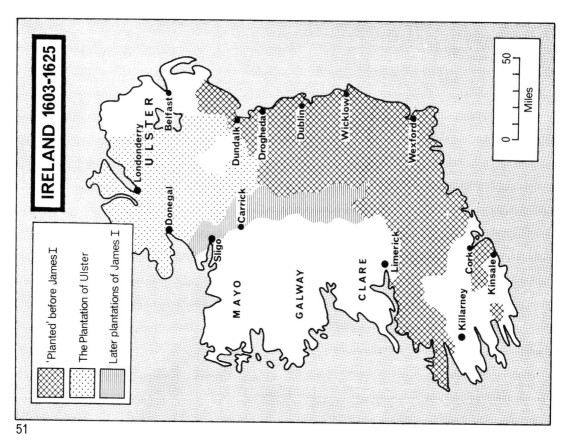

IRELAND 1603–1625

Legend:
- 'Planted' before James I
- The Plantation of Ulster
- Later plantations of James I

ULSTER

- Londonderry
- Belfast
- Donegal
- Dundalk
- Drogheda
- Dublin
- Wicklow
- Wexford
- Sligo
- Carrick
- MAYO
- GALWAY
- CLARE
- Limerick
- Killarney
- Cork
- Kinsale

0 50 Miles

51

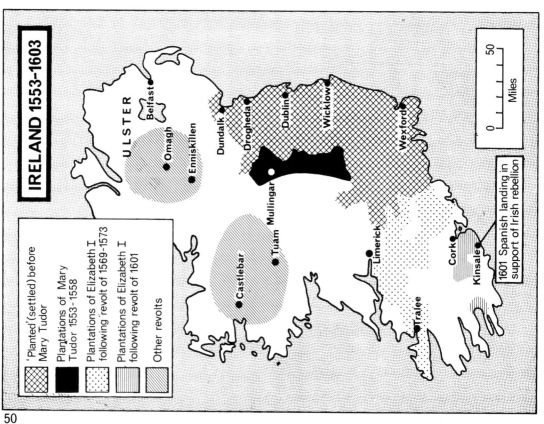

IRELAND 1553–1603

Legend:
- 'Planted' (settled) before Mary Tudor
- Plantations of Mary Tudor 1553–1558
- Plantations of Elizabeth I following 'revolt of 1569–1573
- Plantations of Elizabeth I following revolt of 1601
- Other revolts

ULSTER

- Belfast
- Omagh
- Enniskillen
- Dundalk
- Drogheda
- Dublin
- Wicklow
- Wexford
- Mullingar
- Castlebar
- Tuam
- Limerick
- Tralee
- Cork
- Kinsale

1601 Spanish landing in support of Irish rebellion

0 50 Miles

50

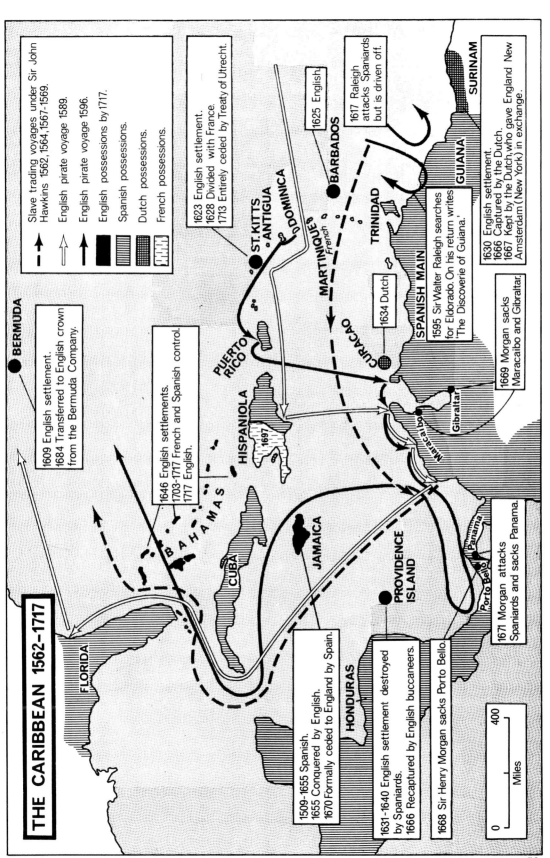

THE CARIBBEAN 1562–1717

Slave trading voyages under Sir John Hawkins 1562,1564,1567-1569.

English pirate voyage 1589.

English pirate voyage 1596.

English possessions by 1717.

Spanish possessions.

Dutch possessions.

French possessions.

BERMUDA
1609 English settlement.
1684 Transferred to English crown from the Bermuda Company.

1623 English settlement.
1628 Divided with France.
1713 Entirely ceded by Treaty of Utrecht.

ST. KITTS
ANTIGUA
DOMINICA
MARTINIQUE French
BARBADOS
1625 English.

1617 Raleigh attacks Spaniards but is driven off.

SURINAM

PUERTO RICO

HISPANIOLA
1697

BAHAMAS
1646 English settlements.
1703-1717 French and Spanish control.
1717 English.

CUBA

JAMAICA

PROVIDENCE ISLAND

CURACAO
1634 Dutch.

TRINIDAD

SPANISH MAIN

1595 Sir Walter Raleigh searches for Eldorado. On his return writes 'The Discoverie of Guiana.'

GUIANA
1630 English settlement.
1666 Captured by the Dutch.
1667 Kept by the Dutch,who gave England New Amsterdam (New York) in exchange.

Maracaibo
Gibraltar
1669 Morgan sacks Maracaibo and Gibraltar.

Porto Bello
Panama
1671 Morgan attacks Spaniards and sacks Panama.

HONDURAS

FLORIDA

1509-1655 Spanish.
1655 Conquered by English.
1670 Formally ceded to England by Spain.

1631-1640 English settlement destroyed by Spaniards.
1666 Recaptured by English buccaneers.

1668 Sir Henry Morgan sacks Porto Bello.

0   400
Miles

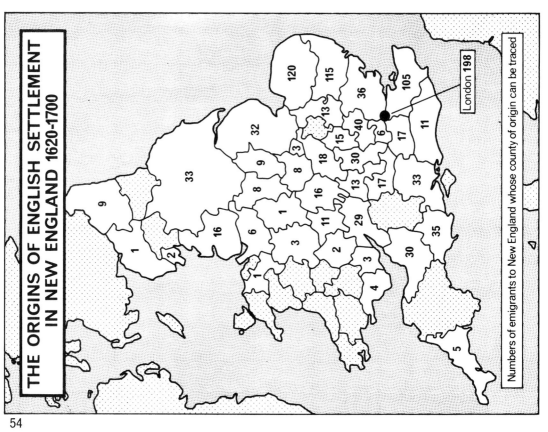

THE ORIGINS OF ENGLISH SETTLEMENT IN NEW ENGLAND 1620–1700

London 198

Numbers of emigrants to New England whose county of origin can be traced

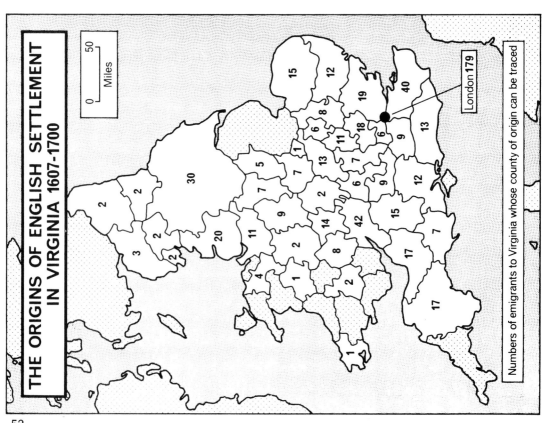

THE ORIGINS OF ENGLISH SETTLEMENT IN VIRGINIA 1607–1700

London 179

0   50
Miles

Numbers of emigrants to Virginia whose county of origin can be traced

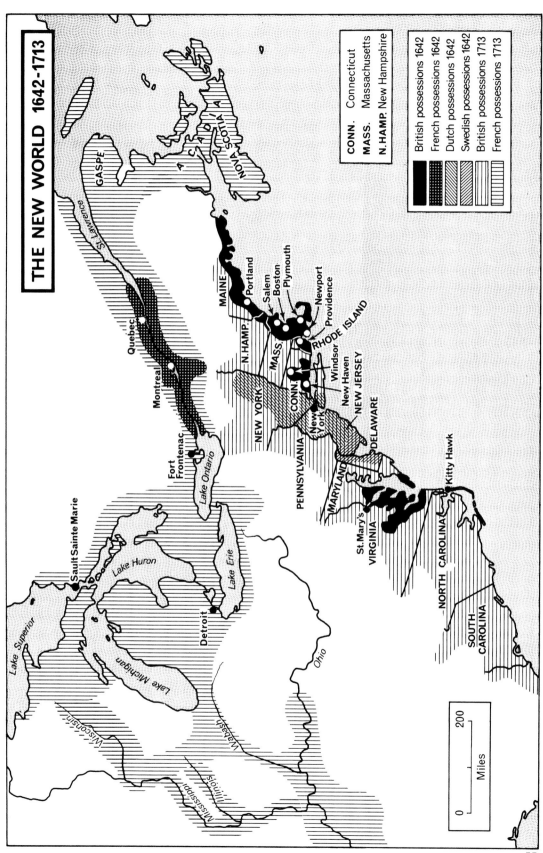

THE NEW WORLD 1642–1713

CONN. Connecticut
MASS. Massachusetts
N.HAMP. New Hampshire

British possessions 1642
French possessions 1642
Dutch possessions 1642
Swedish possessions 1642
British possessions 1713
French possessions 1713

GASPE

NOVA SCOTIA

CANADA

St. Lawrence

Quebec

Montreal

Fort Frontenac

Lake Ontario

Sault Sainte Marie

Lake Superior

Lake Michigan

Lake Huron

Lake Erie

Detroit

Wisconsin

Mississippi

Illinois

Wabash

Ohio

MAINE

Portland
Salem
Boston
Plymouth
Newport
Providence

N.HAMP.

MASS.

RHODE ISLAND

Windsor
New Haven

NEW YORK

CONN.

New York

NEW JERSEY

DELAWARE

PENNSYLVANIA

MARYLAND

St. Mary's

VIRGINIA

Kitty Hawk

NORTH CAROLINA

SOUTH CAROLINA

0   200
        Miles

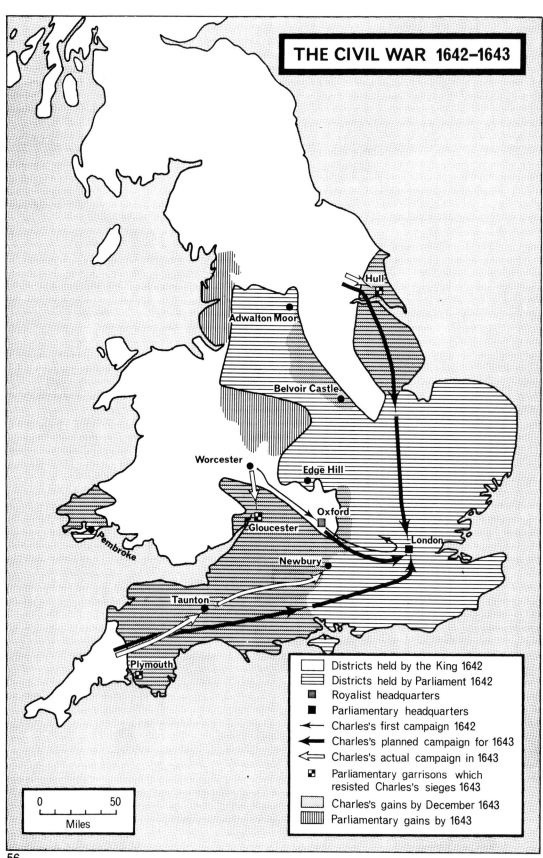

THE CIVIL WAR 1642–1643

Adwalton Moor

Belvoir Castle

Worcester

Edge Hill

Oxford

Gloucester

London

Newbury

Pembroke

Taunton

Plymouth

Hull

Districts held by the King 1642
Districts held by Parliament 1642
Royalist headquarters
Parliamentary headquarters
Charles's first campaign 1642
Charles's planned campaign for 1643
Charles's actual campaign in 1643
Parliamentary garrisons which resisted Charles's sieges 1643
Charles's gains by December 1643
Parliamentary gains by 1643

0   50
Miles

THE CIVIL WAR 1644–1646

In May 1646 King Charles surrendered to the Scottish Army at Newark.
In February 1647 the Scots sold the King to Parliament for £400,000.
He was beheaded on 30 January 1649.

Carlisle

Marston Moor

Hull

Preston
Bolton
Liverpool
Stockport
Sandal Castle
Hulme
Nantwich
Newark
Belvoir Castle
Shrewsbury
Ashby
Lichfield
Naseby
Holmby House
Banbury
Cropredy Bridge
Gloucester
Oxford
Donnington Castle
Bridgewater
Taunton
Lyme Regis
Corfe Castle
Plymouth

The Eastern Association : main recruiting ground for Parliamentary Army 1643
← Campaign of Prince Rupert to Marston Moor.
← Parliamentary advances to Marston Moor, where the Royalists were defeated 2 July 1644
Area controlled by Parliament in December 1644.
Area gained by Parliament by December 1645.
Districts held by the King in May 1646.
Area gained by Parliament by December 1646.

0   50
Miles

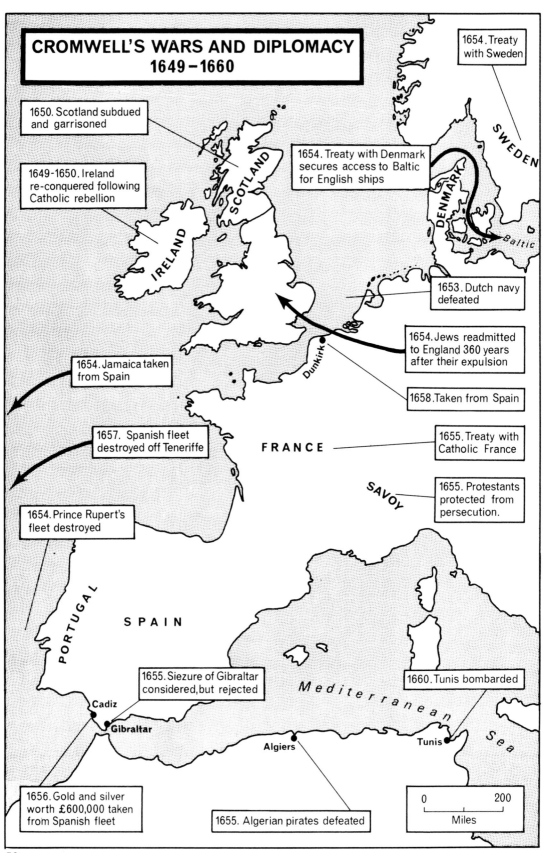

CROMWELL'S WARS AND DIPLOMACY 1649–1660

1654. Treaty with Sweden

1650. Scotland subdued and garrisoned

1649-1650. Ireland re-conquered following Catholic rebellion

1654. Treaty with Denmark secures access to Baltic for English ships

SWEDEN

DENMARK

Baltic

SCOTLAND

IRELAND

1653. Dutch navy defeated

1654. Jamaica taken from Spain

Dunkirk

1654. Jews readmitted to England 360 years after their expulsion

1658. Taken from Spain

1657. Spanish fleet destroyed off Teneriffe

FRANCE

1655. Treaty with Catholic France

SAVOY

1655. Protestants protected from persecution.

1654. Prince Rupert's fleet destroyed

PORTUGAL

SPAIN

Mediterranean Sea

1655. Siezure of Gibraltar considered, but rejected

1660. Tunis bombarded

Cadiz

Gibraltar

Algiers

Tunis

1656. Gold and silver worth £600,000 taken from Spanish fleet

1655. Algerian pirates defeated

0   200
Miles

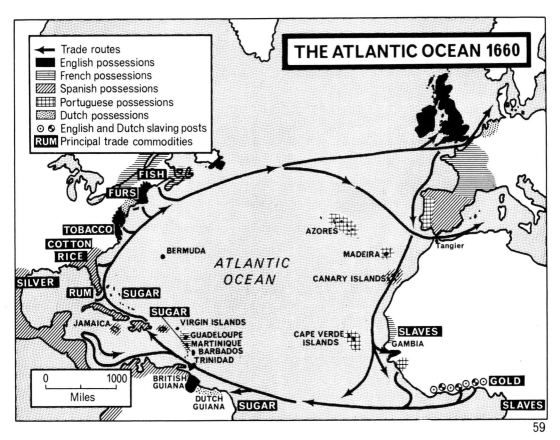

THE ATLANTIC OCEAN 1660

Trade routes
English possessions
French possessions
Spanish possessions
Portuguese possessions
Dutch possessions
⊙ ⊕ English and Dutch slaving posts
RUM Principal trade commodities

FISH
FURS
TOBACCO
COTTON
RICE
SILVER
RUM
SUGAR
SUGAR
JAMAICA
VIRGIN ISLANDS
GUADELOUPE
MARTINIQUE
BARBADOS
TRINIDAD
BERMUDA
AZORES
MADEIRA
ATLANTIC
OCEAN
CANARY ISLANDS
CAPE VERDE
ISLANDS
Tangier
SLAVES
GAMBIA
GOLD
SLAVES
BRITISH
GUIANA
DUTCH
GUIANA
SUGAR

0   1000
Miles

59

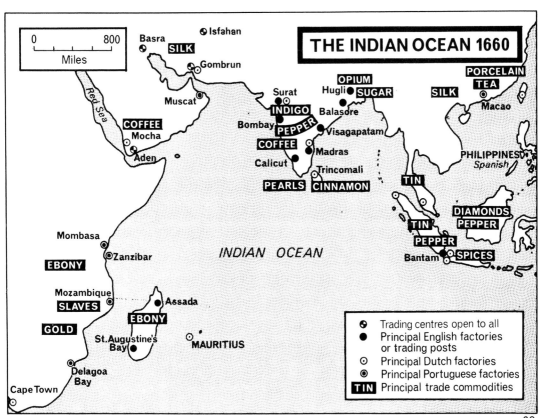

THE INDIAN OCEAN 1660

0   800
Miles

Isfahan
Basra
SILK
Gombrun
Red Sea
Muscat
COFFEE
Mocha
Aden
Surat
INDIGO
Bombay
PEPPER
COFFEE
Calicut
Hugli
OPIUM
SUGAR
Balasore
Visagapatam
Madras
Trincomali
PEARLS CINNAMON
SILK
PORCELAIN
TEA
Macao
PHILIPPINES
Spanish
TIN
DIAMONDS
PEPPER
TIN
PEPPER
Bantam
SPICES
Mombasa
Zanzibar
EBONY
INDIAN OCEAN
Mozambique
SLAVES
Assada
EBONY
GOLD
St.Augustine's
Bay
MAURITIUS
Delagoa
Bay
Cape Town

⊙ Trading centres open to all
● Principal English factories
  or trading posts
⊙ Principal Dutch factories
◉ Principal Portuguese factories
TIN Principal trade commodities

60

THE THREE DUTCH WARS

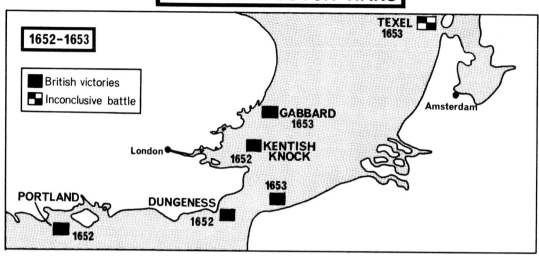

1652-1653

■ British victories
◪ Inconclusive battle

TEXEL ◪
1653

Amsterdam

■ GABBARD
1653

London ●
1652

■ KENTISH
KNOCK

1653

PORTLAND
1652

DUNGENESS
1652

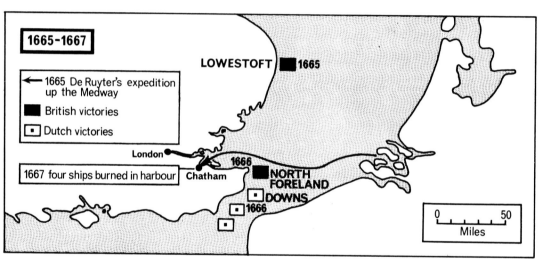

1665-1667

← 1665 De Ruyter's expedition up the Medway

■ British victories

▣ Dutch victories

1667 four ships burned in harbour

LOWESTOFT ■ 1665

London ●

Chatham

1666
■ NORTH
FORELAND
▣ DOWNS
▣ 1666
▣

0 ⎯⎯ 50
Miles

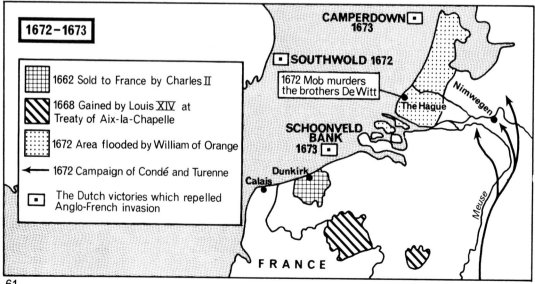

1672-1673

▦ 1662 Sold to France by Charles II

▧ 1668 Gained by Louis XIV at Treaty of Aix-la-Chapelle

▒ 1672 Area flooded by William of Orange

← 1672 Campaign of Condé and Turenne

▣ The Dutch victories which repelled Anglo-French invasion

CAMPERDOWN ▣
1673

▣ SOUTHWOLD 1672

1672 Mob murders the brothers De Witt

The Hague

Nimwegen

SCHOONVELD
BANK
1673 ▣

Dunkirk

Calais

Meuse

F R A N C E

61

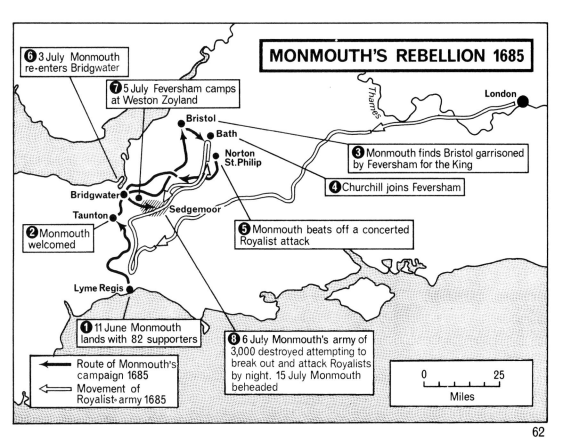

MONMOUTH'S REBELLION 1685

6 3 July Monmouth re-enters Bridgwater

7 5 July Feversham camps at Weston Zoyland

3 Monmouth finds Bristol garrisoned by Feversham for the King

4 Churchill joins Feversham

2 Monmouth welcomed

5 Monmouth beats off a concerted Royalist attack

1 11 June Monmouth lands with 82 supporters

8 6 July Monmouth's army of 3,000 destroyed attempting to break out and attack Royalists by night. 15 July Monmouth beheaded

London

Thames

Bristol
Bath
Norton St.Philip

Bridgwater
Taunton
Sedgemoor

Lyme Regis

→ Route of Monmouth's campaign 1685
⇦ Movement of Royalist army 1685

0 ___ 25
Miles

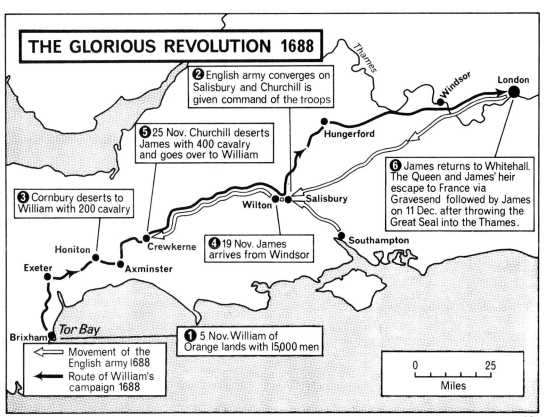

THE GLORIOUS REVOLUTION 1688

2 English army converges on Salisbury and Churchill is given command of the troops

5 25 Nov. Churchill deserts James with 400 cavalry and goes over to William

3 Cornbury deserts to William with 200 cavalry

6 James returns to Whitehall. The Queen and James' heir escape to France via Gravesend followed by James on 11 Dec. after throwing the Great Seal into the Thames.

4 19 Nov. James arrives from Windsor

1 5 Nov. William of Orange lands with 15,000 men

Thames
Windsor
London

Hungerford

Wilton
Salisbury

Southampton

Honiton
Crewkerne

Exeter
Axminster

Brixham
Tor Bay

⇦ Movement of the English army 1688
→ Route of William's campaign 1688

0 ___ 25
Miles

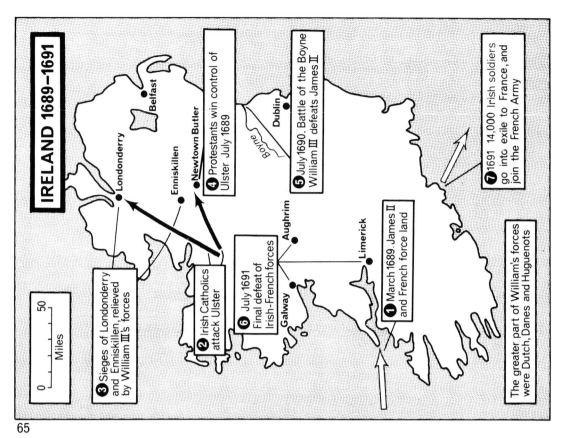

IRELAND 1689–1691

❶ March 1689. James II and French force land

❷ Irish Catholics attack Ulster

❸ Sieges of Londonderry and Enniskillen, relieved by William III's forces

❹ Protestants win control of Ulster July 1689

❺ July 1690. Battle of the Boyne William III defeats James II

❻ July 1691 Final defeat of Irish–French forces

❼ 1691 14,000 Irish soldiers go into exile to France, and join the French Army

The greater part of William's forces were Dutch, Danes and Huguenots

Londonderry · Belfast · Enniskillen · Newtown Butler · Dublin · Boyne · Aughrim · Galway · Limerick

0 — 50 Miles

65

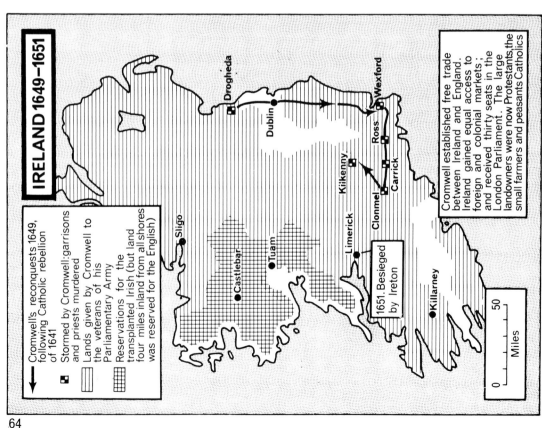

IRELAND 1649–1651

→ Cromwell's reconquests 1649, following Catholic rebellion of 1641

■ Stormed by Cromwell: garrisons and priests murdered

▥ Lands given by Cromwell to the veterans of his Parliamentary Army

▦ Reservations for the transplanted Irish (but land four miles inland from all shores was reserved for the English)

1651. Besieged by Ireton

Cromwell established free trade between Ireland and England. Ireland gained equal access to foreign and colonial markets; and received thirty seats in the London Parliament. The large landowners were now Protestants, the small farmers and peasants Catholics

Sligo · Castlebar · Tuam · Drogheda · Dublin · Kilkenny · Wexford · Ross · Carrick · Clonmel · Limerick · Killarney

0 — 50 Miles

64

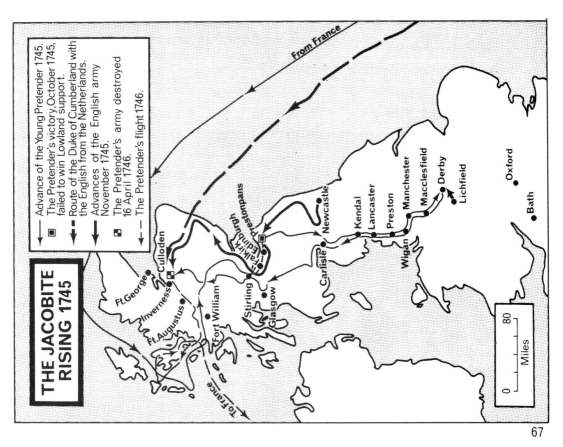

THE JACOBITE RISING 1745

Legend:
- → Advance of the Young Pretender 1745.
- ■ The Pretender's victory, October 1745, failed to win Lowland support.
- ▬▬ Route of the Duke of Cumberland with the English from the Netherlands.
- → Advances of the English army November 1745.
- ⊡ The Pretender's army destroyed 16 April 1746.
- ----- The Pretender's flight 1746.

From France

To France

Ft.George
Culloden
Inverness
Ft.Augustus
Fort William
Stirling
Glasgow
Prestonpans
Falkirk
Edinburgh
Newcastle
Carlisle
Kendal
Lancaster
Preston
Wigan
Manchester
Macclesfield
Derby
Lichfield
Oxford
Bath

0 — 80 Miles

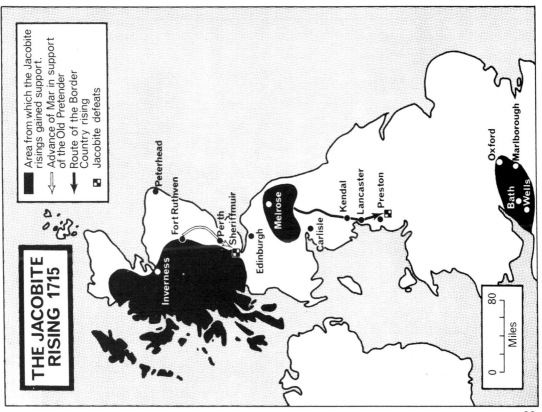

THE JACOBITE RISING 1715

Legend:
- ■ Area from which the Jacobite risings gained support.
- ⇨ Advance of Mar in support of the Old Pretender
- → Route of the Border Country rising
- ⊡ Jacobite defeats

Peterhead
Fort Ruthven
Inverness
Perth
Sheriffmuir
Edinburgh
Melrose
Carlisle
Kendal
Lancaster
Preston
Oxford
Marlborough
Bath
Wells

0 — 80 Miles

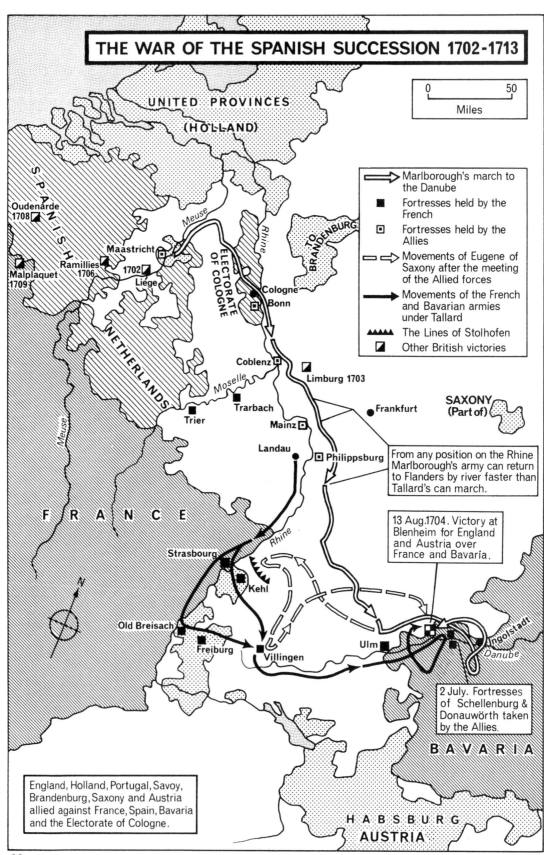

THE WAR OF THE SPANISH SUCCESSION 1702-1713

0   50
Miles

→ Marlborough's march to the Danube

■ Fortresses held by the French

▣ Fortresses held by the Allies

⇨ Movements of Eugene of Saxony after the meeting of the Allied forces

➡ Movements of the French and Bavarian armies under Tallard

▲▲▲▲▲ The Lines of Stolhofen

◪ Other British victories

UNITED PROVINCES
(HOLLAND)

S P A N I S H

Oudenarde
1708

Malplaquet
1709

Ramillies
1706

Maastricht
1702

Liège

NETHERLANDS

Meuse

Meuse

Rhine

ELECTORATE OF COLOGNE

BRANDENBURG

TO BRANDENBURG

Cologne
Bonn

Coblenz

Limburg 1703

Moselle

Trarbach

Trier

Mainz

Frankfurt

SAXONY
(Part of)

Landau

Philippsburg

From any position on the Rhine Marlborough's army can return to Flanders by river faster than Tallard's can march.

F R A N C E

Rhine

Strasbourg

Kehl

13 Aug.1704. Victory at Blenheim for England and Austria over France and Bavaria.

Old Breisach

Freiburg

Villingen

Ulm

Ingolstadt

Danube

2 July. Fortresses of Schellenburg & Donauwörth taken by the Allies.

B A V A R I A

England, Holland, Portugal, Savoy, Brandenburg, Saxony and Austria allied against France, Spain, Bavaria and the Electorate of Cologne.

H A B S B U R G
AUSTRIA

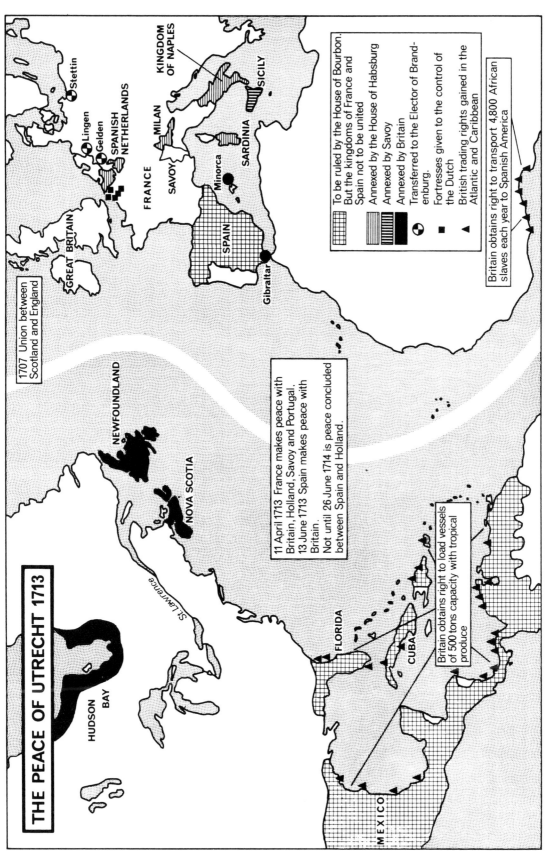

THE PEACE OF UTRECHT 1713

1707 Union between Scotland and England

11 April 1713 France makes peace with Britain, Holland, Savoy and Portugal.
13 June 1713 Spain makes peace with Britain.
Not until 26 June 1714 is peace concluded between Spain and Holland.

Britain obtains right to load vessels of 500 tons capacity with tropical produce

Britain obtains right to transport 4,800 African slaves each year to Spanish America

HUDSON BAY

St. Lawrence

NEWFOUNDLAND

NOVA SCOTIA

FLORIDA

CUBA

MEXICO

GREAT BRITAIN

Stettin

Lingen

Gelden

SPANISH NETHERLANDS

FRANCE

MILAN

SAVOY

SARDINIA

Minorca

SPAIN

Gibraltar

KINGDOM OF NAPLES

SICILY

To be ruled by the House of Bourbon. But the kingdoms of France and Spain not to be united

Annexed by the House of Habsburg

Annexed by Savoy

Annexed by Britain

Transferred to the Elector of Brandenburg.

Fortresses given to the control of the Dutch

British trading rights gained in the Atlantic and Caribbean

69

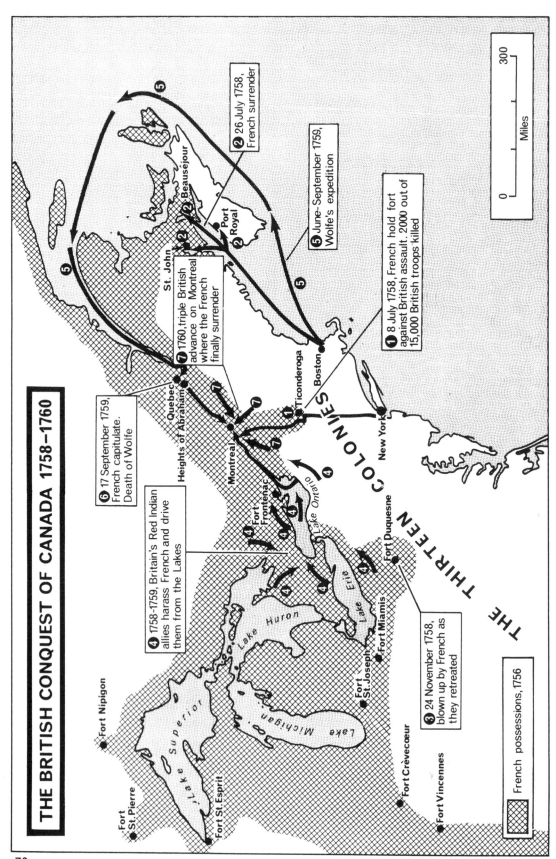

THE BRITISH CONQUEST OF CANADA 1758–1760

1 8 July 1758, French hold fort against British assault. 2000 out of 15,000 British troops killed

2 26 July 1758, French surrender

3 24 November 1758, blown up by French as they retreated

4 1758–1759, Britain's Red Indian allies harass French and drive them from the Lakes

5 June–September 1759, Wolfe's expedition

6 17 September 1759, French capitulate. Death of Wolfe

7 1760, triple British advance on Montreal where the French finally surrender

French possessions, 1756

0   300

Miles

THE THIRTEEN COLONIES

Lake Superior
Lake Michigan
Lake Huron
Lake Erie
Lake Ontario

Fort St. Pierre
Fort St. Esprit
Fort Nipigon
Fort Crèvecœur
Fort Vincennes
Fort St. Joseph
Fort Miamis
Fort Duquesne
Fort Frontenac
Montreal
Quebec
Heights of Abraham
St. John
Beauséjour
Port Royal
Ticonderoga
Boston
New York

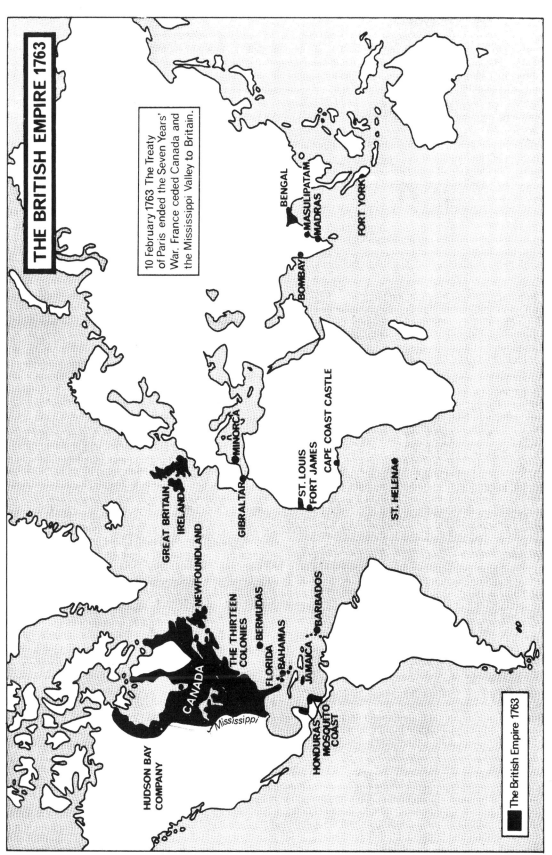

THE BRITISH EMPIRE 1763

10 February 1763 The Treaty of Paris ended the Seven Years' War. France ceded Canada and the Mississippi Valley to Britain.

BENGAL
MASULIPATAM
MADRAS
FORT YORK
BOMBAY

GREAT BRITAIN
IRELAND
NEWFOUNDLAND
GIBRALTAR
MINORCA

ST. LOUIS
FORT JAMES
CAPE COAST CASTLE

ST. HELENA

HUDSON BAY COMPANY

CANADA
Mississippi

THE THIRTEEN COLONIES
BERMUDAS
FLORIDA
BAHAMAS
JAMAICA
BARBADOS
HONDURAS
MOSQUITO COAST

■ The British Empire 1763

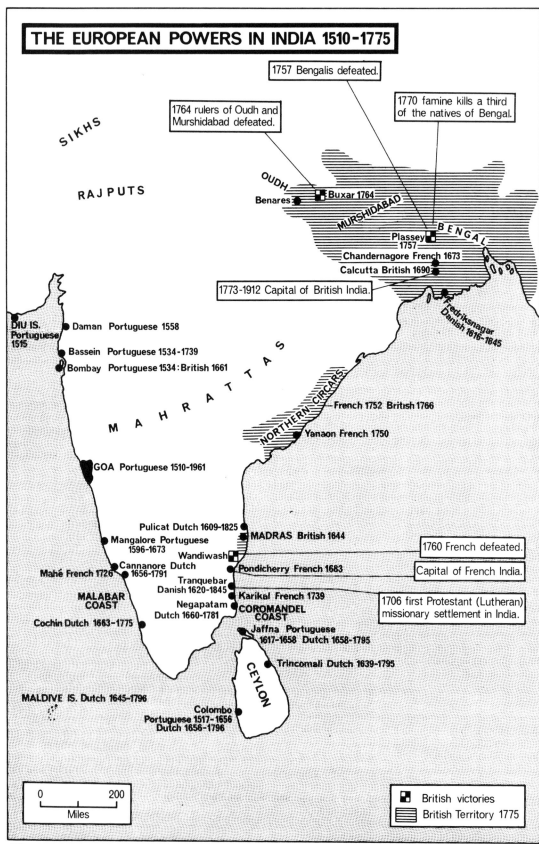

THE EUROPEAN POWERS IN INDIA 1510-1775

1757 Bengalis defeated.

1770 famine kills a third of the natives of Bengal.

1764 rulers of Oudh and Murshidabad defeated.

SIKHS

RAJPUTS

OUDH

Benares

Buxar 1764

MURSHIDABAD

BENGAL

Plassey 1757

Chandernagore French 1673

Calcutta British 1690

1773-1912 Capital of British India.

Fredriksnagar Danish 1616-1845

DIU IS. Portuguese 1515

Daman Portuguese 1558

Bassein Portuguese 1534-1739

Bombay Portuguese 1534: British 1661

M A H R A T T A S

NORTHERN CIRCARS

French 1752 British 1766

Yanaon French 1750

GOA Portuguese 1510-1961

Pulicat Dutch 1609-1825

Mangalore Portuguese 1596-1673

MADRAS British 1644

Wandiwash

1760 French defeated.

Mahé French 1726

Cannanore Dutch 1656-1791

Pondicherry French 1683

Capital of French India.

Tranquebar Danish 1620-1845

Karikal French 1739

MALABAR COAST

Negapatam Dutch 1660-1781

COROMANDEL COAST

1706 first Protestant (Lutheran) missionary settlement in India.

Cochin Dutch 1663-1775

Jaffna Portuguese 1617-1658 Dutch 1658-1795

Trincomali Dutch 1639-1795

CEYLON

MALDIVE IS. Dutch 1645-1796

Colombo Portuguese 1517-1656 Dutch 1656-1796

0   200
Miles

British victories
British Territory 1775

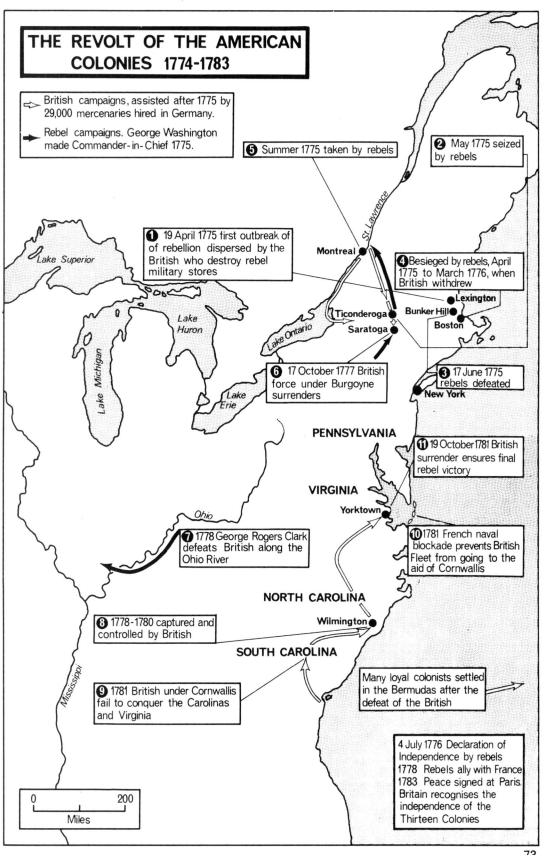

THE REVOLT OF THE AMERICAN COLONIES 1774-1783

British campaigns, assisted after 1775 by 29,000 mercenaries hired in Germany.

Rebel campaigns. George Washington made Commander-in-Chief 1775.

❺ Summer 1775 taken by rebels

❷ May 1775 seized by rebels

❶ 19 April 1775 first outbreak of of rebellion dispersed by the British who destroy rebel military stores

❹ Besieged by rebels, April 1775 to March 1776, when British withdrew

Lake Superior

Lake Huron

Lake Michigan

Lake Erie

Lake Ontario

St. Lawrence

Montreal

Ticonderoga

Saratoga

Lexington

Bunker Hill

Boston

❻ 17 October 1777 British force under Burgoyne surrenders

❸ 17 June 1775 rebels defeated

New York

PENNSYLVANIA

⓫ 19 October 1781 British surrender ensures final rebel victory

VIRGINIA

Ohio

Yorktown

❼ 1778 George Rogers Clark defeats British along the Ohio River

❿ 1781 French naval blockade prevents British Fleet from going to the aid of Cornwallis

NORTH CAROLINA

Wilmington

❽ 1778-1780 captured and controlled by British

SOUTH CAROLINA

Mississippi

❾ 1781 British under Cornwallis fail to conquer the Carolinas and Virginia

Many loyal colonists settled in the Bermudas after the defeat of the British

4 July 1776 Declaration of Independence by rebels 1778 Rebels ally with France 1783 Peace signed at Paris. Britain recognises the independence of the Thirteen Colonies

0   200
Miles

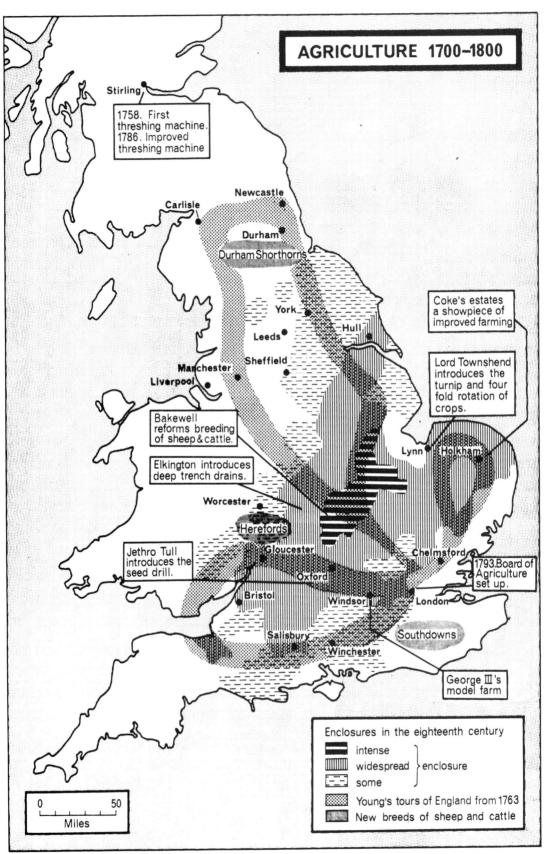

AGRICULTURE 1700–1800

1758. First threshing machine. 1786. Improved threshing machine

Stirling

Newcastle

Carlisle

Durham
Durham Shorthorns

York

Leeds

Hull

Sheffield

Manchester

Liverpool

Coke's estates a showpiece of improved farming

Lord Townshend introduces the turnip and four fold rotation of crops.

Bakewell reforms breeding of sheep & cattle.

Elkington introduces deep trench drains.

Lynn   Holkham

Worcester

Herefords

Jethro Tull introduces the seed drill.

Gloucester

Chelmsford

1793. Board of Agriculture set up.

Oxford

Bristol

Windsor

London

Salisbury

Southdowns

Winchester

George III's model farm

Enclosures in the eighteenth century

▬▬▬ intense
▥▥▥ widespread } enclosure
- - - some

Young's tours of England from 1763
New breeds of sheep and cattle

0   50
Miles

74

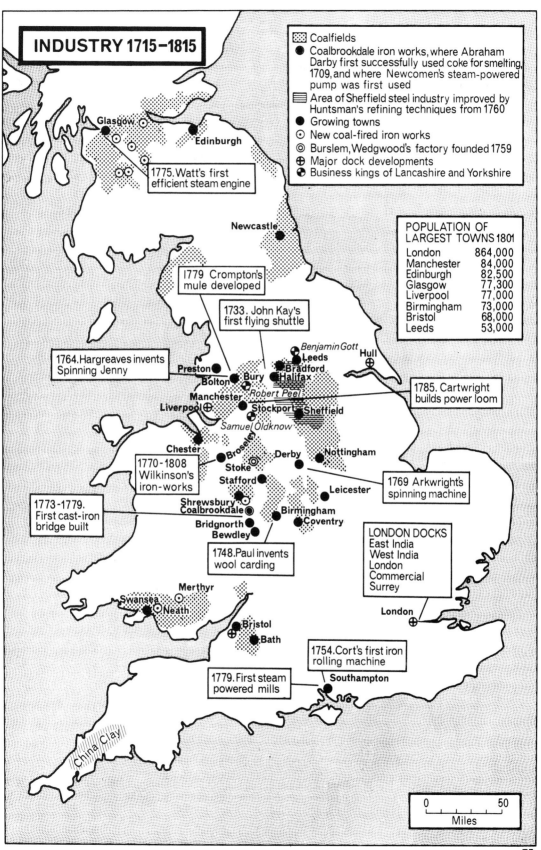

INDUSTRY 1715–1815

▨ Coalfields
● Coalbrookdale iron works, where Abraham Darby first successfully used coke for smelting, 1709, and where Newcomen's steam-powered pump was first used
▤ Area of Sheffield steel industry improved by Huntsman's refining techniques from 1760
● Growing towns
⊙ New coal-fired iron works
◎ Burslem, Wedgwood's factory founded 1759
⊕ Major dock developments
◑ Business kings of Lancashire and Yorkshire

1775. Watt's first efficient steam engine

1779 Crompton's mule developed

1733. John Kay's first flying shuttle

1764. Hargreaves invents Spinning Jenny

Benjamin Gott

1785. Cartwright builds power loom

Robert Peel

Samuel Oldknow

1770-1808 Wilkinson's iron-works

1773-1779. First cast-iron bridge built

1769 Arkwright's spinning machine

1748. Paul invents wool carding

LONDON DOCKS
East India
West India
London
Commercial
Surrey

1754. Cort's first iron rolling machine

1779. First steam powered mills

Glasgow
Edinburgh
Newcastle
Preston
Bolton   Bury
Manchester
Liverpool
Stockport
Chester
Broseley
Stoke
Stafford
Shrewsbury
Coalbrookdale
Bridgnorth
Bewdley
Leeds
Bradford
Halifax
Hull
Sheffield
Derby
Nottingham
Leicester
Birmingham
Coventry
Merthyr
Swansea
Neath
Bristol
Bath
Southampton
London

China Clay

0   50
Miles

75

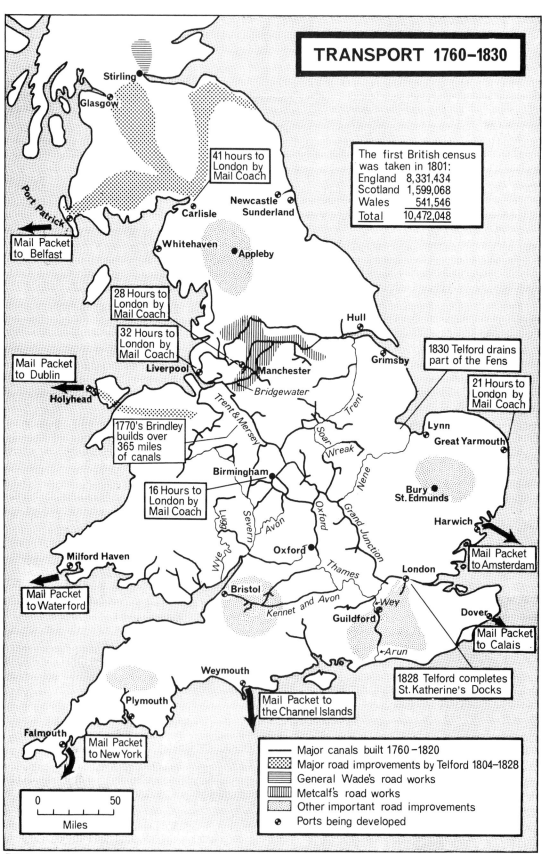

TRANSPORT 1760–1830

The first British census was taken in 1801:
England 8,331,434
Scotland 1,599,068
Wales 541,546
Total 10,472,048

Stirling

Glasgow

Port Patrick

Mail Packet to Belfast

41 hours to London by Mail Coach

Carlisle

Newcastle
Sunderland

Whitehaven

Appleby

28 Hours to London by Mail Coach

32 Hours to London by Mail Coach

Mail Packet to Dublin

Holyhead

Liverpool

Manchester

Bridgewater

Hull

Grimsby

1830 Telford drains part of the Fens

21 Hours to London by Mail Coach

1770's Brindley builds over 365 miles of canals

Trent & Mersey

Trent

Soar

Wreak

Lynn

Great Yarmouth

16 Hours to London by Mail Coach

Birmingham

Nene

Bury St. Edmunds

Harwich

Lugg

Severn

Avon

Oxford

Grand Junction

Milford Haven

Wye

Oxford

Mail Packet to Amsterdam

Mail Packet to Waterford

Bristol

Kennet and Avon

Thames

Wey

London

Guildford

Dover

Mail Packet to Calais

Arun

Weymouth

1828 Telford completes St. Katherine's Docks

Plymouth

Mail Packet to the Channel Islands

Falmouth

Mail Packet to New York

—— Major canals built 1760–1820
Major road improvements by Telford 1804–1828
General Wade's road works
Metcalf's road works
Other important road improvements
● Ports being developed

0   50
Miles

76

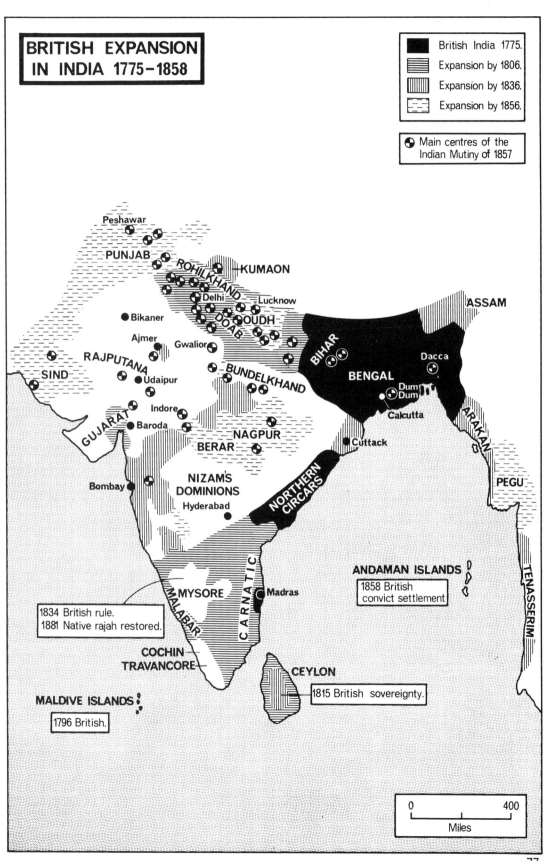

BRITISH EXPANSION IN INDIA 1775–1858

British India 1775.
Expansion by 1806.
Expansion by 1836.
Expansion by 1856.

Main centres of the Indian Mutiny of 1857

Peshawar
PUNJAB
ROHILKHAND
KUMAON
Delhi
Lucknow
Bikaner
DOAB
OUDH
Ajmer
Gwalior
RAJPUTANA
Udaipur
BUNDELKHAND
BIHAR
Dacca
ASSAM
SIND
BENGAL
Indore
Dum Dum
Baroda
GUJARAT
NAGPUR
Calcutta
ARAKAN
BERAR
Cuttack
PEGU
Bombay
NIZAM'S DOMINIONS
NORTHERN CIRCARS
Hyderabad

ANDAMAN ISLANDS
1858 British convict settlement

TENASSERIM

MYSORE
MALABAR
CARNATIC
Madras

1834 British rule.
1881 Native rajah restored.

COCHIN
TRAVANCORE

CEYLON
1815 British sovereignty.

MALDIVE ISLANDS
1796 British.

0   400
Miles

77

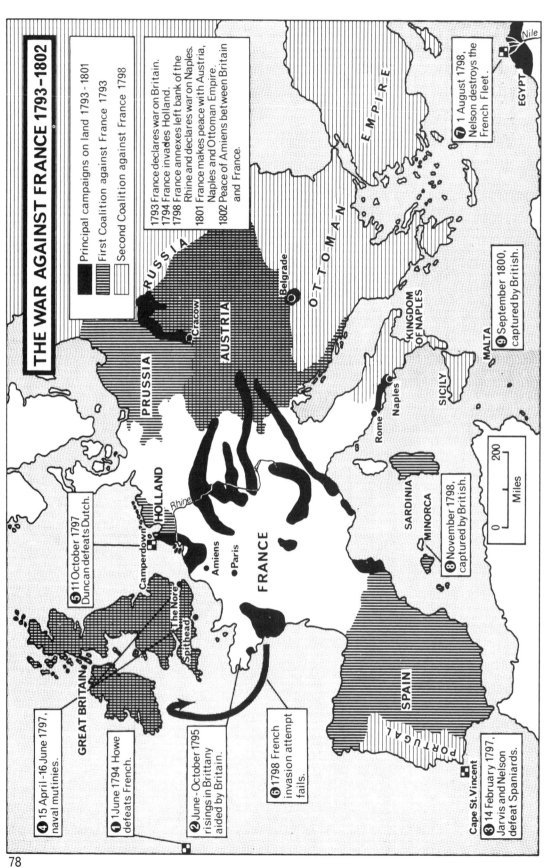

THE WAR AGAINST FRANCE 1793–1802

■ Principal campaigns on land 1793 – 1801
▥ First Coalition against France 1793
▨ Second Coalition against France 1798

1793 France declares war on Britain.
1794 France invades Holland.
1798 France annexes left bank of the Rhine and declares war on Naples.
1801 France makes peace with Austria, Naples and Ottoman Empire.
1802 Peace of Amiens between Britain and France.

4 15 April–16 June 1797, naval mutinies.

1 1 June 1794 Howe defeats French.

2 June–October 1795 risings in Brittany aided by Britain.

6 1798 French invasion attempt fails.

3 14 February 1797, Jarvis and Nelson defeat Spaniards.

Cape St. Vincent

5 11 October 1797 Duncan defeats Dutch.

7 1 August 1798, Nelson destroys the French Fleet.

9 September 1800, captured by British.

8 November 1798, captured by British.

0   200
Miles

Nile

EGYPT

OTTOMAN EMPIRE

RUSSIA

PRUSSIA

AUSTRIA

PRUSSIA

HOLLAND

GREAT BRITAIN

FRANCE

SPAIN

PORTUGAL

SARDINIA

MINORCA

SICILY

MALTA

KINGDOM OF NAPLES

Rome

Naples

Belgrade

Cracow

Paris

Amiens

Rhine

Camperdown

The Nore

Spithead

78

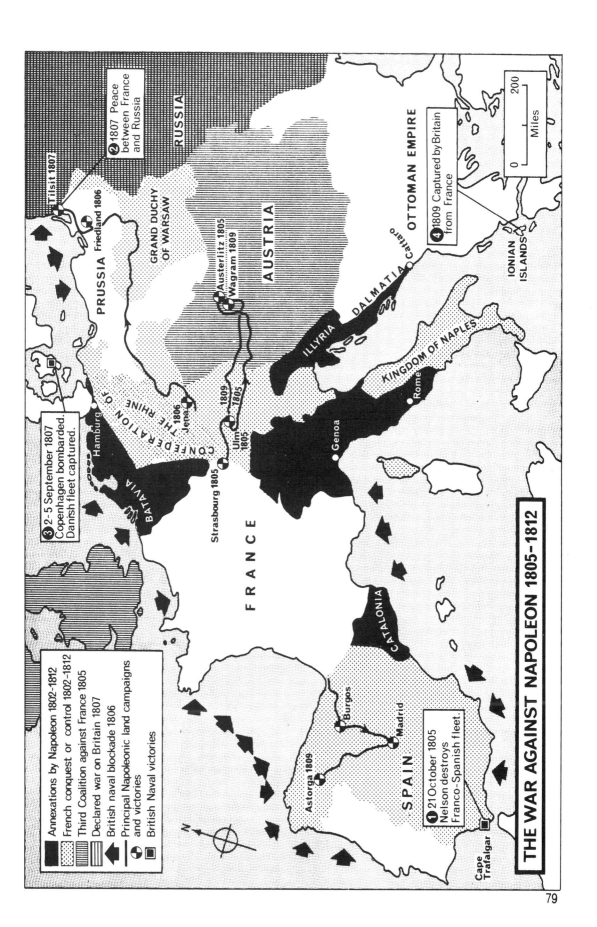

THE WAR AGAINST NAPOLEON 1805–1812

Annexations by Napoleon 1802–1812
French conquest or control 1802–1812
Third Coalition against France 1805
Declared war on Britain 1807
British naval blockade 1806
Principal Napoleonic land campaigns and victories
British Naval victories

2 1807 Peace between France and Russia

4 1809 Captured by Britain from France

3 2–5 September 1807 Copenhagen bombarded. Danish fleet captured.

1 21 October 1805 Nelson destroys Franco-Spanish fleet.

RUSSIA

OTTOMAN EMPIRE

IONIAN ISLANDS

Tilsit 1807

Friedland 1806

PRUSSIA

GRAND DUCHY OF WARSAW

AUSTRIA

Austerlitz 1805

Wagram 1809

DALMATIA

Cattaro

ILLYRIA

KINGDOM OF NAPLES

Rome

Genoa

Jena 1806

1809

1805

Ulm 1805

CONFEDERATION OF THE RHINE

BATAVIA

Hamburg

Strasbourg 1805

FRANCE

CATALONIA

SPAIN

Madrid

Burgos

Astorga 1809

Cape Trafalgar

200

0

Miles

N

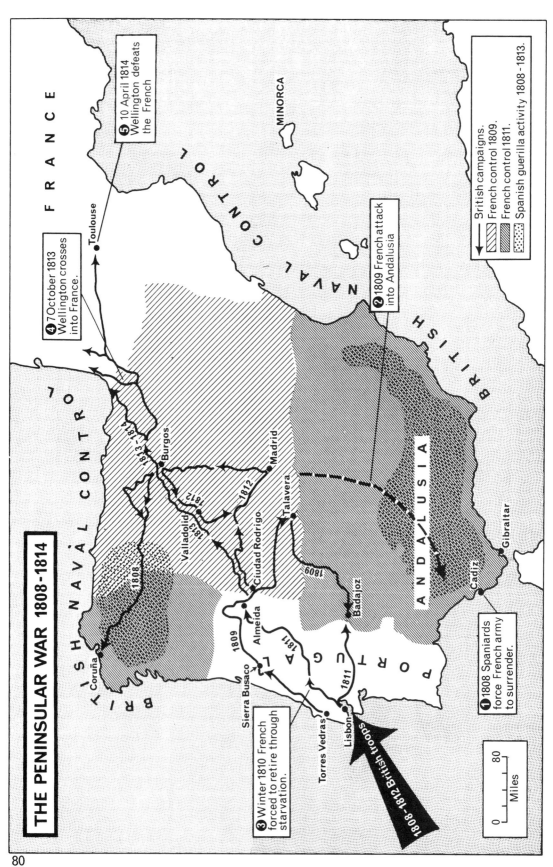

THE PENINSULAR WAR 1808-1814

FRANCE

BRITISH NAVAL CONTROL

TO

MINORCA

ANDALUSIA

PORTUGAL

5 10 April 1814 Wellington defeats the French

4 7 October 1813 Wellington crosses into France.

2 1809 French attack into Andalusia

3 Winter 1810 French forced to retire through starvation.

1 1808 Spaniards force French army to surrender.

Toulouse

Burgos

Madrid

1813-1814

1812

1812

1813

Valladolid

Ciudad Rodrigo

Talavera

1809

Badajoz

Cadiz

Gibraltar

Coruña

1808

Sierra Busaco

Almeida

1809

1811

Torres Vedras

Lisbon

1808-1812 British troops

British campaigns.
French control 1809.
French control 1811.
Spanish guerilla activity 1808 - 1813.

0   80
Miles

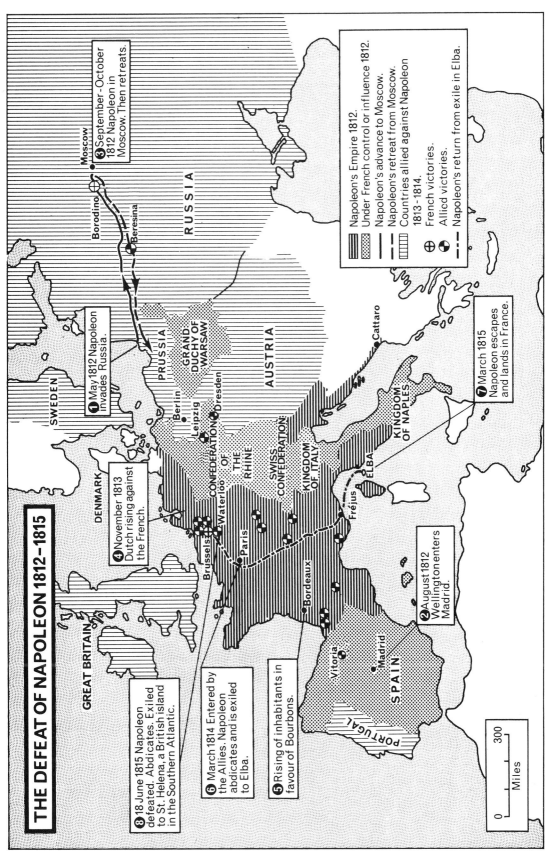

THE DEFEAT OF NAPOLEON 1812–1815

1 May 1812 Napoleon invades Russia.

2 August 1812 Wellington enters Madrid.

3 September–October 1812 Napoleon in Moscow. Then retreats.

4 November 1813 Dutch rising against the French.

5 Rising of inhabitants in favour of Bourbons.

6 March 1814 Entered by the Allies. Napoleon abdicates and is exiled to Elba.

7 March 1815 Napoleon escapes and lands in France.

8 18 June 1815 Napoleon defeated. Abdicates. Exiled to St. Helena, a British island in the Southern Atlantic.

Napoleon's Empire 1812.
Under French control or influence 1812.
Napoleon's advance to Moscow.
Napoleon's retreat from Moscow.
Countries allied against Napoleon 1813–1814.
French victories.
Allied victories.
Napoleon's return from exile in Elba.

GREAT BRITAIN

SWEDEN

DENMARK

RUSSIA

Moscow

Borodino

Beresina

PRUSSIA

GRAND DUCHY OF WARSAW

Berlin

Leipzig

Dresden

CONFEDERATION OF THE RHINE

AUSTRIA

SWISS CONFEDERATION

KINGDOM OF ITALY

Cattaro

KINGDOM OF NAPLES

ELBA

Fréjus

Waterloo

Brussels

Paris

Bordeaux

Vitoria

Madrid

SPAIN

PORTUGAL

0   300

Miles

81

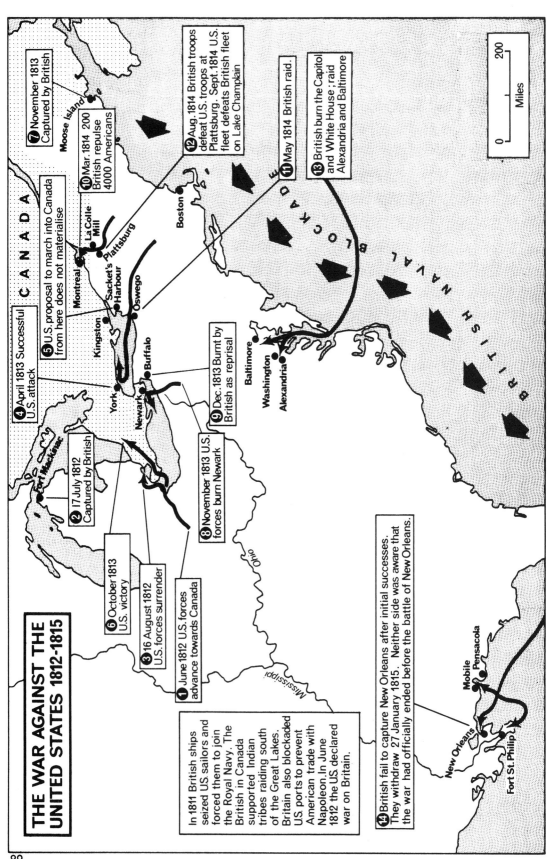

THE WAR AGAINST THE UNITED STATES 1812-1815

In 1811 British ships seized US sailors and forced them to join the Royal Navy. The British in Canada supported Indian tribes raiding south of the Great Lakes. Britain also blockaded US ports to prevent American trade with Napoleon. In June 1812 the US declared war on Britain.

1 June 1812 U.S. forces advance towards Canada

2 17 July 1812 Captured by British

3 16 August 1812 U.S. forces surrender

4 April 1813 Successful U.S. attack

5 U.S. proposal to march into Canada from here does not materialise

6 October 1813 U.S. victory

7 November 1813 Captured by British

8 November 1813 U.S. forces burn Newark

9 Dec. 1813 Burnt by British as reprisal

10 Mar. 1814 200 British repulse 4000 Americans

11 May 1814 British raid.

12 Aug. 1814 British troops defeat U.S. troops at Plattsburg. Sept. 1814 U.S. fleet defeats British fleet on Lake Champlain

13 British burn the Capitol and White House; raid Alexandria and Baltimore

14 British fail to capture New Orleans after initial successes. They withdraw 27 January 1815. Neither side was aware that the war had officially ended before the battle of New Orleans.

BRITISH NAVAL BLOCKADE

Moose Island

La Colle Mill

Plattsburg

Sacket's Harbour

Montreal

Kingston

Oswego

York

Newark

Buffalo

Boston

Baltimore

Washington

Alexandria

Fort Mackinac

Ohio

Mississippi

New Orleans

Mobile

Pensacola

Fort St. Philip

CANADA

0   200
Miles

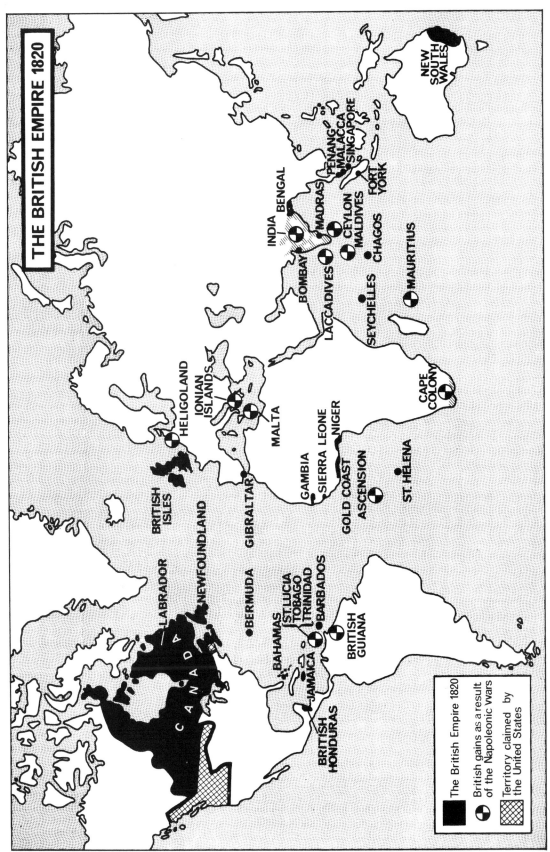

THE BRITISH EMPIRE 1820

NEW SOUTH WALES

PENANG
MALACCA
SINGAPORE

INDIA
BENGAL
MADRAS
BOMBAY
CEYLON
MALDIVES
LACCADIVES
FORT YORK
SEYCHELLES
CHAGOS
MAURITIUS

HELIGOLAND
IONIAN ISLANDS
MALTA

BRITISH ISLES

GIBRALTAR

GAMBIA
SIERRA LEONE
NIGER
GOLD COAST
ASCENSION
ST. HELENA

CAPE COLONY

LABRADOR
NEWFOUNDLAND

BERMUDA

CANADA

BAHAMAS
ST LUCIA
TOBAGO
TRINIDAD
BARBADOS
JAMAICA
BRITISH GUIANA

BRITISH HONDURAS

The British Empire 1820

British gains as a result of the Napoleonic wars

Territory claimed by the United States

83

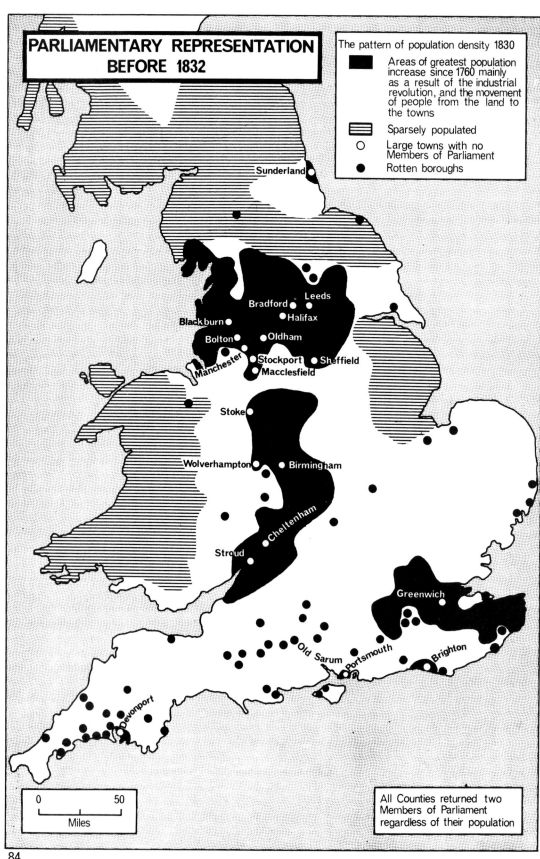

PARLIAMENTARY REPRESENTATION BEFORE 1832

The pattern of population density 1830

■ Areas of greatest population increase since 1760 mainly as a result of the industrial revolution, and the movement of people from the land to the towns

▤ Sparsely populated

○ Large towns with no Members of Parliament

● Rotten boroughs

Sunderland

Bradford
Leeds
Halifax
Blackburn
Bolton
Oldham
Manchester
Stockport
Sheffield
Macclesfield

Stoke

Wolverhampton
Birmingham

Cheltenham

Stroud

Greenwich

Old Sarum
Portsmouth
Brighton

Devonport

0   50
Miles

All Counties returned two Members of Parliament regardless of their population

84

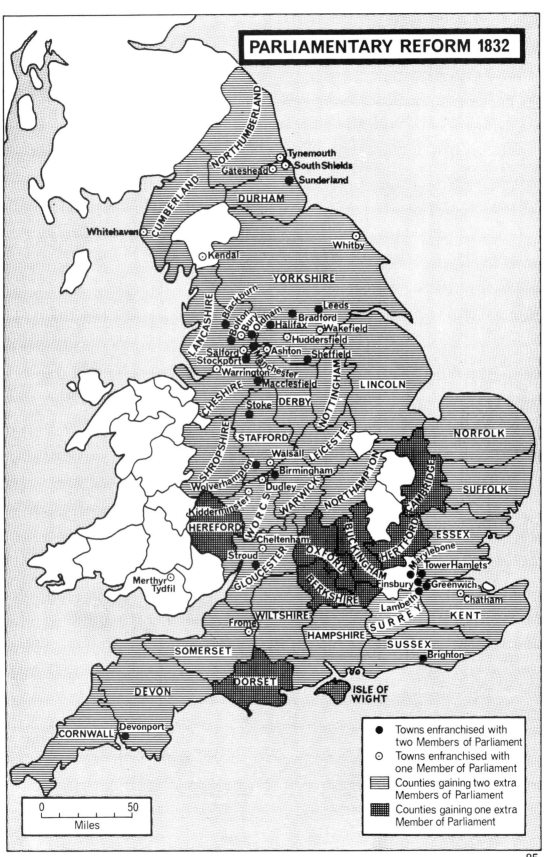

PARLIAMENTARY REFORM 1832

Legend:

- ● Towns enfranchised with two Members of Parliament
- ☉ Towns enfranchised with one Member of Parliament
- ▤ Counties gaining two extra Members of Parliament
- ▦ Counties gaining one extra Member of Parliament

0 — 50 Miles

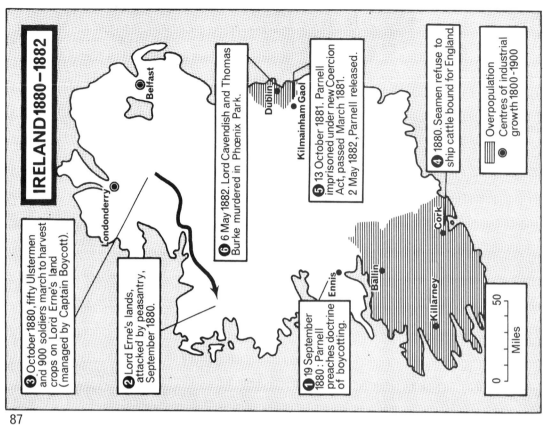

IRELAND 1880–1882

❸ October 1880, fifty Ulstermen and 900 soldiers march to harvest crops on Lord Erne's land (managed by Captain Boycott).

❷ Lord Erne's lands, attacked by peasantry, September 1880.

❶ 19 September 1880 : Parnell preaches doctrine of boycotting.

❻ 6 May 1882. Lord Cavendish and Thomas Burke murdered in Phoenix Park.

❺ 13 October 1881. Parnell imprisoned under new Coercion Act, passed March 1881. 2 May 1882 ,Parnell released.

❹ 1880. Seamen refuse to ship cattle bound for England.

Belfast

Londonderry

Dublin

Kilmainham Gaol

Ennis

Ballin

Cork

Killarney

⫴ Overpopulation
◉ Centres of industrial growth 1800-1900

0   50
Miles

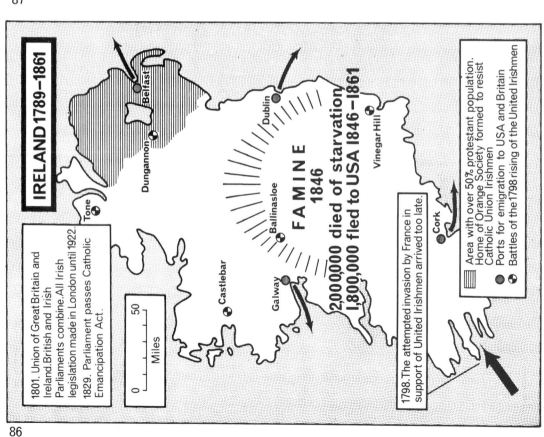

IRELAND 1789–1861

1801. Union of Great Britain and Ireland. British and Irish Parliaments combine. All Irish legislation made in London until 1922.

1829. Parliament passes Catholic Emancipation Act.

0   50
Miles

Tone

Belfast

Dungannon

Castlebar

Galway

Ballinasloe

Dublin

Vinegar Hill

Cork

FAMINE 1846

2,000,000 died of starvation
1,800,000 fled to USA 1846–1861

1798. The attempted invasion by France in support of United Irishmen arrived too late.

⫴ Area with over 50% protestant population. Home of Orange Society formed to resist Catholic Union Irishmen
◐ Ports for emigration to USA and Britain
◑ Battles of the 1798 rising of the United Irishmen

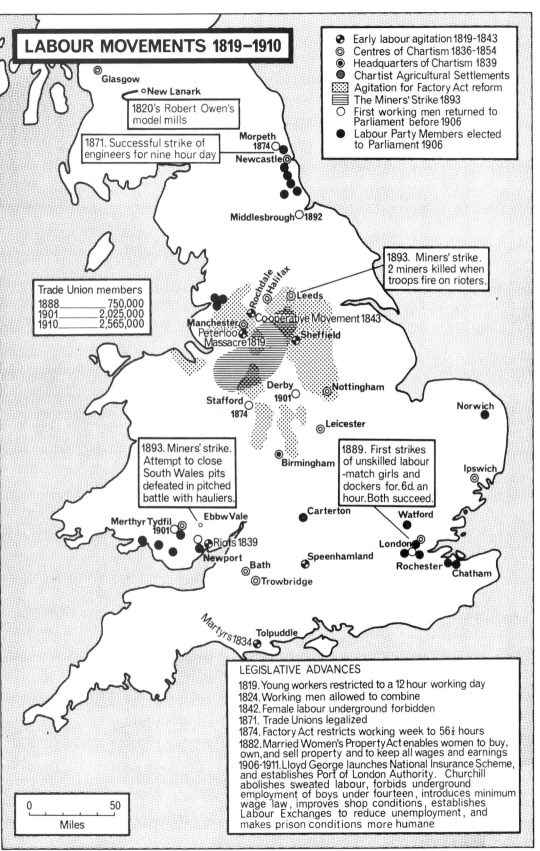

LABOUR MOVEMENTS 1819–1910

Legend:
- ◉ Early labour agitation 1819-1843
- ◎ Centres of Chartism 1836-1854
- ◉ Headquarters of Chartism 1839
- ⊜ Chartist Agricultural Settlements
- ▦ Agitation for Factory Act reform
- ▤ The Miners' Strike 1893
- ○ First working men returned to Parliament before 1906
- ● Labour Party Members elected to Parliament 1906

◎ Glasgow
○ New Lanark

1820's Robert Owen's model mills

1871. Successful strike of engineers for nine hour day

Morpeth 1874 ○
Newcastle ◎

Middlesbrough ○ 1892

1893. Miners' strike. 2 miners killed when troops fire on rioters.

Trade Union members
1888	750,000
1901	2,025,000
1910	2,565,000

Rochdale
Halifax
◎ Leeds

Co-operative Movement 1843

Manchester ◎
Peterloo
Massacre 1819
◉ Sheffield

Derby 1901 ○
◎ Nottingham

Stafford 1874 ○

Norwich ●

◎ Leicester

1893. Miners' strike. Attempt to close South Wales pits defeated in pitched battle with hauliers.

◎ Birmingham

1889. First strikes of unskilled labour -match girls and dockers for 6d. an hour. Both succeed.

Ipswich ◎

Merthyr Tydfil 1901 ○

Ebbw Vale ○

Carterton
Watford ●

○ Riots 1839
Newport

London ◎
Rochester
Chatham

Bath ◎
⊜ Speenhamland

◎ Trowbridge

Martyrs 1834 Tolpuddle

LEGISLATIVE ADVANCES
1819. Young workers restricted to a 12 hour working day
1824. Working men allowed to combine
1842. Female labour underground forbidden
1871. Trade Unions legalized
1874. Factory Act restricts working week to 56½ hours
1882. Married Women's Property Act enables women to buy, own, and sell property and to keep all wages and earnings
1906-1911. Lloyd George launches National Insurance Scheme, and establishes Port of London Authority. Churchill abolishes sweated labour, forbids underground employment of boys under fourteen, introduces minimum wage law, improves shop conditions, establishes Labour Exchanges to reduce unemployment, and makes prison conditions more humane

0   50
Miles

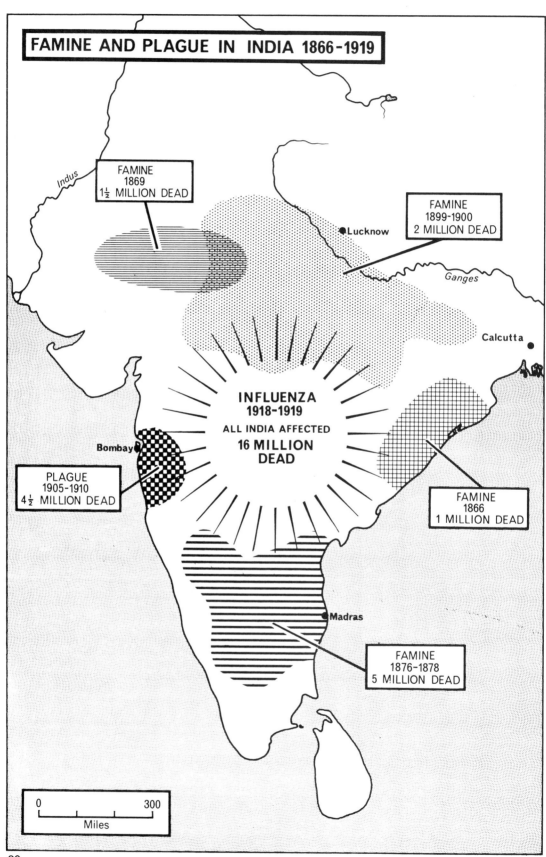

FAMINE AND PLAGUE IN INDIA 1866-1919

FAMINE
1869
1½ MILLION DEAD

FAMINE
1899-1900
2 MILLION DEAD

Lucknow

Ganges

Calcutta

INFLUENZA
1918-1919
ALL INDIA AFFECTED
16 MILLION
DEAD

Bombay

PLAGUE
1905-1910
4½ MILLION DEAD

FAMINE
1866
1 MILLION DEAD

Madras

FAMINE
1876-1878
5 MILLION DEAD

0   300
Miles

Indus

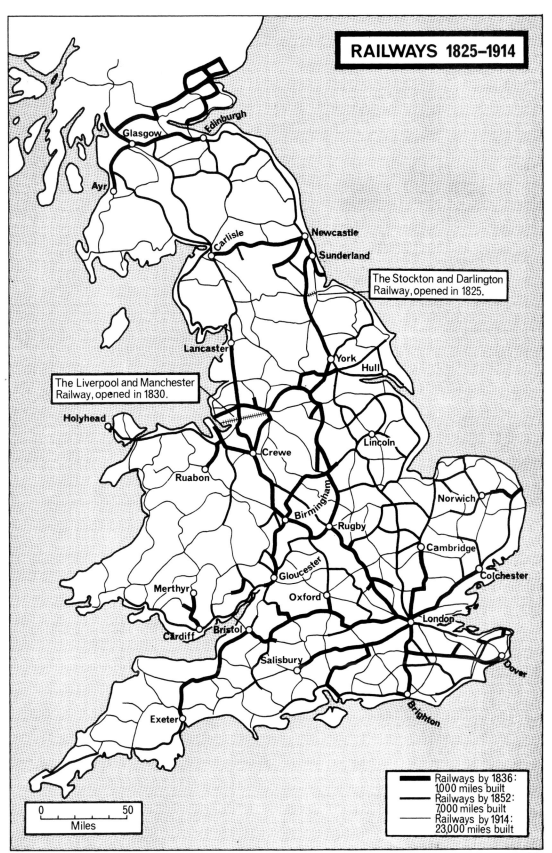

RAILWAYS 1825–1914

The Stockton and Darlington Railway, opened in 1825.

The Liverpool and Manchester Railway, opened in 1830.

Glasgow
Edinburgh
Ayr
Carlisle
Newcastle
Sunderland
Lancaster
York
Hull
Holyhead
Crewe
Lincoln
Ruabon
Birmingham
Norwich
Rugby
Cambridge
Gloucester
Colchester
Merthyr
Oxford
Cardiff
Bristol
London
Salisbury
Dover
Brighton
Exeter

0   50
Miles

Railways by 1836:
1,000 miles built
Railways by 1852:
7,000 miles built
Railways by 1914:
23,000 miles built

90

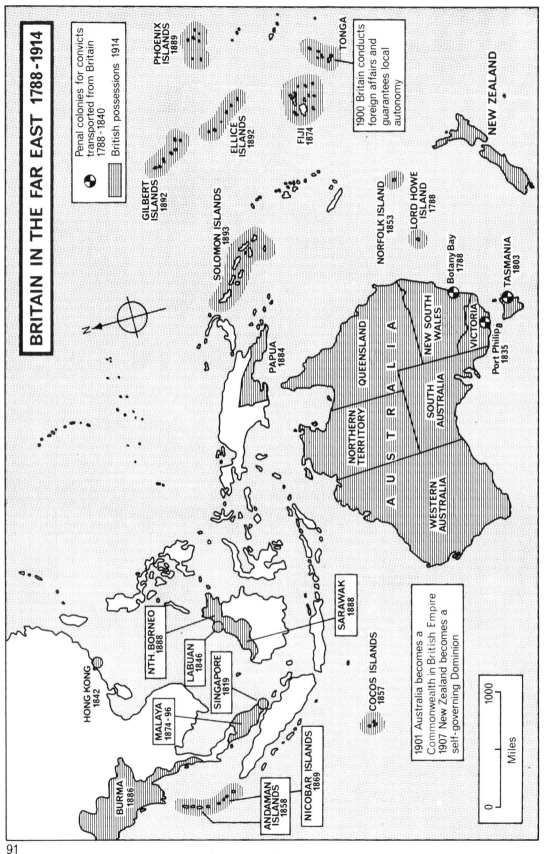

BRITAIN IN THE FAR EAST 1788-1914

Penal colonies for convicts transported from Britain 1788-1840

British possessions 1914

PHOENIX ISLANDS 1889

TONGA

1900 Britain conducts foreign affairs and guarantees local autonomy

NEW ZEALAND

GILBERT ISLANDS 1892

ELLICE ISLANDS 1892

FIJI 1874

SOLOMON ISLANDS 1893

NORFOLK ISLAND 1853

LORD HOWE ISLAND 1788

N

PAPUA 1884

QUEENSLAND

NORTHERN TERRITORY

NEW SOUTH WALES

Botany Bay 1788

A U S T R A L I A

VICTORIA

Port Philip 1835

TASMANIA 1803

WESTERN AUSTRALIA

SOUTH AUSTRALIA

HONG KONG 1842

NTH. BORNEO 1888

LABUAN 1846

SINGAPORE 1819

SARAWAK 1888

COCOS ISLANDS 1857

MALAYA 1874-96

1901 Australia becomes a Commonwealth in British Empire
1907 New Zealand becomes a self-governing Dominion

BURMA 1886

ANDAMAN ISLANDS 1858

NICOBAR ISLANDS 1869

0   1000

Miles

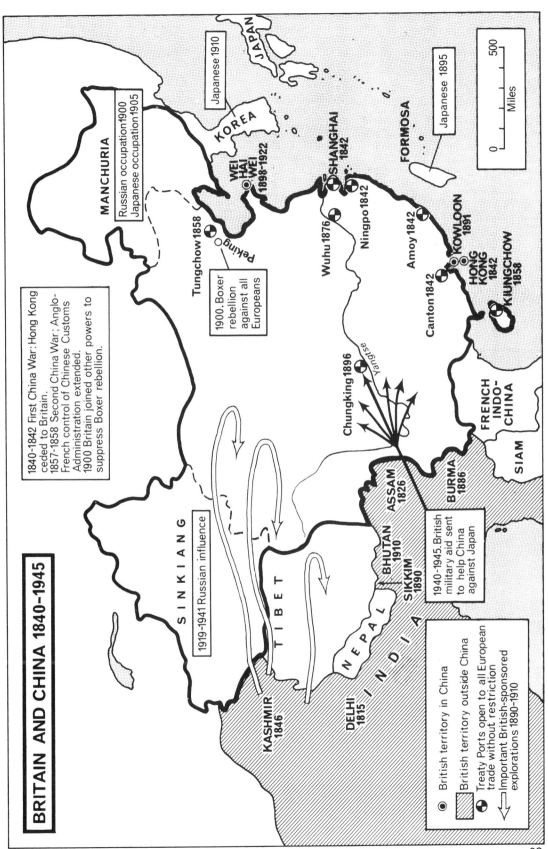

BRITAIN AND CHINA 1840-1945

1840-1842 First China War: Hong Kong ceded to Britain.
1857-1858 Second China War; Anglo-French control of Chinese Customs Administration extended.
1900 Britain joined other powers to suppress Boxer rebellion.

MANCHURIA
Russian occupation 1900
Japanese occupation 1905

JAPAN

Japanese 1910

KOREA

WEI HAI WEI 1898-1922

SHANGHAI 1842

FORMOSA

Japanese 1895

Tungchow 1858

Peking

1900. Boxer rebellion against all Europeans

Wuhu 1876

Ningpo 1842

Amoy 1842

KOWLOON 1891

HONG KONG 1842

KIUNGCHOW 1858

Canton 1842

Chungking 1896

Yangtse

FRENCH INDO-CHINA

SIAM

BURMA 1886

1940-1945. British military aid sent to help China against Japan

SINKIANG

1919-1941 Russian influence

TIBET

BHUTAN 1910

ASSAM 1826

SIKKIM 1890

NEPAL

KASHMIR 1846

INDIA

DELHI 1815

500

0   Miles

● British territory in China

British territory outside China

Treaty Ports open to all European trade without restriction

Important British-sponsored explorations 1890-1910

92

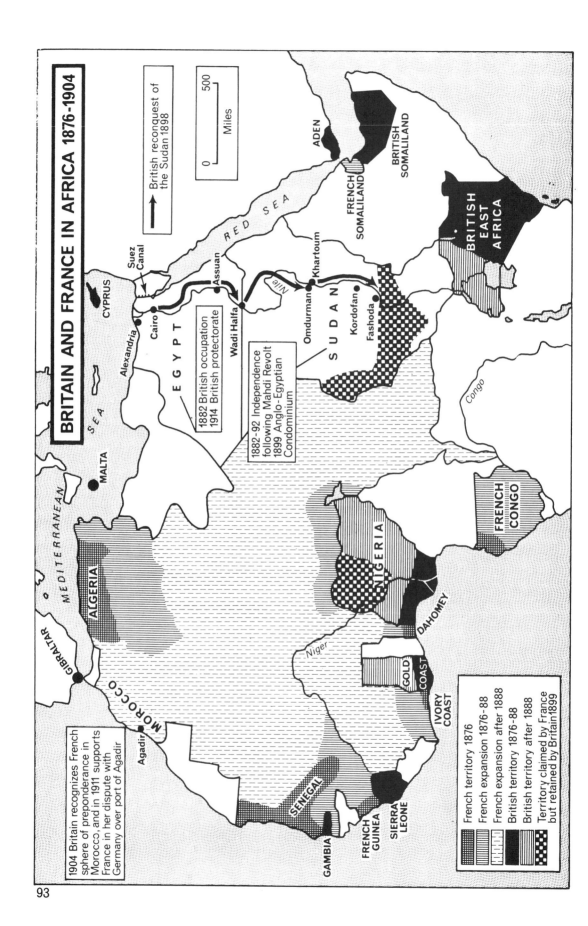

BRITAIN AND FRANCE IN AFRICA 1876-1904

British reconquest of the Sudan 1898

500

0

Miles

→ British reconquest of the Sudan 1898

1882 British occupation
1914 British protectorate

1882-92 Independence following Mahdi Revolt
1899 Anglo-Egyptian Condominium

RED SEA

ADEN

FRENCH SOMALILAND

BRITISH SOMALILAND

BRITISH EAST AFRICA

Suez Canal

Assuan

Cairo

Alexandria

CYPRUS

Wadi Halfa

EGYPT

Nile

Khartoum

Omdurman

Kordofan

Fashoda

SUDAN

Congo

MALTA

SEA

MEDITERRANEAN

FRENCH CONGO

ALGERIA

GIBRALTAR

MOROCCO

Agadir

Niger

NIGERIA

DAHOMEY

GOLD COAST

IVORY COAST

SIERRA LEONE

FRENCH GUINEA

SENEGAL

GAMBIA

1904 Britain recognizes French sphere of preponderance in Morocco, and in 1911 supports France in her dispute with Germany over port of Agadir

French territory 1876
French expansion 1876-88
French expansion after 1888
British territory 1876-88
British territory after 1888
Territory claimed by France but retained by Britain 1899

93

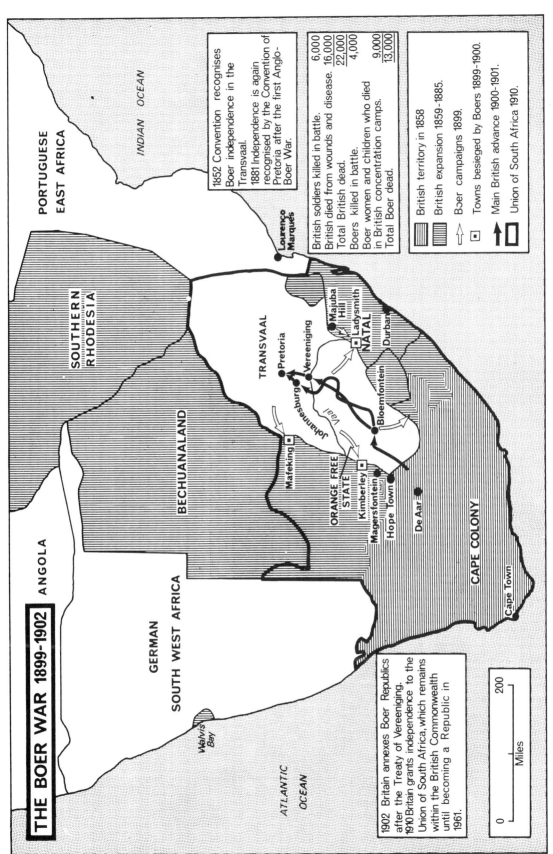

THE BOER WAR 1899-1902

PORTUGUESE
EAST AFRICA

INDIAN OCEAN

ANGOLA

GERMAN
SOUTH WEST AFRICA

ATLANTIC
OCEAN

Walvis
Bay

SOUTHERN
RHODESIA

BECHUANALAND

TRANSVAAL

Pretoria
Johannesburg
Vereeniging
Majuba Hill
Ladysmith
NATAL
Durban

Mafeking

Vaal

Bloemfontein

ORANGE FREE
STATE

Kimberley
Magersfontein
Hope Town
De Aar

CAPE COLONY

Cape Town

Lourenço
Marques

1852 Convention recognises
Boer independence in the
Transvaal.
1881 Independence is again
recognised by the Convention of
Pretoria after the first Anglo-
Boer War.

British soldiers killed in battle.	6,000
British died from wounds and disease.	16,000
Total British dead.	22,000
Boers killed in battle.	4,000
Boer women and children who died in British concentration camps.	9,000
Total Boer dead.	13,000

British territory in 1858

British expansion 1859-1885.

Boer campaigns 1899.

Towns besieged by Boers 1899-1900.

Main British advance 1900-1901.

Union of South Africa 1910.

1902 Britain annexes Boer Republics
after the Treaty of Vereeniging.
1910 Britain grants independence to the
Union of South Africa, which remains
within the British Commonwealth
until becoming a Republic in
1961.

0   Miles   200

94

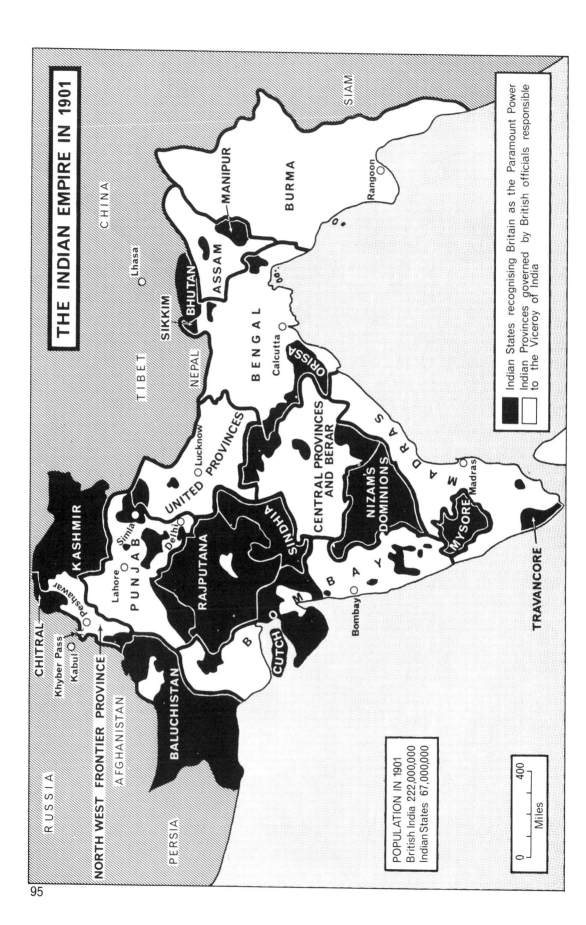

THE INDIAN EMPIRE IN 1901

Indian States recognising Britain as the Paramount Power

Indian Provinces governed by British officials responsible to the Viceroy of India

POPULATION IN 1901
British India 222,000,000
Indian States 67,000,000

0   400
Miles

RUSSIA
PERSIA
AFGHANISTAN
NORTH WEST FRONTIER PROVINCE
CHITRAL
Kabul
Khyber Pass
Peshawar
KASHMIR
BALUCHISTAN
PUNJAB
Lahore
Simla
Delhi
RAJPUTANA
SINDHIA
CUTCH
B
UNITED PROVINCES
Lucknow
TIBET
Lhasa
NEPAL
SIKKIM
BHUTAN
ASSAM
MANIPUR
CHINA
BURMA
Rangoon
SIAM
BENGAL
Calcutta
ORISSA
CENTRAL PROVINCES AND BERAR
NIZAM'S DOMINIONS
MADRAS
Madras
MYSORE
TRAVANCORE
Bombay
B A Y
O F
M

95

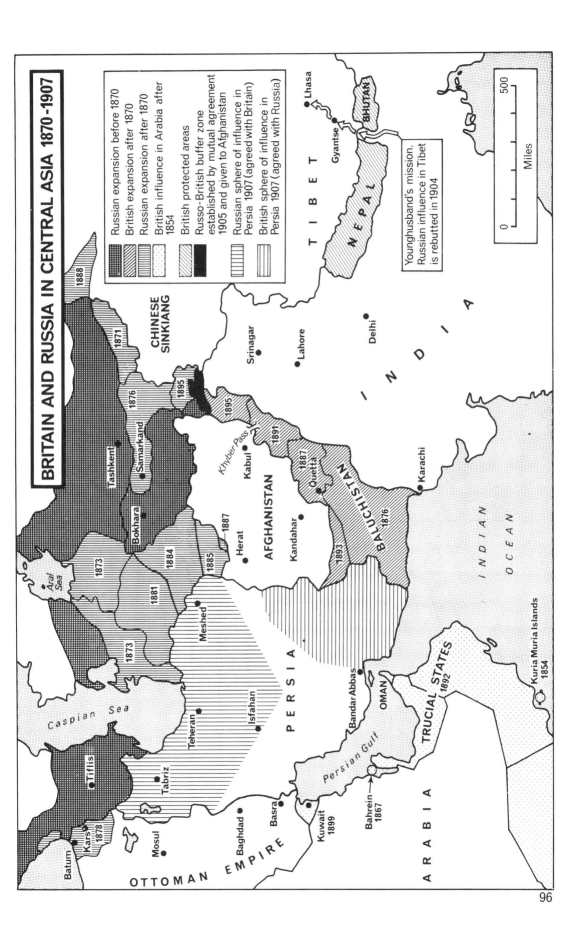

BRITAIN AND RUSSIA IN CENTRAL ASIA 1870-1907

Russian expansion before 1870

British expansion after 1870

Russian expansion after 1870

British influence in Arabia after 1854

British protected areas

Russo-British buffer zone established by mutual agreement 1905 and given to Afghanistan

Russian sphere of influence in Persia 1907 (agreed with Britain)

British sphere of influence in Persia 1907 (agreed with Russia)

Younghusband's mission. Russian influence in Tibet is rebutted in 1904

0   500
Miles

CHINESE SINKIANG

TIBET

BHUTAN

●Lhasa

●Gyantse

NEPAL

1888

1871

1876

1895

1895

Srinagar●

Lahore●

Delhi●

INDIA

1891

Khyber Pass

Kabul●

1887

Quetta●

●Karachi

Tashkent●

Samarkand●

Bokhara■

1887

Herat●

AFGHANISTAN

Kandahar●

BALUCHISTAN

1876

1893

1873

1884

1885

Aral Sea

1881

Meshed●

PERSIA

1873

INDIAN OCEAN

Caspian Sea

Teheran●

Isfahan●

Bandar Abbas●

Kuria Muria Islands
1854

Tabriz●

●Tiflis

TRUCIAL STATES
1892

Persian Gulf

OMAN

Kars●
1878

Baghdad●

Basra●

Kuwait
1899

Bahrein
1867

ARABIA

Batum

Mosul●

OTTOMAN EMPIRE

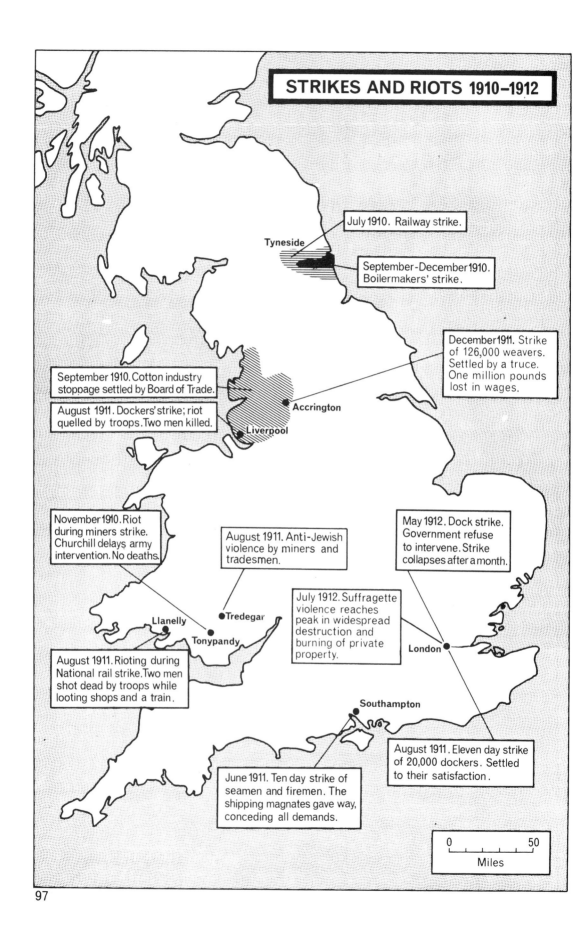

STRIKES AND RIOTS 1910–1912

July 1910. Railway strike.

September–December 1910. Boilermakers' strike.

Tyneside

December 1911. Strike of 126,000 weavers. Settled by a truce. One million pounds lost in wages.

September 1910. Cotton industry stoppage settled by Board of Trade.

August 1911. Dockers' strike; riot quelled by troops. Two men killed.

Accrington

Liverpool

November 1910. Riot during miners strike. Churchill delays army intervention. No deaths.

August 1911. Anti-Jewish violence by miners and tradesmen.

May 1912. Dock strike. Government refuse to intervene. Strike collapses after a month.

July 1912. Suffragette violence reaches peak in widespread destruction and burning of private property.

Llanelly

Tredegar

Tonypandy

August 1911. Rioting during National rail strike. Two men shot dead by troops while looting shops and a train.

London

Southampton

August 1911. Eleven day strike of 20,000 dockers. Settled to their satisfaction.

June 1911. Ten day strike of seamen and firemen. The shipping magnates gave way, conceding all demands.

0					50

Miles

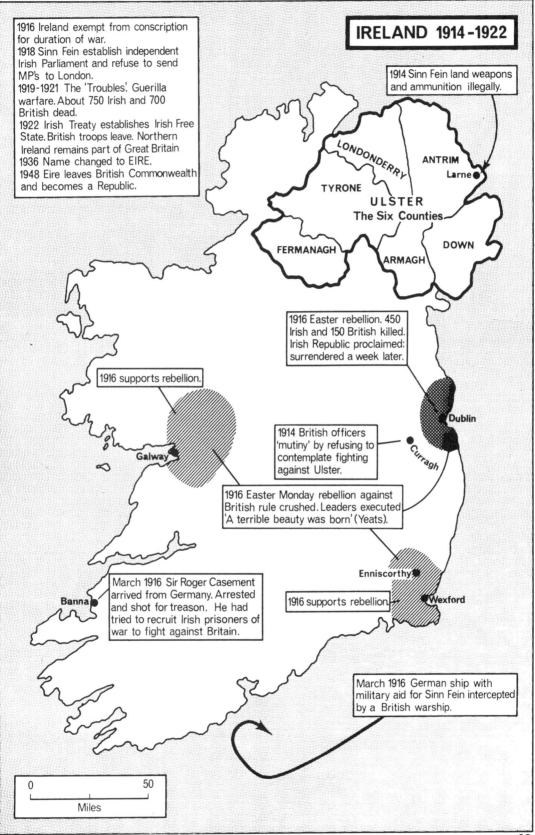

IRELAND 1914-1922

1916 Ireland exempt from conscription for duration of war.
1918 Sinn Fein establish independent Irish Parliament and refuse to send MP's to London.
1919-1921 The 'Troubles'. Guerilla warfare. About 750 Irish and 700 British dead.
1922 Irish Treaty establishes Irish Free State. British troops leave. Northern Ireland remains part of Great Britain
1936 Name changed to EIRE.
1948 Eire leaves British Commonwealth and becomes a Republic.

1914 Sinn Fein land weapons and ammunition illegally.

LONDONDERRY

ANTRIM

Larne

TYRONE

ULSTER
The Six Counties

FERMANAGH

ARMAGH

DOWN

1916 Easter rebellion. 450 Irish and 150 British killed. Irish Republic proclaimed: surrendered a week later.

1916 supports rebellion.

Galway

1914 British officers 'mutiny' by refusing to contemplate fighting against Ulster.

Dublin

Curragh

1916 Easter Monday rebellion against British rule crushed. Leaders executed 'A terrible beauty was born' (Yeats).

March 1916 Sir Roger Casement arrived from Germany. Arrested and shot for treason. He had tried to recruit Irish prisoners of war to fight against Britain.

Banna

Enniscorthy

1916 supports rebellion.

Wexford

March 1916 German ship with military aid for Sinn Fein intercepted by a British warship.

0   50
Miles

98

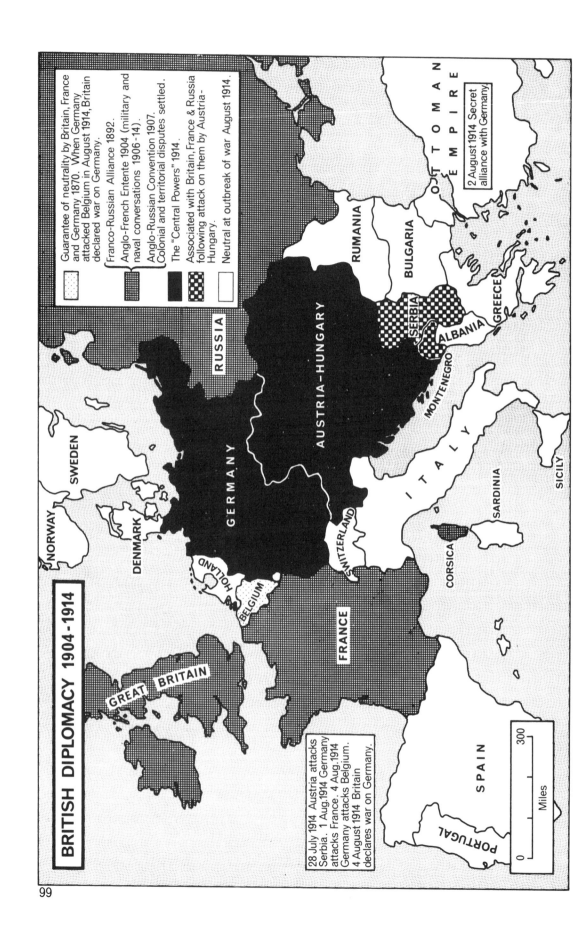

BRITISH DIPLOMACY 1904-1914

Guarantee of neutrality by Britain, France and Germany 1870. When Germany attacked Belgium in August 1914, Britain declared war on Germany.

Franco-Russian Alliance 1892.

Anglo-French Entente 1904 (military and naval conversations 1906-14).

Anglo-Russian Convention 1907. Colonial and territorial disputes settled.

The "Central Powers" 1914.

Associated with Britain, France & Russia following attack on them by Austria-Hungary.

Neutral at outbreak of war August 1914.

2 August 1914 Secret alliance with Germany.

28 July 1914 Austria attacks Serbia. 1 Aug.1914 Germany attacks France. 4 Aug.1914 Germany attacks Belgium. 4 August 1914 Britain declares war on Germany.

NORWAY

SWEDEN

DENMARK

HOLLAND

BELGIUM

GREAT BRITAIN

GERMANY

RUSSIA

AUSTRIA-HUNGARY

SWITZERLAND

FRANCE

ITALY

RUMANIA

BULGARIA

SERBIA

ALBANIA

MONTENEGRO

GREECE

OTTOMAN EMPIRE

SPAIN

PORTUGAL

CORSICA

SARDINIA

SICILY

Miles

0   300

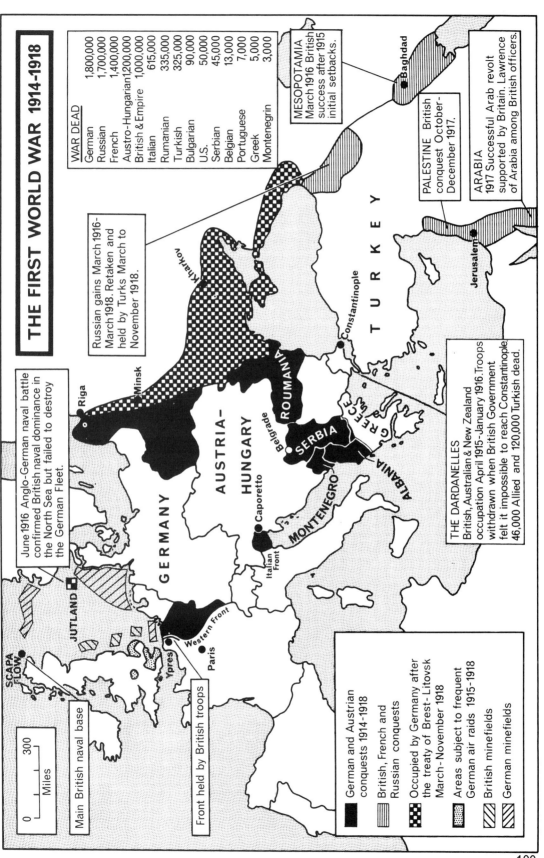

THE FIRST WORLD WAR 1914-1918

WAR DEAD
German	1,800,000
Russian	1,700,000
French	1,400,000
Austro-Hungarian	1,200,000
British & Empire	1,000,000
Italian	615,000
Rumanian	335,000
Turkish	325,000
Bulgarian	90,000
U.S.	50,000
Serbian	45,000
Belgian	13,000
Portuguese	7,000
Greek	5,000
Montenegrin	3,000

MESOPOTAMIA
March 1916 British
success after 1915
initial setbacks.

PALESTINE British
conquest October-
December 1917.

ARABIA
1917 Successful Arab revolt
supported by Britain. Lawrence
of Arabia among British officers.

Russian gains March 1916-
March 1918. Retaken and
held by Turks March to
November 1918.

June 1916 Anglo-German naval battle
confirmed British naval dominance in
the North Sea but failed to destroy
the German Fleet.

THE DARDANELLES
British, Australian & New Zealand
occupation April 1915-January 1916. Troops
withdrawn when British Government
felt it impossible to reach Constantinople.
46,000 Allied and 120,000 Turkish dead.

Main British naval base

Front held by British troops

Baghdad

Jerusalem

Constantinople

T U R K E Y

G R E E C E

ALBANIA

MONTENEGRO

SERBIA

ROUMANIA

Belgrade

Caporetto

Italian
Front

AUSTRIA-
HUNGARY

GERMANY

Western Front

Paris

Ypres

JUTLAND

SCAPA
FLOW

Riga

Minsk

Kharkov

0   300
Miles

Legend
- German and Austrian conquests 1914-1918
- British, French and Russian conquests
- Occupied by Germany after the treaty of Brest-Litovsk March-November 1918
- Areas subject to frequent German air raids 1915-1918
- British minefields
- German minefields

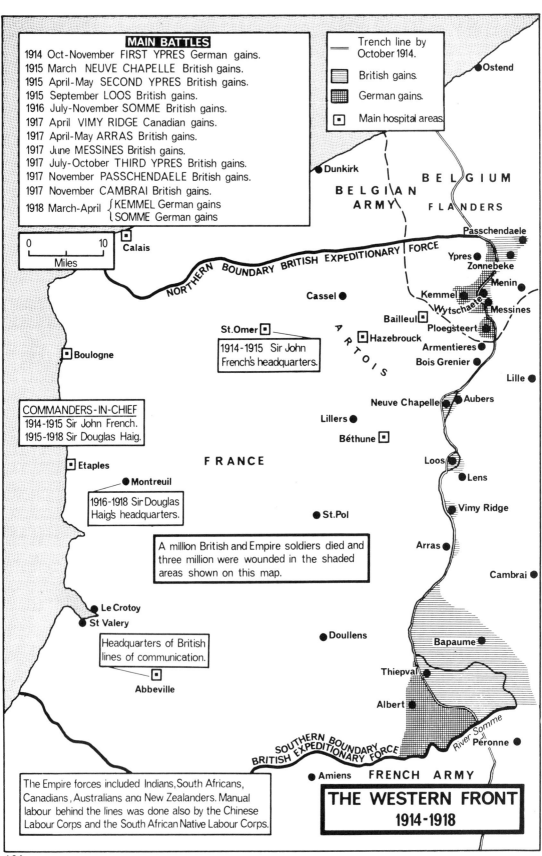

MAIN BATTLES

1914 Oct-November FIRST YPRES German gains.
1915 March NEUVE CHAPELLE British gains.
1915 April-May SECOND YPRES British gains.
1915 September LOOS British gains.
1916 July-November SOMME British gains.
1917 April VIMY RIDGE Canadian gains.
1917 April-May ARRAS British gains.
1917 June MESSINES British gains.
1917 July-October THIRD YPRES British gains.
1917 November PASSCHENDAELE British gains.
1917 November CAMBRAI British gains.
1918 March-April { KEMMEL German gains
                  { SOMME German gains

Trench line by October 1914.

British gains.

German gains.

Main hospital areas.

0   10
Miles

Calais

NORTHERN BOUNDARY BRITISH EXPEDITIONARY FORCE

Ostend

B E L G I U M

BELGIAN
ARMY

F L A N D E R S

Dunkirk

Passchendaele

Ypres
Zonnebeke
Menin
Kemmel
Wytschaete
Messines
Bailleul
Ploegsteert
Armentieres
Bois Grenier

Cassel

St.Omer
Hazebrouck

1914-1915 Sir John French's headquarters.

A
R
T
O
I
S

Boulogne

Lille

Neuve Chapelle
Aubers

COMMANDERS-IN-CHIEF
1914-1915 Sir John French.
1915-1918 Sir Douglas Haig.

Lillers

Béthune

F R A N C E

Loos

Lens

Etaples

Montreuil

1916-1918 Sir Douglas Haig's headquarters.

St.Pol

Vimy Ridge

A million British and Empire soldiers died and three million were wounded in the shaded areas shown on this map.

Arras

Cambrai

Le Crotoy
St Valery

Doullens

Bapaume

Headquarters of British lines of communication.

Thiepval

Abbeville

Albert

River Somme
Péronne

SOUTHERN BOUNDARY
BRITISH EXPEDITIONARY FORCE

Amiens   F R E N C H   A R M Y

The Empire forces included Indians, South Africans, Canadians, Australians and New Zealanders. Manual labour behind the lines was done also by the Chinese Labour Corps and the South African Native Labour Corps.

THE WESTERN FRONT 1914-1918

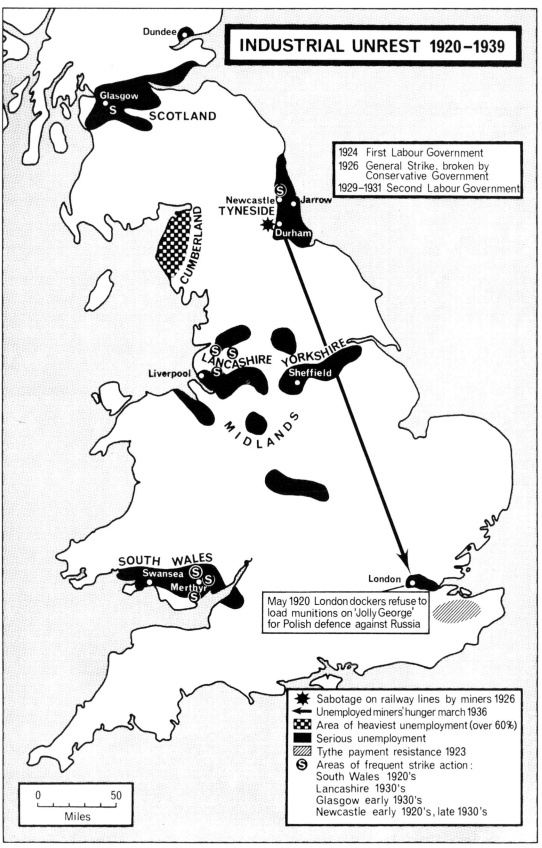

INDUSTRIAL UNREST 1920–1939

Dundee

Glasgow
S

SCOTLAND

1924 First Labour Government
1926 General Strike, broken by
Conservative Government
1929–1931 Second Labour Government

CUMBERLAND

Newcastle S Jarrow
TYNESIDE
Durham

LANCASHIRE YORKSHIRE
Liverpool S S
S Sheffield

M I D L A N D S

SOUTH WALES
Swansea S
Merthyr S
S

London

May 1920 London dockers refuse to
load munitions on 'Jolly George'
for Polish defence against Russia

★ Sabotage on railway lines by miners 1926
← Unemployed miners' hunger march 1936
▨ Area of heaviest unemployment (over 60%)
■ Serious unemployment
▨ Tythe payment resistance 1923
Ⓢ Areas of frequent strike action:
South Wales 1920's
Lancashire 1930's
Glasgow early 1930's
Newcastle early 1920's, late 1930's

0   50
Miles

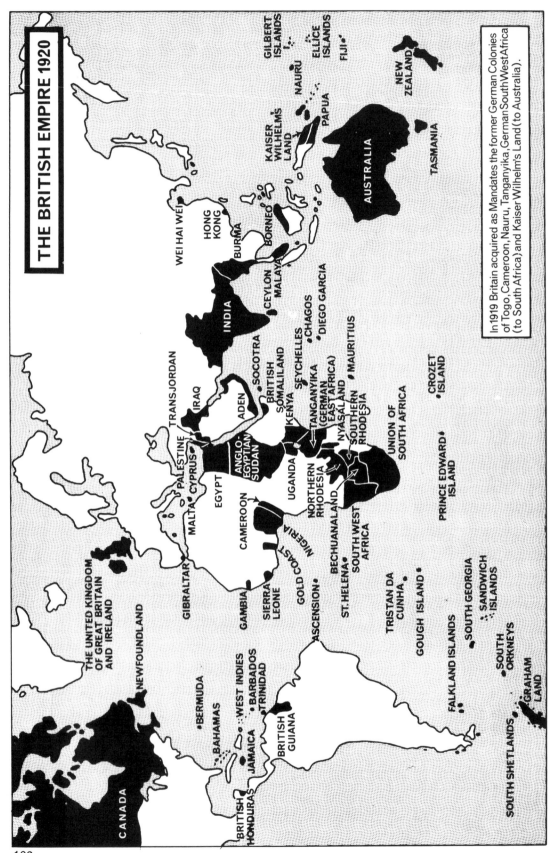

THE BRITISH EMPIRE 1920

In 1919 Britain acquired as Mandates the former German Colonies of Togo, Cameroon, Nauru, Tanganyika, German South West Africa (to South Africa) and Kaiser Wilhelm's Land (to Australia).

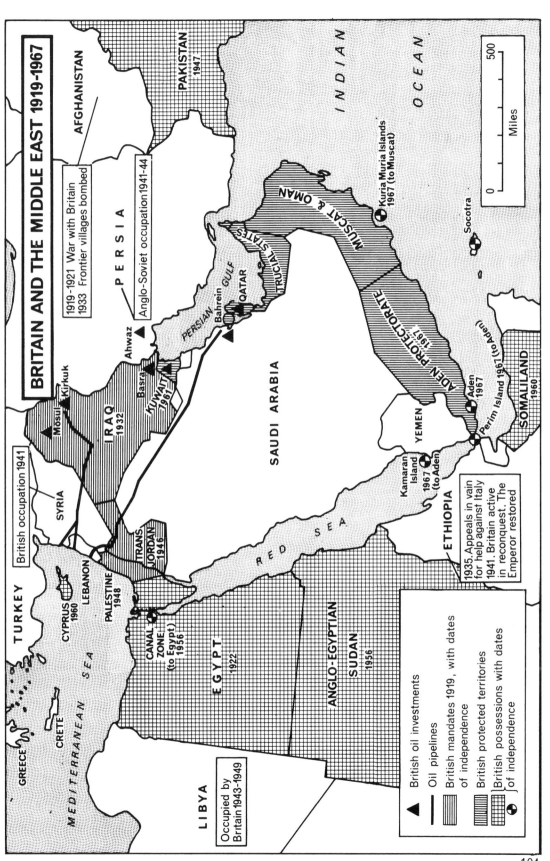

BRITAIN AND THE MIDDLE EAST 1919-1967

AFGHANISTAN

1919-1921 War with Britain
1933 Frontier villages bombed

Anglo-Soviet occupation 1941-44

PERSIA

PAKISTAN
1947

Ahwaz

Kirkuk

Mosul

IRAQ
1932

Basra

KUWAIT
1961

Bahrein

QATAR

PERSIAN GULF

TRUCIAL STATES

MUSCAT & OMAN

Kuria Muria Islands
1967 (to Muscat)

Socotra

INDIAN OCEAN

British occupation 1941

SYRIA

TURKEY

CYPRUS
1960

LEBANON

British occupation 1941

TRANS-JORDAN
1946

PALESTINE
1948

SAUDI ARABIA

ADEN PROTECTORATE
1967

Aden
1967

Perim Island 1967 (to Aden)

SOMALILAND
1960

YEMEN

Kamaran
Island
1967
(to Aden)

ETHIOPIA

1935. Appeals in vain
for help against Italy
in reconquest. The
Emperor restored

CANAL
ZONE
(to Egypt)
1956

EGYPT
1922

**ANGLO-EGYPTIAN
SUDAN**
1956

RED SEA

LIBYA

Occupied by
Britain 1943-1949

MEDITERRANEAN SEA

GREECE

CRETE

British oil investments

Oil pipelines

British mandates 1919, with dates
of independence

British protected territories

British possessions with dates
of independence

Miles

0   500

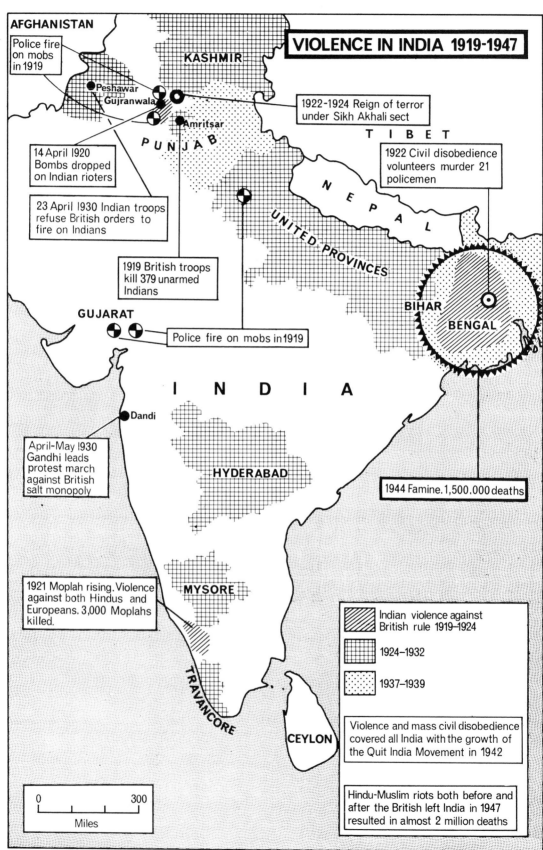

VIOLENCE IN INDIA 1919-1947

AFGHANISTAN

Police fire on mobs in 1919

KASHMIR

Peshawar

Gujranwala

Amritsar

PUNJAB

T I B E T

1922-1924 Reign of terror under Sikh Akhali sect

14 April 1920 Bombs dropped on Indian rioters

1922 Civil disobedience volunteers murder 21 policemen

23 April 1930 Indian troops refuse British orders to fire on Indians

N E P A L

UNITED PROVINCES

1919 British troops kill 379 unarmed Indians

BIHAR

BENGAL

GUJARAT

Police fire on mobs in 1919

I N D I A

Dandi

April-May 1930 Gandhi leads protest march against British salt monopoly

HYDERABAD

1944 Famine. 1,500,000 deaths

1921 Moplah rising. Violence against both Hindus and Europeans. 3,000 Moplahs killed.

MYSORE

Indian violence against British rule 1919–1924

1924–1932

1937–1939

TRAVANCORE

CEYLON

Violence and mass civil disobedience covered all India with the growth of the Quit India Movement in 1942

Hindu-Muslim riots both before and after the British left India in 1947 resulted in almost 2 million deaths

0   300

Miles

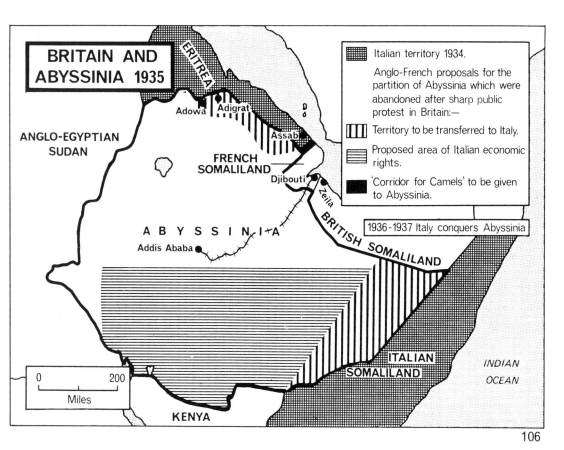

BRITAIN AND ABYSSINIA 1935

ERITREA

ANGLO-EGYPTIAN SUDAN

Adowa · Adigrat

Assab

FRENCH SOMALILAND

Djibouti

Zeila

BRITISH SOMALILAND

A B Y S S I N I A

Addis Ababa ·

ITALIAN SOMALILAND

INDIAN OCEAN

KENYA

0   200
Miles

▦ Italian territory 1934.

Anglo-French proposals for the partition of Abyssinia which were abandoned after sharp public protest in Britain:—

▥ Territory to be transferred to Italy.

▤ Proposed area of Italian economic rights.

■ 'Corridor for Camels' to be given to Abyssinia.

| 1936-1937 Italy conquers Abyssinia |

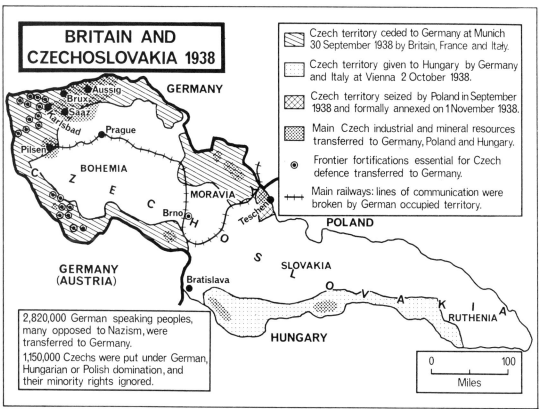

BRITAIN AND CZECHOSLOVAKIA 1938

GERMANY

Aussig
Brux
Saaz
Karlsbad
Prague
Pilsen

BOHEMIA

C Z E C H O S L O V A K I A

MORAVIA

Brno

Teschen

POLAND

GERMANY (AUSTRIA)

Bratislava

SLOVAKIA

RUTHENIA

HUNGARY

2,820,000 German speaking peoples, many opposed to Nazism, were transferred to Germany.

1,150,000 Czechs were put under German, Hungarian or Polish domination, and their minority rights ignored.

▨ Czech territory ceded to Germany at Munich 30 September 1938 by Britain, France and Italy.

▢ Czech territory given to Hungary by Germany and Italy at Vienna 2 October 1938.

▩ Czech territory seized by Poland in September 1938 and formally annexed on 1 November 1938.

▦ Main Czech industrial and mineral resources transferred to Germany, Poland and Hungary.

⊙ Frontier fortifications essential for Czech defence transferred to Germany.

+++ Main railways: lines of communication were broken by German occupied territory.

0   100
Miles

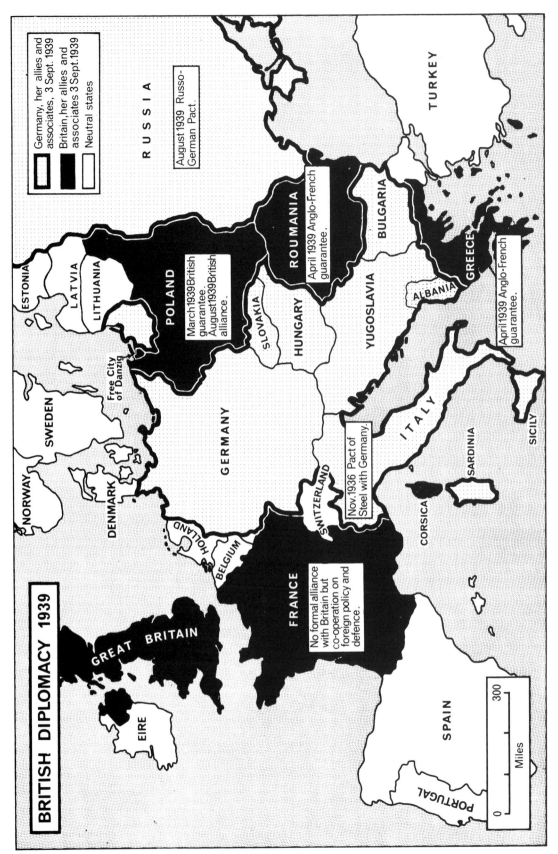

BRITISH DIPLOMACY 1939

Germany, her allies and associates, 3 Sept. 1939

Britain, her allies and associates 3 Sept.1939

Neutral states

August 1939 Russo-German Pact.

RUSSIA

ESTONIA

LATVIA

LITHUANIA

POLAND

March1939British guarantee. August1939British alliance.

ROUMANIA

April 1939 Anglo-French guarantee.

BULGARIA

SLOVAKIA

HUNGARY

YUGOSLAVIA

ALBANIA

GREECE

April1939 Anglo-French guarantee.

SWEDEN

Free City of Danzig

GERMANY

ITALY

TURKEY

NORWAY

DENMARK

HOLLAND

BELGIUM

SWITZERLAND

Nov.1936 Pact of Steel with Germany.

FRANCE

No formal alliance with Britain but co-operation on foreign policy and defence.

CORSICA

SARDINIA

SICILY

GREAT BRITAIN

EIRE

SPAIN

PORTUGAL

0   300

Miles

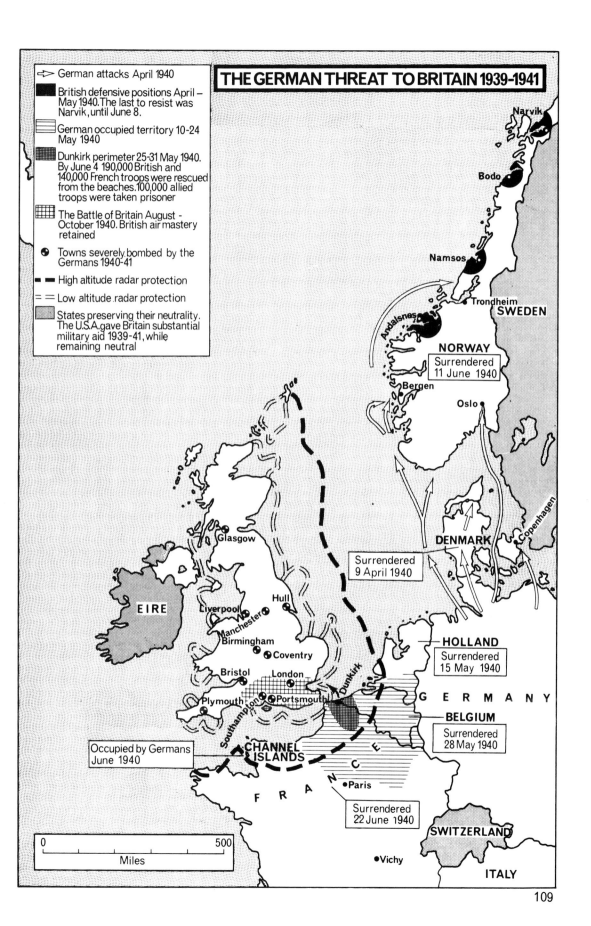

THE GERMAN THREAT TO BRITAIN 1939-1941

Legend:

- German attacks April 1940
- British defensive positions April – May 1940. The last to resist was Narvik, until June 8.
- German occupied territory 10-24 May 1940
- Dunkirk perimeter 25-31 May 1940. By June 4 190,000 British and 140,000 French troops were rescued from the beaches. 100,000 allied troops were taken prisoner
- The Battle of Britain August - October 1940. British air mastery retained
- ⊕ Towns severely bombed by the Germans 1940-41
- High altitude radar protection
- = Low altitude radar protection
- States preserving their neutrality. The U.S.A. gave Britain substantial military aid 1939-41, while remaining neutral

Narvik

Bodo

Namsos

Andalsnes · Trondheim

SWEDEN

NORWAY
Surrendered
11 June 1940

Bergen

Oslo

DENMARK
Surrendered
9 April 1940

Copenhagen

Glasgow

EIRE

Liverpool   Hull
Manchester ⊕
Birmingham
⊕ Coventry

Bristol   London
Plymouth   ⊕ Portsmouth
Southampton

CHANNEL ISLANDS
Occupied by Germans June 1940

Dunkirk

HOLLAND
Surrendered
15 May 1940

GERMANY

BELGIUM
Surrendered
28 May 1940

F R A N C E

· Paris

Surrendered
22 June 1940

SWITZERLAND

· Vichy

ITALY

0   500
Miles

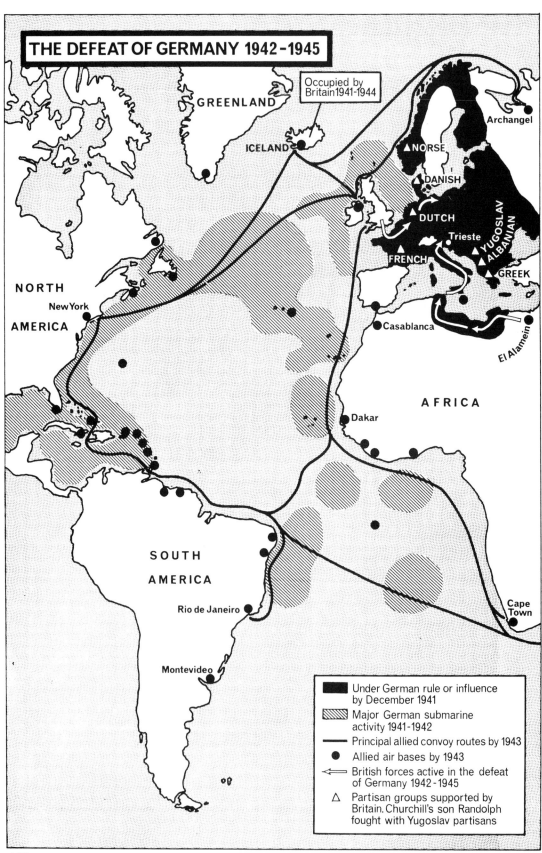

THE DEFEAT OF GERMANY 1942-1945

GREENLAND

Occupied by Britain 1941-1944

Archangel

ICELAND

△ NORSE

△ DANISH

△ DUTCH

△ YUGOSLAV

Trieste

△ ALBANIAN

NORTH

△ FRENCH

△ GREEK

New York

AMERICA

Casablanca

El Alamein

AFRICA

Dakar

SOUTH

AMERICA

Cape Town

Rio de Janeiro

Montevideo

■ Under German rule or influence by December 1941

▨ Major German submarine activity 1941-1942

— Principal allied convoy routes by 1943

● Allied air bases by 1943

⇐ British forces active in the defeat of Germany 1942-1945

△ Partisan groups supported by Britain. Churchill's son Randolph fought with Yugoslav partisans

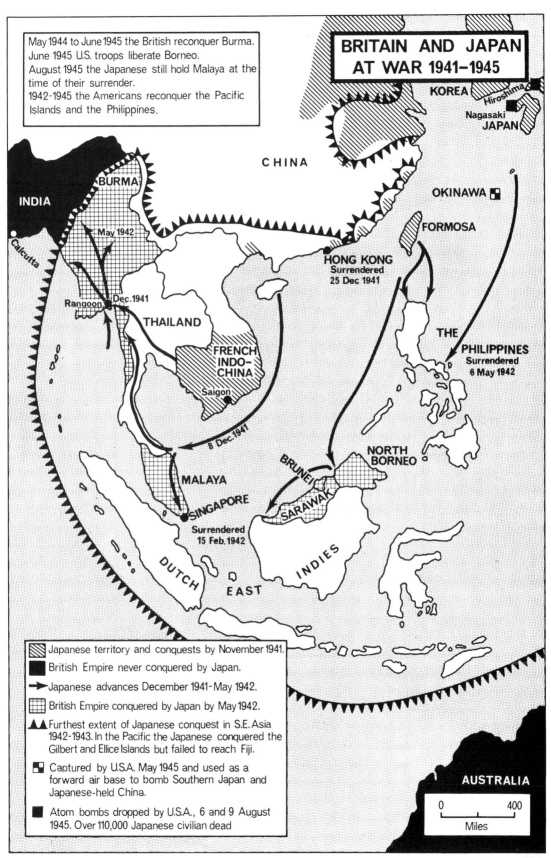

BRITAIN AND JAPAN AT WAR 1941–1945

May 1944 to June 1945 the British reconquer Burma.
June 1945 U.S. troops liberate Borneo.
August 1945 the Japanese still hold Malaya at the time of their surrender.
1942-1945 the Americans reconquer the Pacific Islands and the Philippines.

KOREA

Hiroshima

Nagasaki
JAPAN

CHINA

OKINAWA

FORMOSA

BURMA

INDIA

Calcutta

May 1942

Rangoon Dec.1941

THAILAND

HONG KONG
Surrendered
25 Dec 1941

THE
PHILIPPINES
Surrendered
6 May 1942

FRENCH
INDO-
CHINA

Saigon

8 Dec 1941

NORTH
BORNEO

BRUNEI

MALAYA

SARAWAK

SINGAPORE
Surrendered
15 Feb.1942

DUTCH

EAST

INDIES

AUSTRALIA

Japanese territory and conquests by November 1941.

British Empire never conquered by Japan.

Japanese advances December 1941-May 1942.

British Empire conquered by Japan by May 1942.

Furthest extent of Japanese conquest in S.E. Asia 1942-1943. In the Pacific the Japanese conquered the Gilbert and Ellice Islands but failed to reach Fiji.

Captured by U.S.A. May 1945 and used as a forward air base to bomb Southern Japan and Japanese-held China.

Atom bombs dropped by U.S.A., 6 and 9 August 1945. Over 110,000 Japanese civilian dead

0   400
Miles

111

Legend

- British occupation zones in Germany and Austria 1945–48.
- European Free Trade Association (EFTA) 1958.
- Associate Members of EFTA.
- The "Iron Curtain".
- European Common Market established by the Treaty of Rome 1957. Britain's first application in 1962 rejected. Second application made in 1967.
- Members of the North Atlantic Treaty Organisation (NATO) established 1949. The USA and Canada are also members. Turkey was admitted 1951.

0 ——— 400
Miles

SWEDEN

NORWAY

FINLAND
February 1947 Anglo–Soviet Peace Treaty limits Army to 34,000 men and Air Force to 60 machines

DENMARK

U. S. S. R.

EIRE

GREAT BRITAIN

NETHERLANDS

Berlin

POLAND

GERMAN DEMOCRATIC REPUBLIC

GERMAN

BELGIUM

LUXEMBOURG

FEDERAL

REPUBLIC

CZECHOSLOVAKIA

FRANCE

SWITZ

AUSTRIA

HUNGARY

RUMANIA

YUGOSLAVIA

BULGARIA

ITALY

ALBANIA

GREECE

PORTUGAL

SPAIN

GIBRALTAR
Anglo–Spanish dispute over sovereignty

BRITAIN AND EUROPE 1945–1965

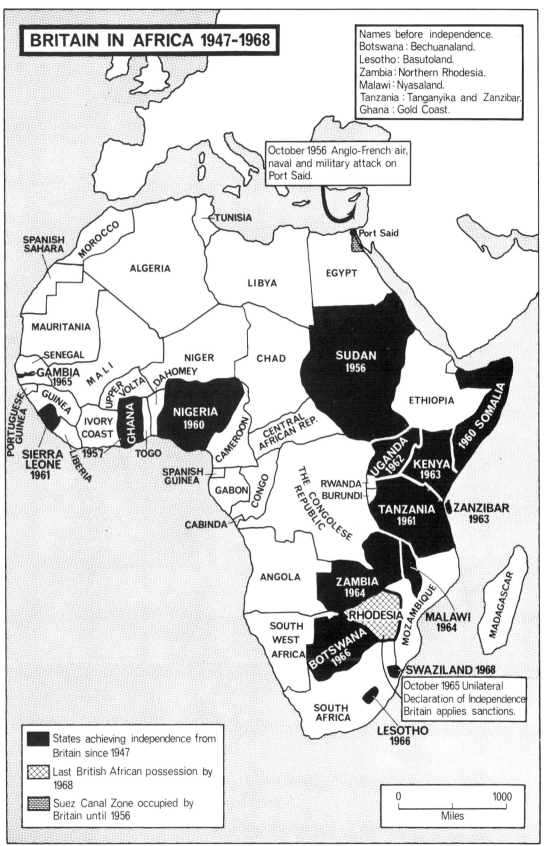

BRITAIN IN AFRICA 1947-1968

Names before independence.
Botswana : Bechuanaland.
Lesotho : Basutoland.
Zambia : Northern Rhodesia.
Malawi : Nyasaland.
Tanzania : Tanganyika and Zanzibar.
Ghana : Gold Coast.

October 1956 Anglo-French air,
naval and military attack on
Port Said.

TUNISIA

SPANISH
SAHARA
MOROCCO

Port Said

ALGERIA

LIBYA

EGYPT

MAURITANIA

SENEGAL

GAMBIA
1965
MALI
NIGER
CHAD
SUDAN
1956
ETHIOPIA
1960 SOMALIA

GUINEA
UPPER
VOLTA
DAHOMEY
GHANA
NIGERIA
1960

PORTUGUESE
GUINEA
IVORY
COAST
1957
TOGO
CAMEROON
CENTRAL
AFRICAN REP.
UGANDA
1962
KENYA
1963

SIERRA
LEONE
1961
LIBERIA
SPANISH
GUINEA
GABON
CONGO
THE
CONGOLESE
REPUBLIC
RWANDA
BURUNDI
TANZANIA
1961
ZANZIBAR
1963

CABINDA

ANGOLA
ZAMBIA
1964
MADAGASCAR

RHODESIA
MOZAMBIQUE
MALAWI
1964

SOUTH
WEST
AFRICA
BOTSWANA
1966
SWAZILAND 1968

October 1965 Unilateral
Declaration of Independence.
Britain applies sanctions.

SOUTH
AFRICA
LESOTHO
1966

■ States achieving independence from
Britain since 1947

▨ Last British African possession by
1968

▦ Suez Canal Zone occupied by
Britain until 1956

0   1000
Miles

113

UNIVERSITY FOUNDATIONS 1264–1967

Aberdeen 1495

0   50
Miles

Dundee 1967

St. Andrews 1410

1967 Stirling

Glasgow 1451
Strathclyde 1964

Edinburgh 1583

Heriot-Watt 1966

Newcastle 1963

Durham 1832

Lancaster 1964

York 1963

Leeds 1904

Hull 1954

Bradford 1966

Liverpool 1903
Manchester 1851
Salford 1967

Sheffield 1905

Bangor

Keele 1962

Nottingham 1938

1966 Loughborough
Leicester 1957

East Anglia 1964

Aston 1966
Birmingham 1900

University of
Wales 1893

Warwick 1965

Cambridge 1284

Aberystwyth

Essex 1965

Oxford 1264

Swansea

Reading 1926

Brunel 1966

Cardiff

Surrey 1966

London 1836

Bristol 1909

The City University 1966

Kent 1965

Bath 1966

Southampton 1952

Exeter 1955

Sussex 1961

● Founded 1264–1583
◉ Nineteenth century foundations
◑ Founded 1900–1938
◎ Founded 1952–1967

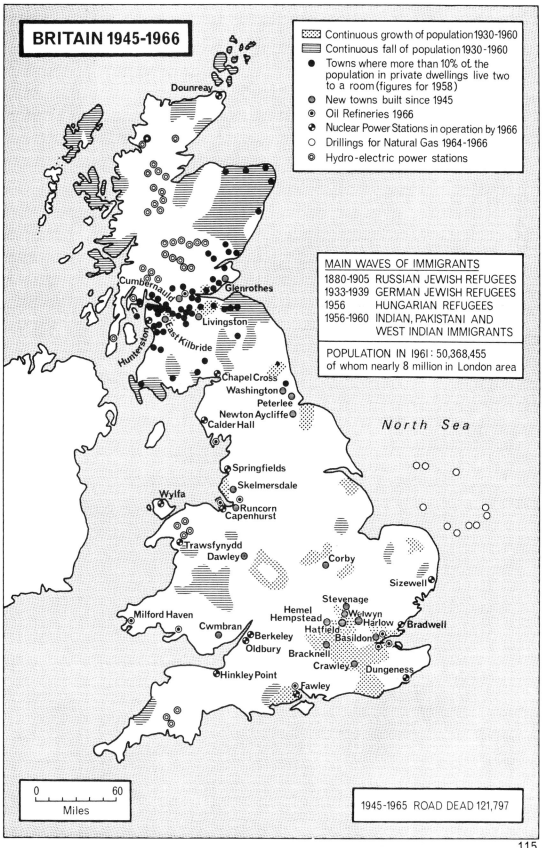

BRITAIN 1945-1966

Legend:
- ▨ Continuous growth of population 1930-1960
- ☰ Continuous fall of population 1930-1960
- ● Towns where more than 10% of the population in private dwellings live two to a room (figures for 1958)
- ⊜ New towns built since 1945
- ⊙ Oil Refineries 1966
- ◓ Nuclear Power Stations in operation by 1966
- ○ Drillings for Natural Gas 1964-1966
- ◉ Hydro-electric power stations

Dounreay

Cumbernauld Glenrothes

Livingston

Hunterston East Kilbride

Chapel Cross
Washington
Peterlee
Newton Aycliffe
Calder Hall

North Sea

Springfields

Skelmersdale

Wylfa
Runcorn
Capenhurst

Trawsfynydd
Dawley Corby

Sizewell

Stevenage
Hemel Welwyn
Hempstead Harlow Bradwell
Milford Haven Hatfield
Cwmbran Basildon
Berkeley
Oldbury Bracknell
Crawley Dungeness
Hinkley Point
Fawley

MAIN WAVES OF IMMIGRANTS
1880-1905	RUSSIAN JEWISH REFUGEES
1933-1939	GERMAN JEWISH REFUGEES
1956	HUNGARIAN REFUGEES
1956-1960	INDIAN, PAKISTANI AND WEST INDIAN IMMIGRANTS

POPULATION IN 1961 : 50,368,455
of whom nearly 8 million in London area

1945-1965 ROAD DEAD 121,797

0 ___ 60
Miles

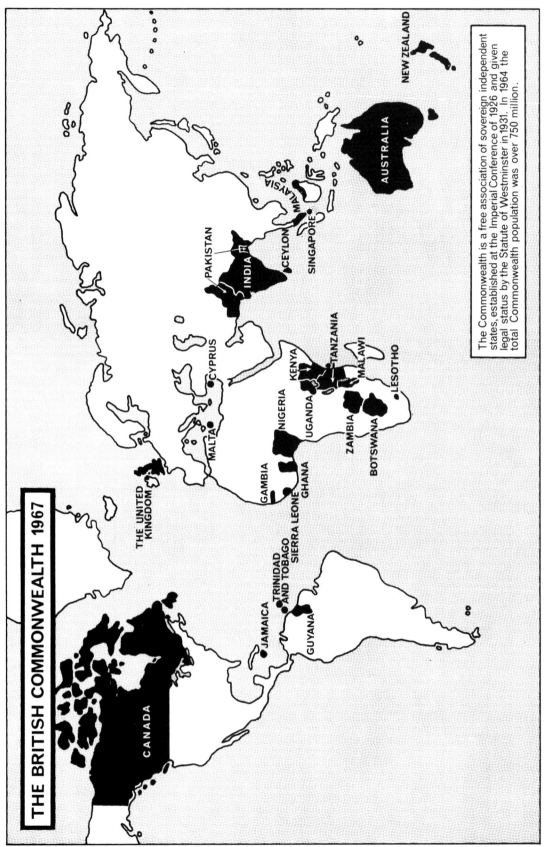

THE BRITISH COMMONWEALTH 1967

The Commonwealth is a free association of sovereign independent states, established at the Imperial Conference of 1926 and given legal status by the Statute of Westminster in 1931. In 1964 the total Commonwealth population was over 750 million.

CANADA

THE UNITED KINGDOM

JAMAICA

TRINIDAD AND TOBAGO

GUYANA

GAMBIA

SIERRA LEONE

GHANA

NIGERIA

MALTA

CYPRUS

PAKISTAN

INDIA

CEYLON

SINGAPORE

MALAYSIA

AUSTRALIA

NEW ZEALAND

UGANDA

KENYA

TANZANIA

MALAWI

ZAMBIA

BOTSWANA

LESOTHO

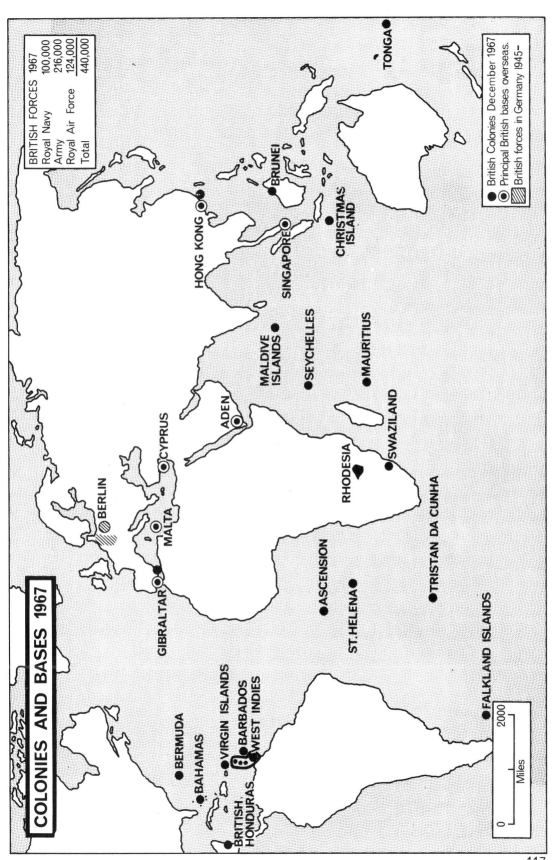

COLONIES AND BASES 1967

BRITISH FORCES 1967	
Royal Navy	100,000
Army	216,000
Royal Air Force	124,000
Total	440,000

● British Colonies December 1967
◉ Principal British bases overseas.
▨ British forces in Germany 1945–

BERMUDA
BAHAMAS
BRITISH HONDURAS
VIRGIN ISLANDS
BARBADOS
WEST INDIES
GIBRALTAR
MALTA
CYPRUS
BERLIN
ADEN
ST. HELENA
ASCENSION
RHODESIA
SWAZILAND
TRISTAN DA CUNHA
FALKLAND ISLANDS
MALDIVE ISLANDS
SEYCHELLES
MAURITIUS
HONG KONG
SINGAPORE
BRUNEI
CHRISTMAS ISLAND
TONGA

0   2000
Miles

THE WESTERN PACIFIC SINCE 1945

ALASKA
49th U.S. STATE

ALEUTIAN
ISLANDS

U.S.S.R.

50th U.S. STATE

HAWAIIAN ISLANDS

MIDWAY

JAPAN

CHINA

JOHNSTON

U.S. MILITARY
ADMINISTRATION

DAITO ●BONIN
OKINAWA
VOLCANO ●MARCUS

Hong
Kong

WAKE

FORMOSA

VIET-
NAM

MARIANAS
ISLANDS
GUAM

U.S. TRUST
TERRITORY

PHILLIPINES

ISLANDS

BIKINI

YAP
PALAU

ENIWETOK
TRUK

Brunei

CAROLINE

MARSHALL ISLANDS

BORNEO

INDONESIA

TO AUSTRALIA

GILBERT
ISLANDS

HOWLAND
BAKER

NEW GUINEA

OCEAN
ISLAND
1900

1892

CANTON ISLAND
1939

SOLOMON
ISLANDS 1893

ELLICE
ISLANDS

PHOENIX
ISLANDS
1937

SANTA CRUZ
ISLANDS 1898

AUSTRALIA

NEW
HEBRIDES 1887
FRENCH

FRENCH

FIJI 1874

SAMOA
TUTUILA

NEW
CALEDONIA

TONGA 1900

TO
NEW
ZEALAND

KERMADEC
TO NEW ZEALAND

COOK

NEW ZEALAND

TO NEW ZEALAND
CHATHAM

British possessions with date
of acquisition.

Anglo-French Condominium.

Anglo-American joint sovereignty.

United States possessions.

Commonwealth possessions.

0   500

Miles
approx.

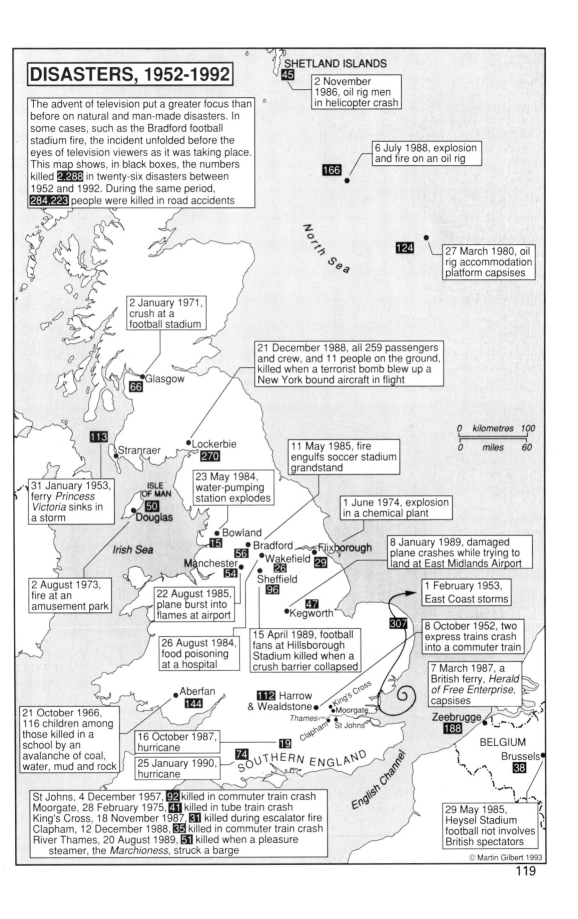

DISASTERS, 1952-1992

The advent of television put a greater focus than before on natural and man-made disasters. In some cases, such as the Bradford football stadium fire, the incident unfolded before the eyes of television viewers as it was taking place. This map shows, in black boxes, the numbers killed **2,288** in twenty-six disasters between 1952 and 1992. During the same period, **284,223** people were killed in road accidents

SHETLAND ISLANDS
45
2 November 1986, oil rig men in helicopter crash

6 July 1988, explosion and fire on an oil rig
166

124
27 March 1980, oil rig accommodation platform capsises

North Sea

2 January 1971, crush at a football stadium

21 December 1988, all 259 passengers and crew, and 11 people on the ground, killed when a terrorist bomb blew up a New York bound aircraft in flight

66 •Glasgow

113
•Stranraer

•Lockerbie
270

11 May 1985, fire engulfs soccer stadium grandstand

23 May 1984, water-pumping station explodes

31 January 1953, ferry *Princess Victoria* sinks in a storm

ISLE OF MAN
50
Douglas

1 June 1974, explosion in a chemical plant

Irish Sea

• Bowland
15
• Bradford •Flixborough
56 •Wakefield **29**
Manchester **26**
54
Sheffield
96

8 January 1989, damaged plane crashes while trying to land at East Midlands Airport

1 February 1953, East Coast storms

2 August 1973, fire at an amusement park

22 August 1985, plane burst into flames at airport

•Kegworth
47

307

8 October 1952, two express trains crash into a commuter train

26 August 1984, food poisoning at a hospital

15 April 1989, football fans at Hillsborough Stadium killed when a crush barrier collapsed

7 March 1987, a British ferry, *Herald of Free Enterprise*, capsises

•Aberfan
144

112 Harrow & Wealdstone•
King's Cross
•Moorgate
Thames
Clapham• St Johns

Zeebrugge
188

BELGIUM

21 October 1966, 116 children among those killed in a school by an avalanche of coal, water, mud and rock

16 October 1987, hurricane
19

Brussels•
38

25 January 1990, hurricane
74
SOUTHERN ENGLAND

English Channel

29 May 1985, Heysel Stadium football riot involves British spectators

St Johns, 4 December 1957, **92** killed in commuter train crash
Moorgate, 28 February 1975, **41** killed in tube train crash
King's Cross, 18 November 1987, **31** killed during escalator fire
Clapham, 12 December 1988, **35** killed in commuter train crash
River Thames, 20 August 1989, **51** killed when a pleasure
    steamer, the *Marchioness*, struck a barge

© Martin Gilbert 1993

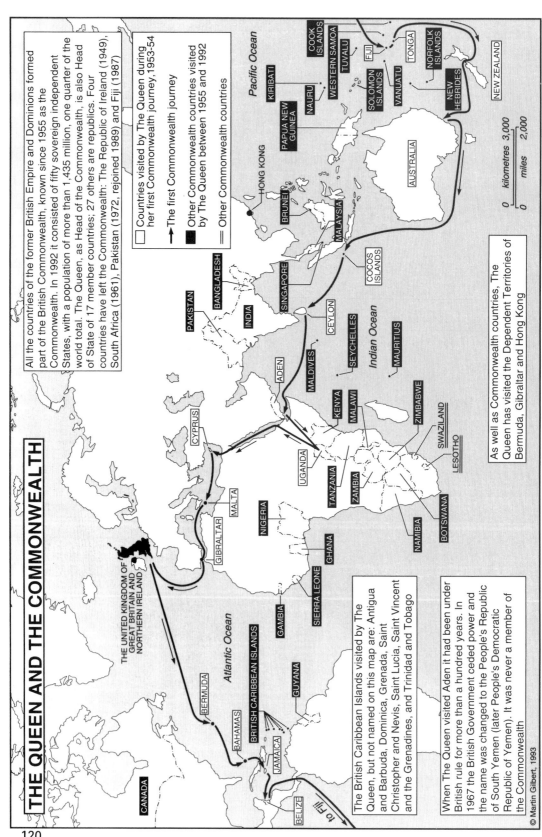

THE QUEEN AND THE COMMONWEALTH

All the countries of the former British Empire and Dominions formed part of the British Commonwealth, known since 1955 as the Commonwealth. In 1992 it consisted of fifty sovereign independent States, with a population of more than 1,435 million, one quarter of the world total. The Queen, as Head of the Commonwealth, is also Head of State of 17 member countries; 27 others are republics. Four countries have left the Commonwealth: The Republic of Ireland (1949), South Africa (1961), Pakistan (1972, rejoined 1989) and Fiji (1987)

☐ Countries visited by The Queen during her first Commonwealth journey, 1953–54

➤ The first Commonwealth journey

■ Other Commonwealth countries visited by The Queen between 1955 and 1992

= Other Commonwealth countries

Pacific Ocean

COOK ISLANDS
WESTERN SAMOA
TUVALU
TONGA
NORFOLK ISLANDS
FIJI
KIRIBATI
SOLOMON ISLANDS
VANUATU
NAURU
NEW HEBRIDES
PAPUA NEW GUINEA
NEW ZEALAND
HONG KONG
AUSTRALIA
BRUNEI
MALAYSIA
SINGAPORE
COCOS ISLANDS
BANGLADESH
CEYLON
SEYCHELLES
PAKISTAN
INDIA
Indian Ocean
MAURITIUS
ADEN
MALDIVES
KENYA
ZIMBABWE
MALAWI
SWAZILAND
TANZANIA
LESOTHO
ZAMBIA
CYPRUS
MALTA
NIGERIA
BOTSWANA
GIBRALTAR
NAMIBIA
GHANA
SIERRA LEONE
GAMBIA
GUYANA
THE UNITED KINGDOM OF GREAT BRITAIN AND NORTHERN IRELAND
BERMUDA
Atlantic Ocean
BAHAMAS
BRITISH CARIBBEAN ISLANDS
JAMAICA
CANADA
BELIZE
to Fiji

0 kilometres 3,000
0 miles 2,000

As well as Commonwealth countries, The Queen has visited the Dependent Territories of Bermuda, Gibraltar and Hong Kong

The British Caribbean Islands visited by The Queen, but not named on this map are: Antigua and Barbuda, Dominica, Grenada, Saint Christopher and Nevis, Saint Lucia, Saint Vincent and the Grenadines, and Trinidad and Tobago

When The Queen visited Aden it had been under British rule for more than a hundred years. In 1967 the British Government ceded power and the name was changed to the People's Republic of South Yemen (later People's Democratic Republic of Yemen). It was never a member of the Commonwealth

© Martin Gilbert, 1993

120

OLD ENEMIES, NEW NATIONS: STATE VISITS 1955-1992

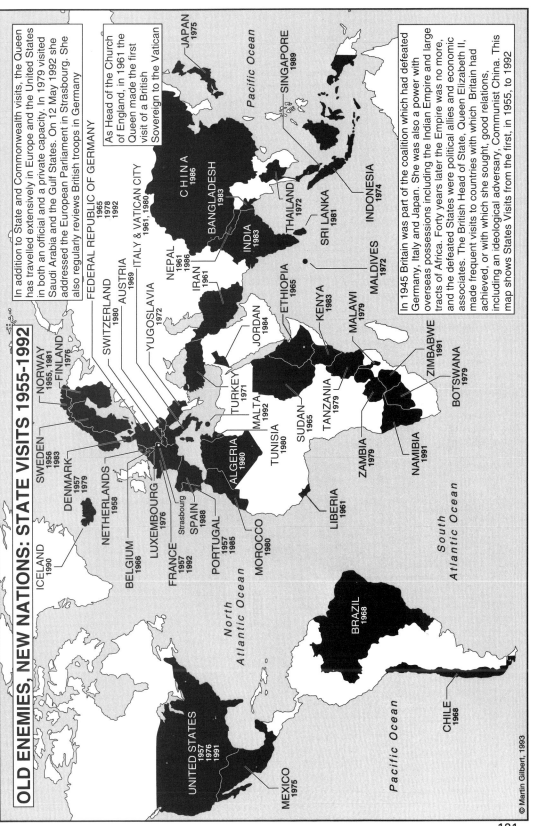

In addition to State and Commonwealth visits, the Queen has travelled extensively in Europe and the United States in both an official and a private capacity. In 1979 visited Saudi Arabia and the Gulf States. On 12 May 1992 she addressed the European Parliament in Strasbourg. She also regularly reviews British troops in Germany.

As Head of the Church of England, in 1961 the Queen made the first visit of a British Sovereign to the Vatican.

In 1945 Britain was part of the coalition which had defeated Germany, Italy and Japan. She was also a power with overseas possessions including the Indian Empire and large tracts of Africa. Forty years later the Empire was no more, and the defeated States were political allies and economic associates. The British Head of State, Queen Elizabeth II, made frequent visits to countries with which Britain had achieved, or with which she sought, good relations, including an ideological adversary, Communist China. This map shows States Visits from the first, in 1955, to 1992

© Martin Gilbert, 1993

121

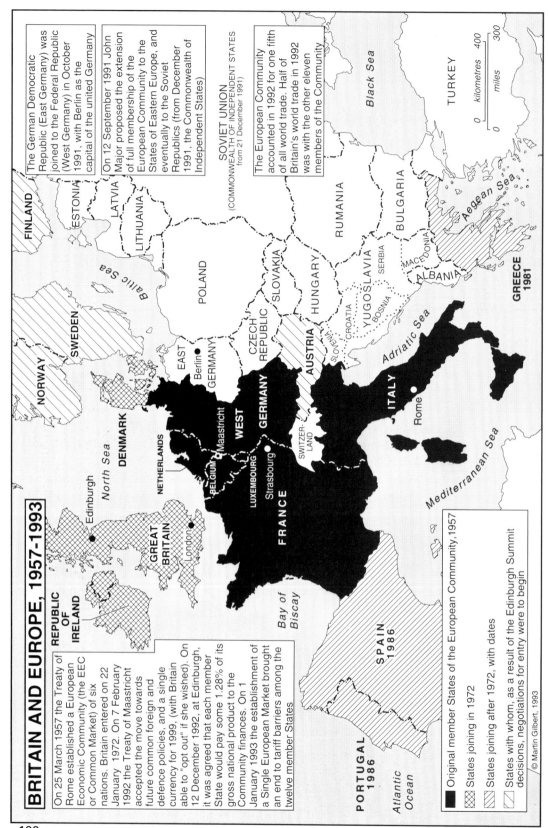

BRITAIN AND EUROPE, 1957-1993

On 25 March 1957 the Treaty of Rome established a European Economic Community (the EEC or Common Market) of six nations. Britain entered on 22 January 1972. On 7 February 1992 the Treaty of Maastricht accepted the move towards future common foreign and defence policies, and a single currency for 1999, (with Britain able to "opt out" if she wished). On 12 December 1992, at Edinburgh, it was agreed that each member State would pay some 1.28% of its gross national product to the Community finances. On 1 January 1993 the establishment of a Single European Market brought an end to tariff barriers among the twelve member States

The German Democratic Republic (East Germany) was joined to the Federal Republic (West Germany) in October 1991, with Berlin as the capital of the united Germany

On 12 September 1991 John Major proposed the extension of full membership of the European Community to the States of Eastern Europe, and eventually to the Soviet Republics (from December 1991, the Commonwealth of Independent States)

SOVIET UNION
(COMMONWEALTH OF INDEPENDENT STATES from 21 December 1991)

The European Community accounted in 1992 for one fifth of all world trade. Half of Britain's world trade in 1992 was with the other eleven members of the Community

FINLAND

ESTONIA
LATVIA
LITHUANIA

NORWAY

SWEDEN

Baltic Sea

POLAND

EAST GERMANY
Berlin

DENMARK

North Sea

NETHERLANDS

BELGIUM
Maastricht
LUXEMBOURG
Strasbourg
SWITZER-LAND

WEST GERMANY

CZECH REPUBLIC

SLOVAKIA

AUSTRIA

HUNGARY

RUMANIA

BULGARIA

SERBIA
MACEDONIA
ALBANIA

SLOVENIA
CROATIA
BOSNIA
YUGOSLAVIA

Black Sea

TURKEY

Aegean Sea

GREECE 1981

FRANCE

Bay of Biscay

ITALY
Rome

Adriatic Sea

Mediterranean Sea

GREAT BRITAIN
London

Edinburgh

REPUBLIC OF IRELAND

SPAIN 1986

PORTUGAL 1986

Atlantic Ocean

0   kilometres   400
0   miles   300

Original member States of the European Community, 1957

States joining in 1972

States joining after 1972, with dates

States with whom, as a result of the Edinburgh Summit decisions, negotiations for entry were to begin

© Martin Gilbert, 1993

122

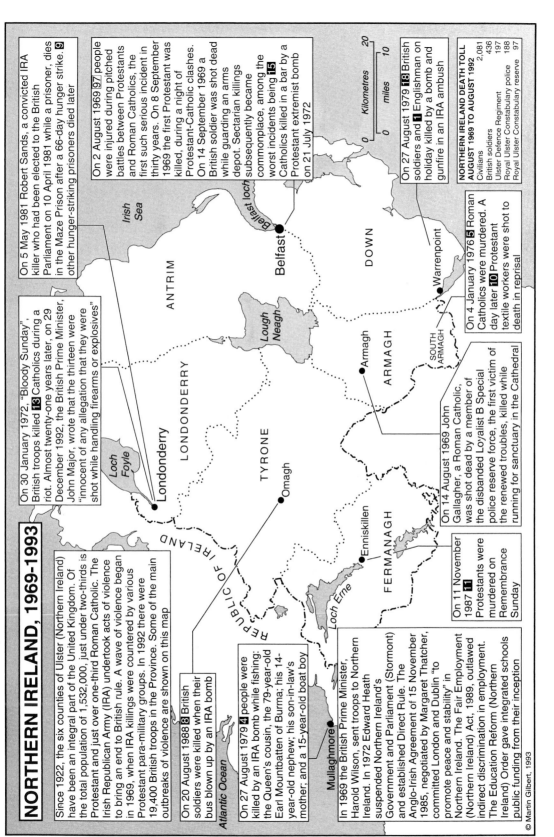

NORTHERN IRELAND, 1969–1993

Since 1922, the six counties of Ulster (Northern Ireland) have been an integral part of the United Kingdom. Of the total population of 1,532,000, just under two-thirds is Protestant and just over one-third Roman Catholic. The Irish Republican Army (IRA) undertook acts of violence to bring an end to British rule. A wave of violence began in 1969, when IRA killings were countered by various Protestant para-military groups. In 1992 there were 19,400 British troops in the Province. Some of the main outbreaks of violence are shown on this map

On 30 January 1972, "Bloody Sunday", British troops killed **13** Catholics during a riot. Almost twenty-one years later, on 29 December 1992, the British Prime Minister, John Major, wrote that the thirteen were "innocent of any allegation that they were shot while handling firearms or explosives"

On 5 May 1981 Robert Sands, a convicted IRA killer who had been elected to the British Parliament on 10 April 1981 while a prisoner, dies in the Maze Prison after a 66-day hunger strike. **9** other hunger-striking prisoners died later

On 2 August 1969 **97** people were injured during pitched battles between Protestants and Roman Catholics, the first such serious incident in thirty years. On 8 September 1969 the first Protestant was killed, during a night of Protestant-Catholic clashes. On 14 September 1969 a British soldier was shot dead while guarding an arms depot. Sectarian killings subsequently became commonplace, among the worst incidents being **15** Catholics killed in a bar by a Protestant extremist bomb on 21 July 1972

On 27 August 1979 **18** British soldiers and **1** Englishman on holiday killed by a bomb and gunfire in an IRA ambush

On 20 August 1988 **8** British soldiers were killed when their bus blown up by an IRA bomb

On 27 August 1979 **4** people were killed by an IRA bomb while fishing: the Queen's cousin, the 79-year-old Earl Mountbatten of Burma; his 14-year-old nephew; his son-in-law's mother; and a 15-year-old boat boy

In 1969 the British Prime Minister, Harold Wilson, sent troops to Northern Ireland. In 1972 Edward Heath suspended Northern Ireland's Government and Parliament (Stormont) and established Direct Rule. The Anglo-Irish Agreement of 15 November 1985, negotiated by Margaret Thatcher, committed London and Dublin "to promote peace and stability" in Northern Ireland. The Fair Employment (Northern Ireland) Act, 1989, outlawed indirect discrimination in employment. The Education Reform (Northern Ireland) Order gave integrated schools public funding from their inception

On 11 November 1987 **11** Protestants were murdered on Remembrance Sunday

On 14 August 1969 John Gallagher, a Roman Catholic, was shot dead by a member of the disbanded Loyalist B Special police reserve force, the first victim of the renewed troubles, killed while running for sanctuary in the Cathedral

On 4 January 1976 **5** Roman Catholics were murdered. A day later **10** Protestant textile workers were shot to death in reprisal

NORTHERN IRELAND DEATH TOLL AUGUST 1969 TO AUGUST 1992

Civilians	2,081
British soldiers	436
Ulster Defence Regiment	197
Royal Ulster Constabulary police	188
Royal Ulster Constabulary reserve	97

Irish Sea

Belfast loch

Belfast

DOWN

ANTRIM

Warrenpoint

Lough Neagh

Armagh

ARMAGH

SOUTH ARMAGH

LONDONDERRY

Londonderry

Loch Foyle

TYRONE

Omagh

REPUBLIC OF IRELAND

Enniskillen

Loch Erne

FERMANAGH

Mullaghmore

Atlantic Ocean

0   10   20 Kilometres
0   miles

© Martin Gilbert, 1993

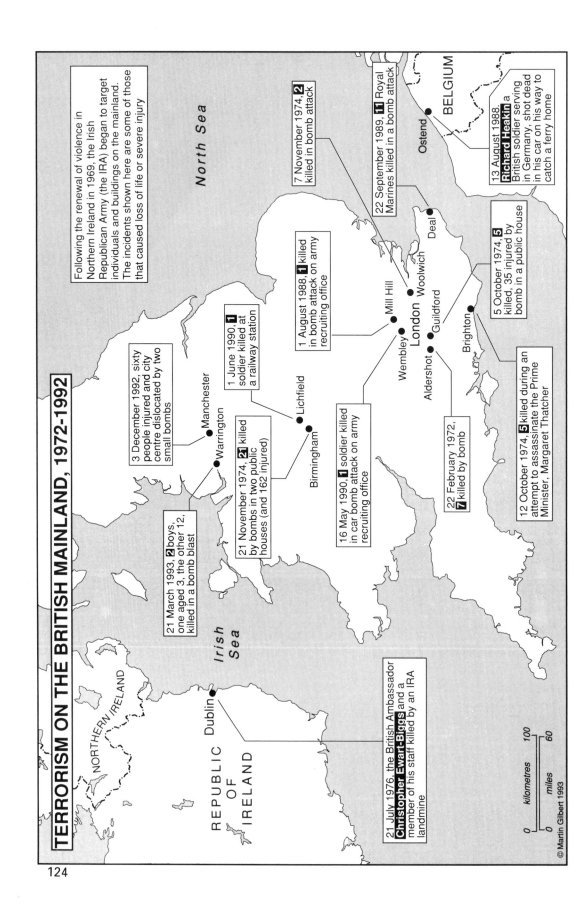

TERRORISM ON THE BRITISH MAINLAND, 1972-1992

Following the renewal of violence in Northern Ireland in 1969, the Irish Republican Army (the IRA) began to target individuals and buildings on the mainland. The incidents shown here are some of those that caused loss of life or severe injury

North Sea

7 November 1974, **2** killed in bomb attack

22 September 1989, **11** Royal Marines killed in a bomb attack

13 August 1988, **Richard Heakin** a British soldier serving in Germany, shot dead in his car on his way to catch a ferry home

BELGIUM

Ostend

Deal

1 August 1988, **1** killed in bomb attack on army recruiting office

Mill Hill
Wembley
Woolwich
London
Guildford
Aldershot
Brighton

5 October 1974, **5** killed, 35 injured by bomb in a public house

1 June 1990, **1** soldier killed at a railway station

3 December 1992, sixty people injured and city centre dislocated by two small bombs

Manchester
Warrington

Lichfield

Birmingham

21 November 1974, **21** killed by bombs in two public houses (and 162 injured)

16 May 1990, **1** soldier killed in car bomb attack on army recruiting office

22 February 1972, **7** killed by bomb

12 October 1984, **5** killed during an attempt to assassinate the Prime Minister, Margaret Thatcher

21 March 1993, **2** boys, one aged 3, the other 12, killed in a bomb blast

Irish Sea

NORTHERN IRELAND

Dublin

REPUBLIC OF IRELAND

21 July 1976, the British Ambassador **Christopher Ewart-Biggs** and a member of his staff killed by an IRA landmine

0   kilometres   100
0   miles   60

© Martin Gilbert 1993

124

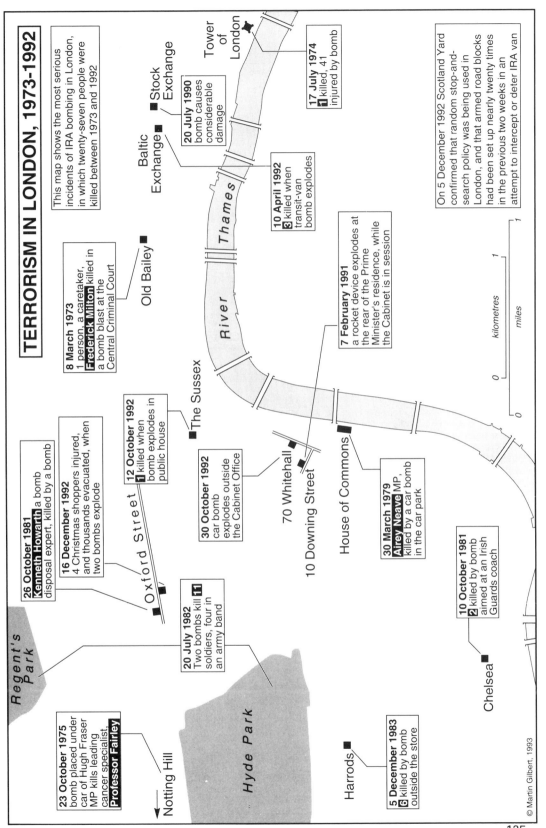

TERRORISM IN LONDON, 1973-1992

This map shows the most serious incidents of IRA bombing in London, in which twenty-seven people were killed between 1973 and 1992

8 March 1973 1 person, a caretaker, **Frederick Milton** killed in a bomb blast at the Central Criminal Court

26 October 1981 Kenneth Howarth a bomb disposal expert, killed by a bomb

16 December 1992 4 Christmas shoppers injured, and thousands evacuated, when two bombs explode

12 October 1992 1 killed when bomb explodes in public house

30 October 1992 car bomb explodes outside the Cabinet Office

20 July 1982 Two bombs kill soldiers, four in an army band 1

23 October 1975 bomb placed under car of Hugh Fraser MP kills leading cancer specialist, **Professor Fairley**

Regent's Park

Notting Hill

Hyde Park

5 December 1983 6 killed by bomb outside the store

Harrods

Chelsea

10 October 1981 2 killed by bomb aimed at an Irish Guards coach

30 March 1979 Airey Neave MP, killed by a car bomb in the car park

House of Commons

10 Downing Street

70 Whitehall

7 February 1991 a rocket device explodes at the rear of the Prime Minister's residence, while the Cabinet is in session

The Sussex

Old Bailey

Oxford Street

River Thames

Baltic Exchange

Stock Exchange

20 July 1990 bomb causes considerable damage

10 April 1992 3 killed when transit-van bomb explodes

Tower of London

17 July 1974 1 killed, 41 injured by bomb

On 5 December 1992 Scotland Yard confirmed that random stop-and-search policy was being used in London, and that armed road blocks had been set up nearly twenty times in the previous two weeks in an attempt to intercept or deter IRA van

0   1   1
kilometres
0   1
miles

© Martin Gilbert, 1993

125

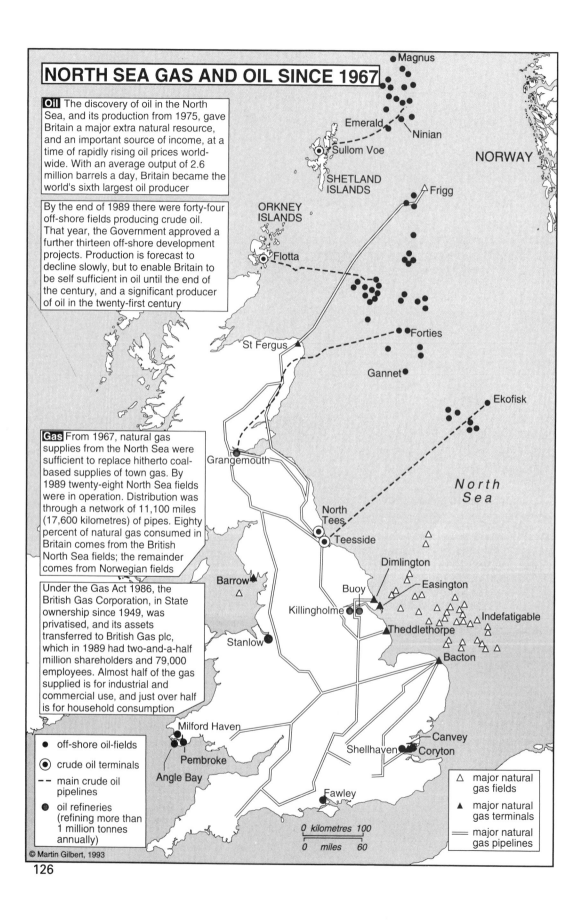

NORTH SEA GAS AND OIL SINCE 1967

Oil The discovery of oil in the North Sea, and its production from 1975, gave Britain a major extra natural resource, and an important source of income, at a time of rapidly rising oil prices world-wide. With an average output of 2.6 million barrels a day, Britain became the world's sixth largest oil producer

By the end of 1989 there were forty-four off-shore fields producing crude oil. That year, the Government approved a further thirteen off-shore development projects. Production is forecast to decline slowly, but to enable Britain to be self sufficient in oil until the end of the century, and a significant producer of oil in the twenty-first century

Gas From 1967, natural gas supplies from the North Sea were sufficient to replace hitherto coal-based supplies of town gas. By 1989 twenty-eight North Sea fields were in operation. Distribution was through a network of 11,100 miles (17,600 kilometres) of pipes. Eighty percent of natural gas consumed in Britain comes from the British North Sea fields; the remainder comes from Norwegian fields

Under the Gas Act 1986, the British Gas Corporation, in State ownership since 1949, was privatised, and its assets transferred to British Gas plc, which in 1989 had two-and-a-half million shareholders and 79,000 employees. Almost half of the gas supplied is for industrial and commercial use, and just over half is for household consumption

Magnus
Emerald
Ninian
Sullom Voe
SHETLAND ISLANDS
NORWAY
Frigg
ORKNEY ISLANDS
Flotta
Forties
St Fergus
Gannet
Ekofisk
North Sea
Grangemouth
North Tees
Teesside
Dimlington
Easington
Buoy
Barrow
Killingholme
Indefatigable
Stanlow
Theddlethorpe
Bacton
Milford Haven
Canvey
Shellhaven
Coryton
Pembroke
Angle Bay
Fawley

- ● off-shore oil-fields
- ◉ crude oil terminals
- – – main crude oil pipelines
- ● oil refineries (refining more than 1 million tonnes annually)

- △ major natural gas fields
- ▲ major natural gas terminals
- = major natural gas pipelines

0 kilometres 100
0 miles 60

© Martin Gilbert, 1993

126

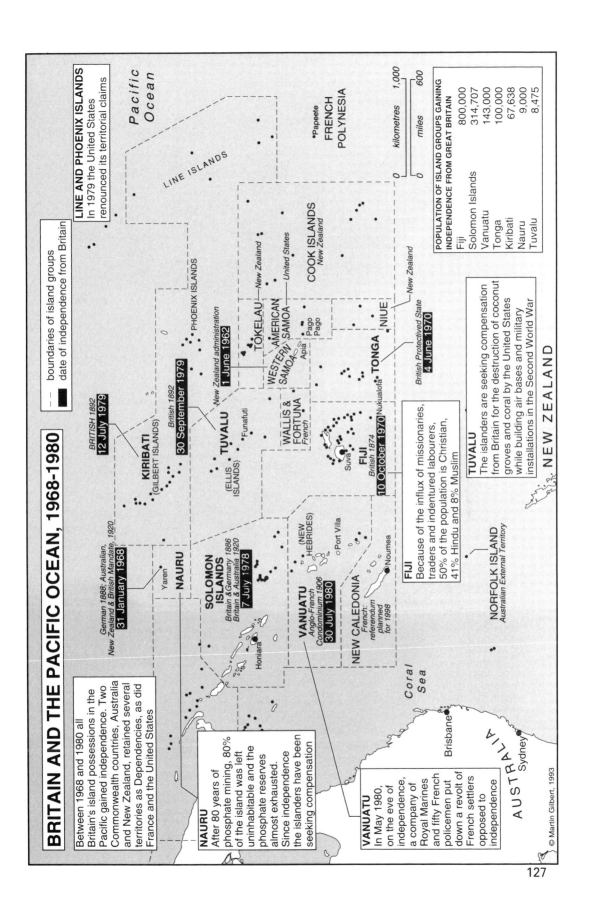

BRITAIN AND THE PACIFIC OCEAN, 1968-1980

Between 1968 and 1980 all Britain's island possessions in the Pacific gained independence. Two Commonwealth countries, Australia and New Zealand, retained several territories as Dependencies, as did France and the United States

LINE AND PHOENIX ISLANDS
In 1979 the United States renounced its territorial claims

--- boundaries of island groups
■ date of independence from Britain

POPULATION OF ISLAND GROUPS GAINING INDEPENDENCE FROM GREAT BRITAIN	
Fiji	800,000
Solomon Islands	314,707
Vanuatu	143,000
Tonga	100,000
Kiribati	67,638
Nauru	9,000
Tuvalu	8,475

Pacific Ocean

LINE ISLANDS

•Papeete FRENCH POLYNESIA

PHOENIX ISLANDS

kilometres 1,000
miles 600
0 0

KIRIBATI (GILBERT ISLANDS)
BRITISH 1892
12 July 1979

British 1892
30 September 1979

TUVALU
(ELLIS ISLANDS)
New Zealand administration
1 June 1962
Funafuti

TOKELAU —*New Zealand*

WESTERN SAMOA
United States
Apia
AMERICAN SAMOA
Pago Pago

COOK ISLANDS
New Zealand

NIUE —*New Zealand*

TONGA
Nukualofa
British Protected State
4 June 1970

German 1888: Australian, New Zealand & British Mandate, 1920
31 January 1968
Yaren
NAURU

NAURU
After 80 years of phosphate mining, 80% of the island was left uninhabitable and the phosphate reserves almost exhausted. Since independence the islanders have been seeking compensation

SOLOMON ISLANDS
Britain & Germany 1886
Britain & Australia 1920
7 July 1978
Honiara

VANUATU
(NEW HEBRIDES)
Anglo-French Condominium 1906
30 July 1980
•Port Villa

NEW CALEDONIA
French: referendum planned for 1998
•Noumea

FIJI
British 1874
Suva
10 October 1970

FIJI
Because of the influx of missionaries, traders and indentured labourers, 50% of the population is Christian, 41% Hindu and 8% Muslim

WALLIS & FORTUNA
French

TUVALU
The islanders are seeking compensation from Britain for the destruction of coconut groves and coral by the United States while building air bases and military installations in the Second World War

NORFOLK ISLAND
Australian External Territory

VANUATU
In May 1980, on the eve of independence, a company of Royal Marines and fifty French policemen put down a revolt of French settlers opposed to independence

Coral Sea

AUSTRALIA
•Brisbane
•Sydney

NEW ZEALAND

© Martin Gilbert, 1993

127

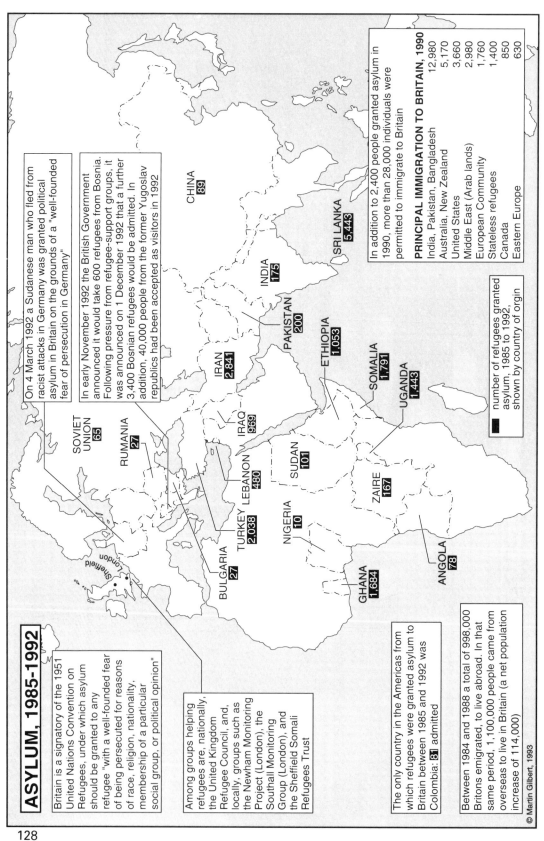

ASYLUM, 1985–1992

Britain is a signatory of the 1951 United Nations Convention on Refugees, under which asylum should be granted to any refugee "with a well-founded fear of being persecuted for reasons of race, religion, nationality, membership of a particular social group, or political opinion"

On 4 March 1992 a Sudanese man who fled from racist attacks in Germany was granted political asylum in Britain on the grounds of a "well-founded fear of persecution in Germany"

In early November 1992 the British Government announced it would take 600 refugees from Bosnia. Following pressure from refugee-support groups, it was announced on 1 December 1992 that a further 3,400 Bosnian refugees would be admitted. In addition, 40,000 people from the former Yugoslav republics had been accepted as visitors in 1992

Among groups helping refugees are, nationally, the United Kingdom Refugee Council, and, locally, groups such as the Newham Monitoring Project (London), the Southall Monitoring Group (London), and the Sheffield Somali Refugees Trust

The only country in the Americas from which refugees were granted asylum to Britain between 1985 and 1992 was Colombia: 81 admitted

Between 1984 and 1988 a total of 998,000 Britons emigrated, to live abroad. In that same period, 1,100,000 people came from overseas to live in Britain (a net population increase of 114,000)

In addition to 2,400 people granted asylum in 1990, more than 28,000 individuals were permitted to immigrate to Britain

PRINCIPAL IMMIGRATION TO BRITAIN, 1990

India, Pakistan, Bangladesh	12,980
Australia, New Zealand	5,170
United States	3,660
Middle East (Arab lands)	2,980
European Community	1,760
Stateless refugees	1,400
Canada	850
Eastern Europe	630

■ number of refugees granted asylum, 1985 to 1992, shown by country of orgin

Sheffield
London

SOVIET UNION 65

RUMANIA 27

BULGARIA 27

TURKEY 2,038

LEBANON 480

IRAQ 969

IRAN 2,841

CHINA 89

SRI LANKA 5,443

INDIA 175

PAKISTAN 200

ETHIOPIA 1,053

SOMALIA 1,791

UGANDA 1,443

SUDAN 101

NIGERIA 10

ZAIRE 167

GHANA 1,684

ANGOLA 78

© Martin Gilbert, 1993

ETHNIC MINORITIES, 1991

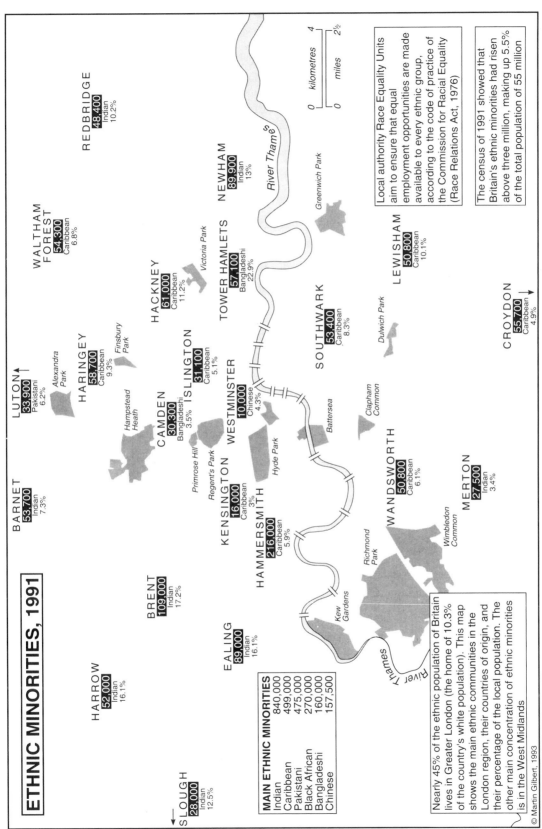

SLOUGH
28,000
Indian
12.5%

HARROW
52,000
Indian
16.1%

BARNET
53,700
Indian
7.3%

LUTON
33,900
Pakistani
6.2%

WALTHAM FOREST
54,300
Caribbean
6.8%

REDBRIDGE
48,400
Indian
10.2%

NEWHAM
89,900
Indian
13%

HARINGEY
58,700
Caribbean
9.3%

HACKNEY
61,000
Caribbean
11.2%

BRENT
109,000
Indian
17.2%

CAMDEN
30,300
Bangladeshi
3.5%

ISLINGTON
31,100
Caribbean
5.1%

WESTMINSTER
10,000
Chinese
4.3%

TOWER HAMLETS
57,100
Bangladeshi
22.9%

EALING
89,000
Indian
16.1%

KENSINGTON
16,000
Caribbean
3%

HAMMERSMITH
216,000
Caribbean
5.9%

WANDSWORTH
50,800
Caribbean
6.1%

SOUTHWARK
53,400
Caribbean
8.3%

LEWISHAM
50,800
Caribbean
10.1%

MERTON
27,500
Indian
3.4%

CROYDON
55,700
Caribbean
4.9%

Alexandra Park
Finsbury Park
Hampstead Heath
Primrose Hill
Regent's Park
Hyde Park
Battersea
Clapham Common
Victoria Park
Greenwich Park
Dulwich Park
Wimbledon Common
Richmond Park
Kew Gardens
River Thames
River Thames

MAIN ETHNIC MINORITIES

Indian	840,000
Caribbean	499,000
Pakistani	475,000
Black African	270,000
Bangladeshi	160,000
Chinese	157,500

Nearly 45% of the ethnic population of Britain lives in Greater London (the home of 10.3% of the country's white population). This map shows the main ethnic communities in the London region, their countries of origin, and their percentage of the local population. The other main concentration of ethnic minorities is in the West Midlands

Local authority Race Equality Units aim to ensure that equal employment opportunities are made available to every ethnic group, according to the code of practice of the Commission for Racial Equality (Race Relations Act, 1976)

The census of 1991 showed that Britain's ethnic minorities had risen above three million, making up 5.5% of the total population of 55 million

0				4
kilometres				
0			2½	
miles				

© Martin Gilbert, 1993

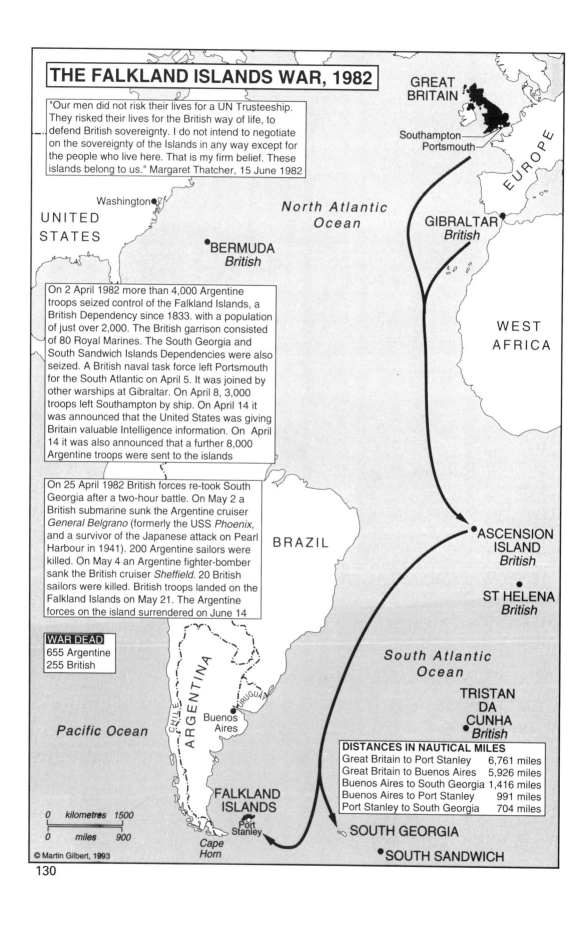

THE FALKLAND ISLANDS WAR, 1982

GREAT BRITAIN

Southampton
Portsmouth

EUROPE

"Our men did not risk their lives for a UN Trusteeship. They risked their lives for the British way of life, to defend British sovereignty. I do not intend to negotiate on the sovereignty of the Islands in any way except for the people who live here. That is my firm belief. These islands belong to us." Margaret Thatcher, 15 June 1982

Washington

UNITED
STATES

North Atlantic
Ocean

GIBRALTAR
British

BERMUDA
British

WEST
AFRICA

On 2 April 1982 more than 4,000 Argentine troops seized control of the Falkland Islands, a British Dependency since 1833. with a population of just over 2,000. The British garrison consisted of 80 Royal Marines. The South Georgia and South Sandwich Islands Dependencies were also seized. A British naval task force left Portsmouth for the South Atlantic on April 5. It was joined by other warships at Gibraltar. On April 8, 3,000 troops left Southampton by ship. On April 14 it was announced that the United States was giving Britain valuable Intelligence information. On April 14 it was also announced that a further 8,000 Argentine troops were sent to the islands

On 25 April 1982 British forces re-took South Georgia after a two-hour battle. On May 2 a British submarine sank the Argentine cruiser *General Belgrano* (formerly the USS *Phoenix*, and a survivor of the Japanese attack on Pearl Harbour in 1941). 200 Argentine sailors were killed. On May 4 an Argentine fighter-bomber sank the British cruiser *Sheffield*. 20 British sailors were killed. British troops landed on the Falkland Islands on May 21. The Argentine forces on the island surrendered on June 14

BRAZIL

ASCENSION
ISLAND
British

ST HELENA
British

WAR DEAD
655 Argentine
255 British

South Atlantic
Ocean

TRISTAN
DA
CUNHA
British

Pacific Ocean

CHILE

ARGENTINA

URUGUAY

Buenos
Aires

DISTANCES IN NAUTICAL MILES
Great Britain to Port Stanley   6,761 miles
Great Britain to Buenos Aires   5,926 miles
Buenos Aires to South Georgia   1,416 miles
Buenos Aires to Port Stanley   991 miles
Port Stanley to South Georgia   704 miles

FALKLAND
ISLANDS

Port
Stanley

Cape
Horn

SOUTH GEORGIA

SOUTH SANDWICH

0   kilometres   1500
0   miles   900

© Martin Gilbert, 1993

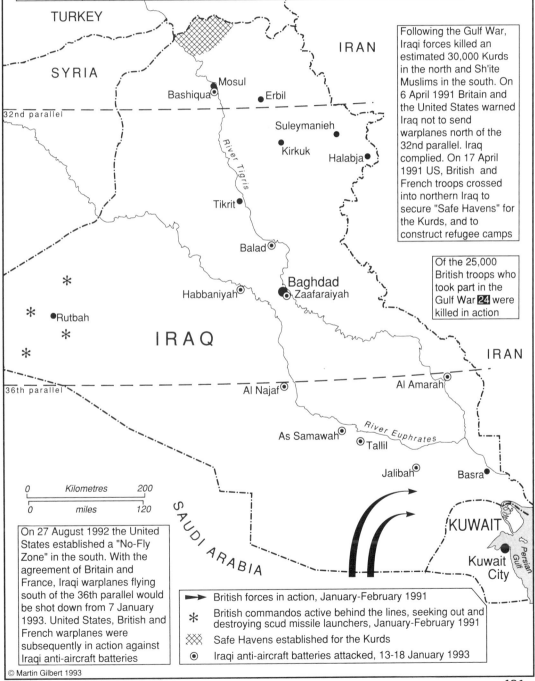

BRITAIN, THE GULF WAR AND ITS AFTERMATH, 1990-1993

On 2 August 1990 Iraqi forces occupied Kuwait. The United Nations Security Council demanded immediate withdrawal. On 29 November 1990 the Security Council authorised UN members to use force to expel Iraq from Kuwait. On 17 January 1991 Allied air forces, British among them, attacked strategic targets throughout Iraq and Iraqi-occupied Kuwait. On 24 February 1991 British forces participated in the land offensive. Four days later Iraq announced a cease-fire

TURKEY

SYRIA

IRAN

Mosul
Bashiqa
Erbil

32nd parallel

Suleymanieh
Kirkuk
Halabja

Tikrit

Balad

Following the Gulf War, Iraqi forces killed an estimated 30,000 Kurds in the north and Sh'ite Muslims in the south. On 6 April 1991 Britain and the United States warned Iraq not to send warplanes north of the 32nd parallel. Iraq complied. On 17 April 1991 US, British and French troops crossed into northern Iraq to secure "Safe Havens" for the Kurds, and to construct refugee camps

Baghdad
Zaafaraiyah
Habbaniyah

*
* ● Rutbah
*
*

IRAQ

IRAN

Of the 25,000 British troops who took part in the Gulf War **24** were killed in action

36th parallel

Al Najaf
Al Amarah

River Euphrates

As Samawah
Tallil

Jalibah
Basra

| 0 | Kilometres | 200 |
| 0 | miles | 120 |

SAUDI ARABIA

KUWAIT

Kuwait City

Persian Gulf

River Tigris

On 27 August 1992 the United States established a "No-Fly Zone" in the south. With the agreement of Britain and France, Iraqi warplanes flying south of the 36th parallel would be shot down from 7 January 1993. United States, British and French warplanes were subsequently in action against Iraqi anti-aircraft batteries

➤ British forces in action, January-February 1991

✳ British commandos active behind the lines, seeking out and destroying scud missile launchers, January-February 1991

▩ Safe Havens established for the Kurds

◉ Iraqi anti-aircraft batteries attacked, 13-18 January 1993

© Martin Gilbert 1993

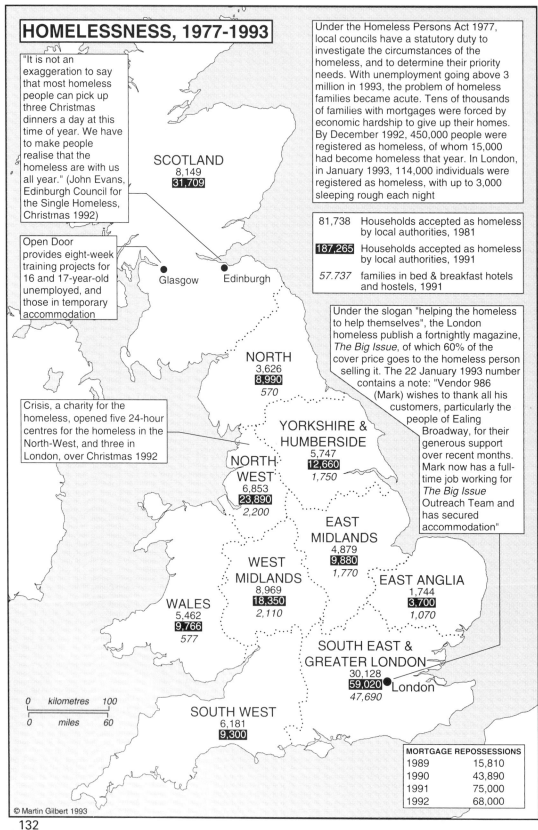

HOMELESSNESS, 1977-1993

"It is not an exaggeration to say that most homeless people can pick up three Christmas dinners a day at this time of year. We have to make people realise that the homeless are with us all year." (John Evans, Edinburgh Council for the Single Homeless, Christmas 1992)

Under the Homeless Persons Act 1977, local councils have a statutory duty to investigate the circumstances of the homeless, and to determine their priority needs. With unemployment going above 3 million in 1993, the problem of homeless families became acute. Tens of thousands of families with mortgages were forced by economic hardship to give up their homes. By December 1992, 450,000 people were registered as homeless, of whom 15,000 had become homeless that year. In London, in January 1993, 114,000 individuals were registered as homeless, with up to 3,000 sleeping rough each night

Open Door provides eight-week training projects for 16 and 17-year-old unemployed, and those in temporary accommodation

81,738	Households accepted as homeless by local authorities, 1981
187,265	Households accepted as homeless by local authorities, 1991
57.737	families in bed & breakfast hotels and hostels, 1991

Under the slogan "helping the homeless to help themselves", the London homeless publish a fortnightly magazine, *The Big Issue*, of which 60% of the cover price goes to the homeless person selling it. The 22 January 1993 number contains a note: "Vendor 986 (Mark) wishes to thank all his customers, particularly the people of Ealing Broadway, for their generous support over recent months. Mark now has a full-time job working for *The Big Issue* Outreach Team and has secured accommodation"

Crisis, a charity for the homeless, opened five 24-hour centres for the homeless in the North-West, and three in London, over Christmas 1992

SCOTLAND
8,149
31,709

● Glasgow ● Edinburgh

NORTH
3,626
8,990
570

YORKSHIRE & HUMBERSIDE
5,747
12,660
1,750

NORTH WEST
6,853
23,890
2,200

EAST MIDLANDS
4,879
9,880
1,770

WEST MIDLANDS
8,969
18,350
2,110

EAST ANGLIA
1,744
3,700
1,070

WALES
5,462
9,766
577

SOUTH EAST & GREATER LONDON
30,128
59,020
47,690
● London

SOUTH WEST
6,181
9,300

| 0 | kilometres | 100 |
| 0 | miles | 60 |

MORTGAGE REPOSSESSIONS	
1989	15,810
1990	43,890
1991	75,000
1992	68,000

© Martin Gilbert 1993

132

HOMES FOR THE HOMELESS, 1992-1993

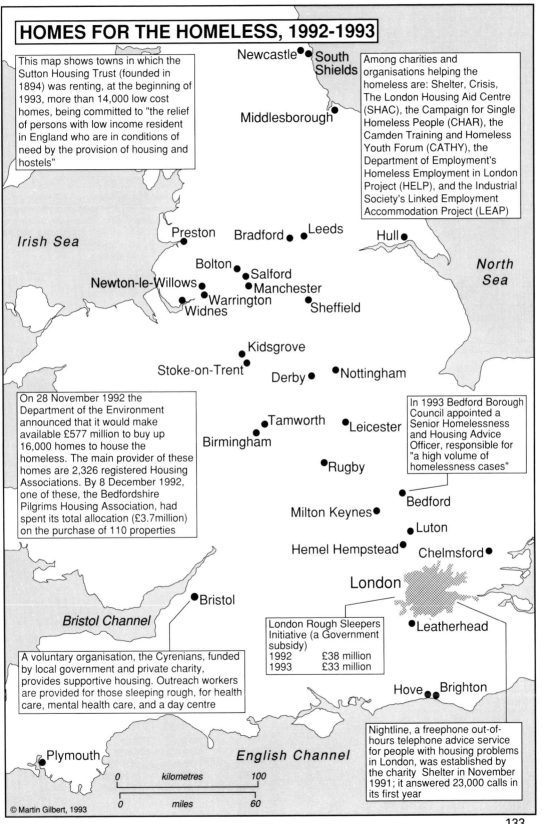

This map shows towns in which the Sutton Housing Trust (founded in 1894) was renting, at the beginning of 1993, more than 14,000 low cost homes, being committed to "the relief of persons with low income resident in England who are in conditions of need by the provision of housing and hostels"

Among charities and organisations helping the homeless are: Shelter, Crisis, The London Housing Aid Centre (SHAC), the Campaign for Single Homeless People (CHAR), the Camden Training and Homeless Youth Forum (CATHY), the Department of Employment's Homeless Employment in London Project (HELP), and the Industrial Society's Linked Employment Accommodation Project (LEAP)

Newcastle • • South Shields

Middlesborough

Preston   Bradford • • Leeds   Hull •

Irish Sea

Bolton
Newton-le-Willows • • Salford
Warrington • Manchester
Widnes   Sheffield

North Sea

Kidsgrove
Stoke-on-Trent   Derby • • Nottingham

On 28 November 1992 the Department of the Environment announced that it would make available £577 million to buy up 16,000 homes to house the homeless. The main provider of these homes are 2,326 registered Housing Associations. By 8 December 1992, one of these, the Bedfordshire Pilgrims Housing Association, had spent its total allocation (£3.7million) on the purchase of 110 properties

Tamworth • Leicester
Birmingham

• Rugby

In 1993 Bedford Borough Council appointed a Senior Homelessness and Housing Advice Officer, responsible for "a high volume of homelessness cases"

Milton Keynes • • Bedford
• Luton
Hemel Hempstead • Chelmsford •

London

• Bristol

Bristol Channel

A voluntary organisation, the Cyrenians, funded by local government and private charity, provides supportive housing. Outreach workers are provided for those sleeping rough, for health care, mental health care, and a day centre

London Rough Sleepers Initiative (a Government subsidy)
1992   £38 million
1993   £33 million

• Leatherhead

Hove • • Brighton

Plymouth

English Channel

Nightline, a freephone out-of-hours telephone advice service for people with housing problems in London, was established by the charity Shelter in November 1991; it answered 23,000 calls in its first year

| 0 | kilometres | 100 |
| 0 | miles | 60 |

© Martin Gilbert, 1993

133

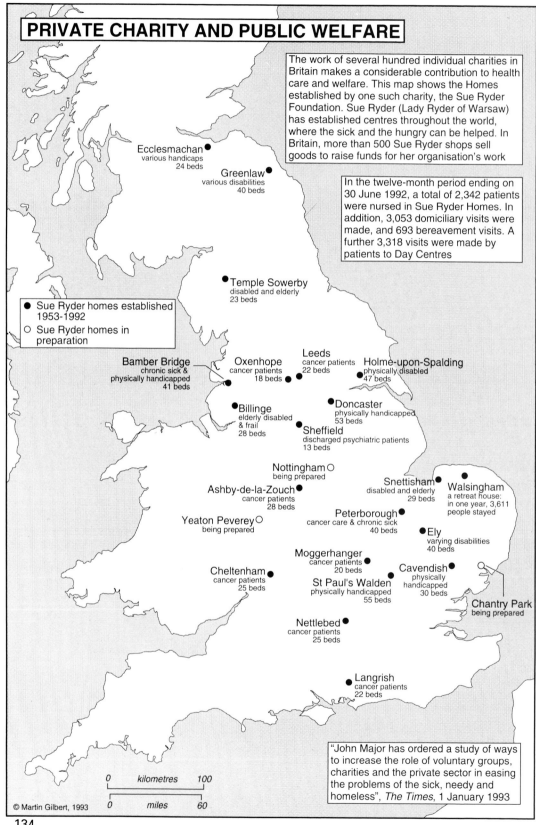

PRIVATE CHARITY AND PUBLIC WELFARE

The work of several hundred individual charities in Britain makes a considerable contribution to health care and welfare. This map shows the Homes established by one such charity, the Sue Ryder Foundation. Sue Ryder (Lady Ryder of Warsaw) has established centres throughout the world, where the sick and the hungry can be helped. In Britain, more than 500 Sue Ryder shops sell goods to raise funds for her organisation's work

In the twelve-month period ending on 30 June 1992, a total of 2,342 patients were nursed in Sue Ryder Homes. In addition, 3,053 domiciliary visits were made, and 693 bereavement visits. A further 3,318 visits were made by patients to Day Centres

Ecclesmachan
various handicaps
24 beds

Greenlaw
various disabilities
40 beds

Temple Sowerby
disabled and elderly
23 beds

● Sue Ryder homes established 1953-1992
○ Sue Ryder homes in preparation

Bamber Bridge
chronic sick &
physically handicapped
41 beds

Oxenhope
cancer patients
18 beds

Leeds
cancer patients
22 beds

Holme-upon-Spalding
physically disabled
47 beds

Billinge
elderly disabled
& frail
28 beds

Doncaster
physically handicapped
53 beds

Sheffield
discharged psychiatric patients
13 beds

Nottingham ○
being prepared

Snettisham
disabled and elderly
29 beds

Walsingham
a retreat house:
in one year, 3,611
people stayed

Ashby-de-la-Zouch
cancer patients
28 beds

Yeaton Peverey ○
being prepared

Peterborough
cancer care & chronic sick
40 beds

Ely
varying disabilities
40 beds

Moggerhanger
cancer patients
20 beds

Cavendish
physically
handicapped
30 beds

Cheltenham
cancer patients
25 beds

St Paul's Walden
physically handicapped
55 beds

Chantry Park
being prepared

Nettlebed
cancer patients
25 beds

Langrish
cancer patients
22 beds

"John Major has ordered a study of ways to increase the role of voluntary groups, charities and the private sector in easing the problems of the sick, needy and homeless", *The Times*, 1 January 1993

0   kilometres   100

0   miles   60

© Martin Gilbert, 1993

134

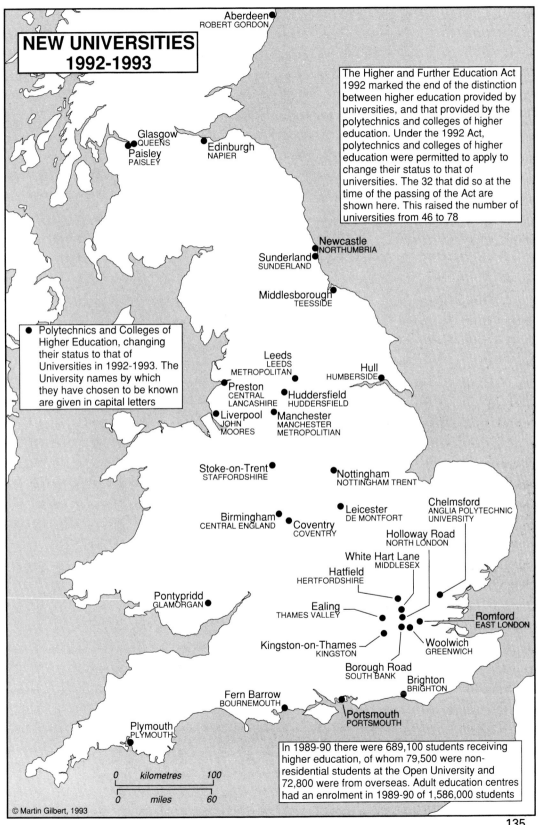

NEW UNIVERSITIES 1992-1993

Aberdeen
ROBERT GORDON

The Higher and Further Education Act 1992 marked the end of the distinction between higher education provided by universities, and that provided by the polytechnics and colleges of higher education. Under the 1992 Act, polytechnics and colleges of higher education were permitted to apply to change their status to that of universities. The 32 that did so at the time of the passing of the Act are shown here. This raised the number of universities from 46 to 78

Glasgow
QUEENS
Paisley
PAISLEY

Edinburgh
NAPIER

Newcastle
NORTHUMBRIA

Sunderland
SUNDERLAND

Middlesborough
TEESSIDE

• Polytechnics and Colleges of Higher Education, changing their status to that of Universities in 1992-1993. The University names by which they have chosen to be known are given in capital letters

Leeds
LEEDS
METROPOLITAN

Hull
HUMBERSIDE

Preston
CENTRAL
LANCASHIRE

Huddersfield
HUDDERSFIELD

Liverpool
JOHN
MOORES

Manchester
MANCHESTER
METROPOLITIAN

Stoke-on-Trent
STAFFORDSHIRE

Nottingham
NOTTINGHAM TRENT

Chelmsford
ANGLIA POLYTECHNIC
UNIVERSITY

Birmingham
CENTRAL ENGLAND

Coventry
COVENTRY

Leicester
DE MONTFORT

Holloway Road
NORTH LONDON

White Hart Lane
MIDDLESEX

Hatfield
HERTFORDSHIRE

Pontypridd
GLAMORGAN

Ealing
THAMES VALLEY

Romford
EAST LONDON

Kingston-on-Thames
KINGSTON

Woolwich
GREENWICH

Borough Road
SOUTH BANK

Brighton
BRIGHTON

Fern Barrow
BOURNEMOUTH

Portsmouth
PORTSMOUTH

Plymouth
PLYMOUTH

In 1989-90 there were 689,100 students receiving higher education, of whom 79,500 were non-residential students at the Open University and 72,800 were from overseas. Adult education centres had an enrolment in 1989-90 of 1,586,000 students

0 — kilometres — 100

0 — miles — 60

© Martin Gilbert, 1993

135

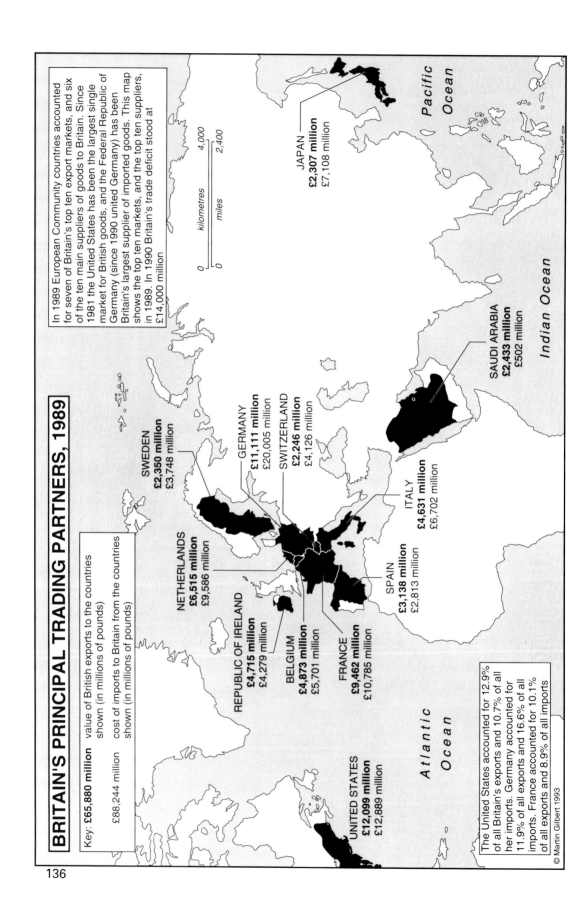

BRITAIN'S PRINCIPAL TRADING PARTNERS, 1989

Key: **£65,880 million** value of British exports to the countries shown (in millions of pounds)

£88,244 million cost of imports to Britain from the countries shown (in millions of pounds)

In 1989 European Community countries accounted for seven of Britain's top ten export markets, and six of the ten main suppliers of goods to Britain. Since 1981 the United States has been the largest single market for British goods, and the Federal Republic of Germany (since 1990 united Germany) has been Britain's largest supplier of imported goods. This map shows the top ten markets, and the top ten suppliers, in 1989. In 1990 Britain's trade deficit stood at £14,000 million

The United States accounted for 12.9% of all Britain's exports and 10.7% of all her imports. Germany accounted for 11.9% of all exports and 16.6% of all imports. France accounted for 10.1% of all exports and 8.9% of all imports

UNITED STATES
£12,099 million
£12,889 million

SWEDEN
£2,350 million
£3,748 million

GERMANY
£11,111 million
£20,005 million

SWITZERLAND
£2,246 million
£4,126 million

NETHERLANDS
£6,515 million
£9,586 million

REPUBLIC OF IRELAND
£4,715 million
£4,279 million

BELGIUM
£4,873 million
£5,701 million

FRANCE
£9,462 million
£10,785 million

ITALY
£4,631 million
£6,702 million

SPAIN
£3,138 million
£2,813 million

SAUDI ARABIA
£2,433 million
£502 million

JAPAN
£2,307 million
£7,108 million

Atlantic Ocean

Pacific Ocean

Indian Ocean

kilometres 4,000

miles 2,400

0

0

© Martin Gilbert 1993

136

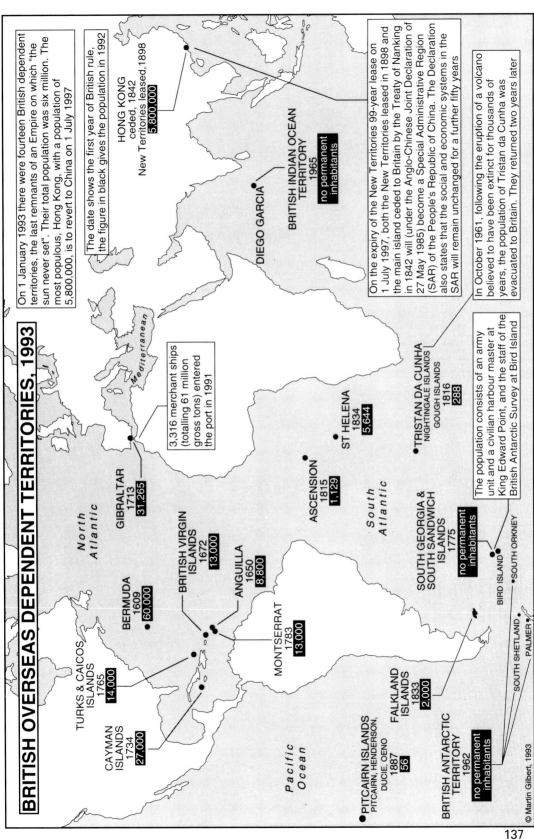

BRITISH OVERSEAS DEPENDENT TERRITORIES, 1993

On 1 January 1993 there were fourteen British dependent territories, the last remnants of an Empire on which "the sun never set". Their total population was six million. The most populous, Hong Kong, with a population of 5,800,000, is to revert to China on 1 July 1997

The date shows the first year of British rule, the figure in black gives the population in 1992

HONG KONG
ceded, 1842
New Territories leased, 1898
5,800,000

BRITISH INDIAN OCEAN TERRITORY
1965
no permanent inhabitants

DIEGO GARCIA

On the expiry of the New Territories 99-year lease on 1 July 1997, both the New Territories leased in 1898 and the main island ceded to Britain by the Treaty of Nanking in 1842 will (under the Anglo-Chinese Joint Declaration of 27 May 1985) become a Special Administrative Region (SAR) of the People's Republic of China. The Declaration also states that the social and economic systems in the SAR will remain unchanged for a further fifty years

In October 1961, following the eruption of a volcano believed to have been extinct for thousands of years, the population of Tristan da Cunha was evacuated to Britain. They returned two years later

Mediterranean

3,316 merchant ships (totalling 61 million gross tons) entered the port in 1991

GIBRALTAR
1713
31,265

North Atlantic

ST HELENA
1834
5,644

ASCENSION
1815
1,129

South Atlantic

TRISTAN DA CUNHA
1816
NIGHTINGALE ISLANDS
GOUGH ISLANDS
288

The population consists of an army unit and a civilian harbour master at King Edward Point, and the staff of the British Antarctic Survey at Bird Island

BERMUDA
1609
60,000

TURKS & CAICOS ISLANDS
1765
14,000

CAYMAN ISLANDS
1734
27,000

BRITISH VIRGIN ISLANDS
1672
13,000

ANGUILLA
1650
8,800

MONTSERRAT
1783
13,000

Pacific Ocean

FALKLAND ISLANDS
1833
2,000

SOUTH GEORGIA & SOUTH SANDWICH ISLANDS
1775
no permanent inhabitants

BIRD ISLAND

SOUTH ORKNEY

PITCAIRN ISLANDS
PITCAIRN, HENDERSON, DUCIE, OENO
1887
56

BRITISH ANTARCTIC TERRITORY
1962
no permanent inhabitants

SOUTH SHETLAND

PALMER

© Martin Gilbert, 1993

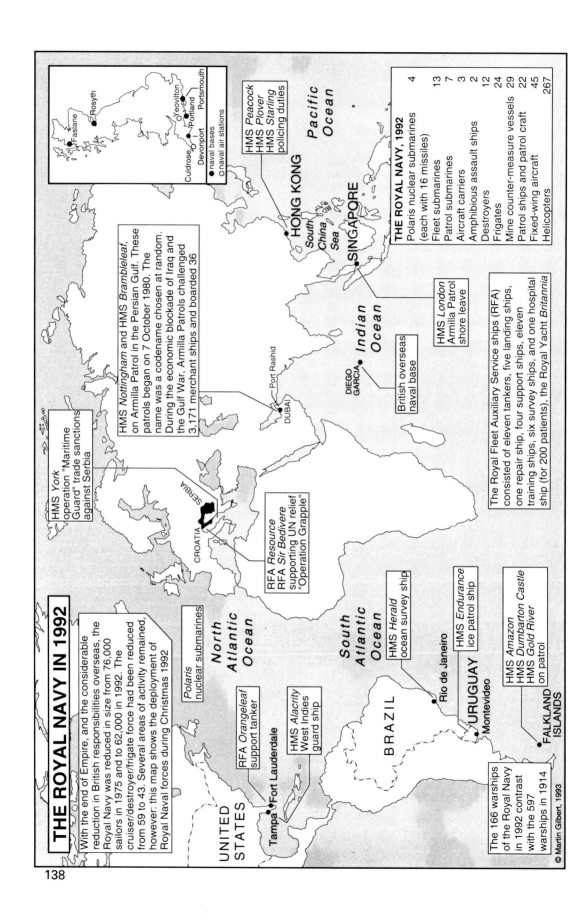

THE ROYAL NAVY IN 1992

With the end of Empire, and the considerable reduction in British responsibilities overseas, the Royal Navy was reduced in size from 76,000 sailors in 1975 and to 62,000 in 1992. The cruiser/destroyer/frigate force had been reduced from 59 to 43. Several areas of activity remained, however: this map shows the deployment of Royal Naval forces during Christmas 1992

THE ROYAL NAVY, 1992

Polaris nuclear submarines (each with 16 missiles)	4
Fleet submarines	13
Patrol submarines	7
Aircraft carriers	3
Amphibious assault ships	2
Destroyers	12
Frigates	24
Mine counter-measure vessels	29
Patrol ships and patrol craft	22
Fixed-wing aircraft	45
Helicopters	267

The Royal Fleet Auxiliary Service ships (RFA) consisted of eleven tankers, five landing ships, one repair ship, four support ships, eleven training ships, six survey ships, and one hospital ship (for 200 patients), the Royal Yacht *Britannia*

HMS *York*
operation "Maritime Guard" trade sanctions against Serbia

HMS *Nottingham* and HMS *Brambleleaf*, on Armilla Patrol in the Persian Gulf. These patrols began on 7 October 1980. The name was a codename chosen at random. During the economic blockade of Iraq and the Gulf War, Armilla Patrols challenged 3,171 merchant ships and boarded 36

HMS *Peacock*
HMS *Plover*
HMS *Starling*
policing duties

HMS *London*
Armilla Patrol
shore leave

RFA *Resource*
RFA *Sir Bedivere*
supporting UN relief
"Operation Grapple"

British overseas
naval base

Polaris
nuclear submarines

RFA *Orangeleaf*
support tanker

HMS *Alacrity*
West Indies
guard ship

HMS *Herald*
ocean survey ship

HMS *Endurance*
ice patrol ship

HMS *Amazon*
HMS *Dumbarton Castle*
HMS *Gold River*
on patrol

The 166 warships of the Royal Navy in 1992 contrast with the 597 warships in 1914

*North
Atlantic
Ocean*

*South
Atlantic
Ocean*

*Indian
Ocean*

*Pacific
Ocean*

*South
China
Sea*

UNITED
STATES

BRAZIL

URUGUAY

FALKLAND
ISLANDS

SERBIA

CROATIA

HONG KONG

SINGAPORE

Tampa

Fort Lauderdale

Rio de Janeiro

Montevideo

DUBAI

Port Rashid

DIEGO
GARCIA

Rosyth

Faslane

Yeovilton

Portland

Portsmouth

Culdrose

Devonport

● naval bases
○ naval air stations

© Martin Gilbert, 1993

BRITISH FORCES OVERSEAS, 1992-1993

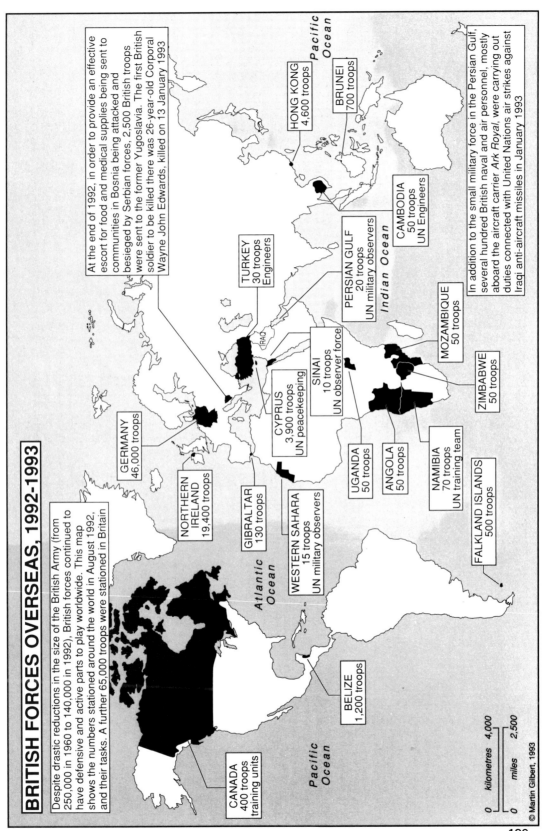

Despite drastic reductions in the size of the British Army (from 250,000 in 1960 to 140,000 in 1992), British forces continued to have defensive and active parts to play worldwide. This map shows the numbers stationed around the world in August 1992, and their tasks. A further 65,000 troops were stationed in Britain

At the end of 1992, in order to provide an effective escort for food and medical supplies being sent to communities in Bosnia being attacked and besieged by Serbian forces, 2,500 British troops were sent to the former Yugoslavia. The first British soldier to be killed there was 26-year-old Corporal Wayne John Edwards, killed on 13 January 1993

In addition to the small military force in the Persian Gulf, several hundred British naval and air personnel, mostly aboard the aircraft carrier *Ark Royal*, were carrying out duties connected with United Nations air strikes against Iraqi anti-aircraft missiles in January 1993

HONG KONG
4,600 troops

BRUNEI
700 troops

CAMBODIA
50 troops
UN Engineers

TURKEY
30 troops
Engineers

PERSIAN GULF
20 troops
UN military observers

MOZAMBIQUE
50 troops

ZIMBABWE
50 troops

CYPRUS
3,900 troops
UN peacekeeping

SINAI
10 troops
UN observer force

UGANDA
50 troops

ANGOLA
50 troops

NAMIBIA
70 troops
UN training team

FALKLAND ISLANDS
500 troops

GERMANY
46,000 troops

NORTHERN IRELAND
19,400 troops

GIBRALTAR
130 troops

WESTERN SAHARA
15 troops
UN military observers

BELIZE
1,200 troops

CANADA
400 troops
training units

Pacific Ocean

Atlantic Ocean

Indian Ocean

Pacific Ocean

IRAQ

0   kilometres   4,000
0   miles   2,500

© Martin Gilbert, 1993

139

TOWARDS A SINGLE EUROPEAN MARKET, OCTOBER-DECEMBER 1992

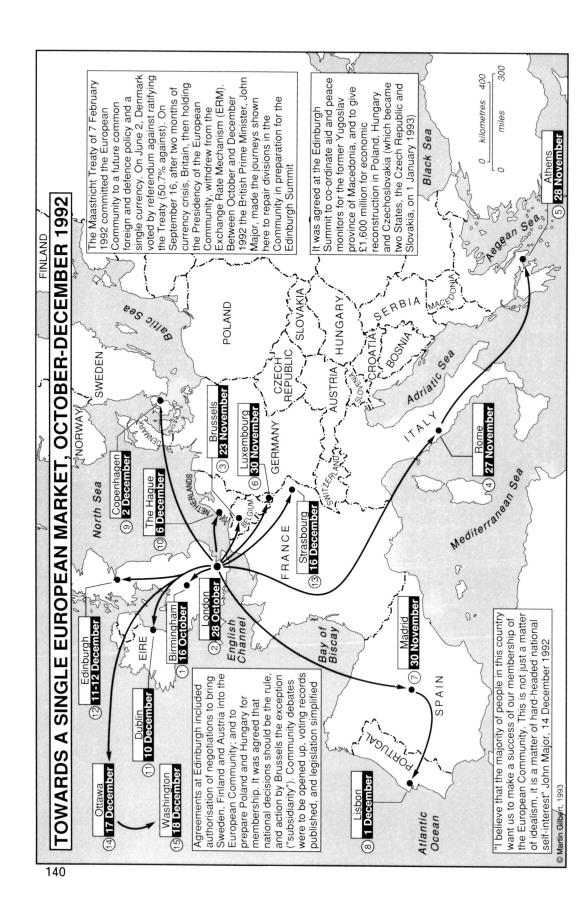

The Maastricht Treaty of 7 February 1992 committed the European Community to a future common foreign and defence policy and a single currency. On June 2, Denmark voted by referendum against ratifying the Treaty (50.7% against). On September 16, after two months of currency crisis, Britain, then holding the Presidency of the European Community, withdrew from the Exchange Rate Mechanism (ERM). Between October and December 1992 the British Prime Minister, John Major, made the journeys shown here to repair divisions in the Community in preparation for the Edinburgh Summit

It was agreed at the Edinburgh Summit to co-ordinate aid and peace monitors for the former Yugoslav province of Macedonia, and to give £1,600 million for economic reconstruction in Poland, Hungary and Czechoslovakia (which became two States, the Czech Republic and Slovakia, on 1 January 1993)

Agreements at Edinburgh included authorisation of negotiations to bring Sweden, Finland and Austria into the European Community; and to prepare Poland and Hungary for membership. It was agreed that national decisions should be the rule, and action by Brussels the exception ("subsidiarity"). Community debates were to be opened up, voting records published, and legislation simplified

"I believe that the majority of people in this country want us to make a success of our membership of the European Community. This is not just a matter of idealism, it is a matter of hard-headed national self-interest" John Major, 14 December 1992

① Birmingham **16 October**
② London **28 October**
③ Brussels **23 November**
④ Rome **27 November**
⑤ Athens **28 November**
⑥ Luxembourg **30 November**
⑦ Madrid **30 November**
⑧ Lisbon **1 December**
⑨ Copenhagen **2 December**
⑩ The Hague **6 December**
⑪ Dublin **10 December**
⑫ Edinburgh **11-12 December**
⑬ Strasbourg **16 December**
⑭ Ottawa **17 December**
⑮ Washington **18 December**

FINLAND
SWEDEN
NORWAY
DENMARK
NETHERLANDS
BELGIUM
EIRE
POLAND
CZECH REPUBLIC
SLOVAKIA
GERMANY
AUSTRIA
HUNGARY
SWITZERLAND
SLOVENIA
CROATIA
BOSNIA
SERBIA
MACEDONIA
FRANCE
ITALY
SPAIN
PORTUGAL

Baltic Sea
North Sea
English Channel
Bay of Biscay
Atlantic Ocean
Mediterranean Sea
Adriatic Sea
Aegean Sea
Black Sea

0 kilometres 400
0 miles 300

© Martin Gilbert, 1993

140

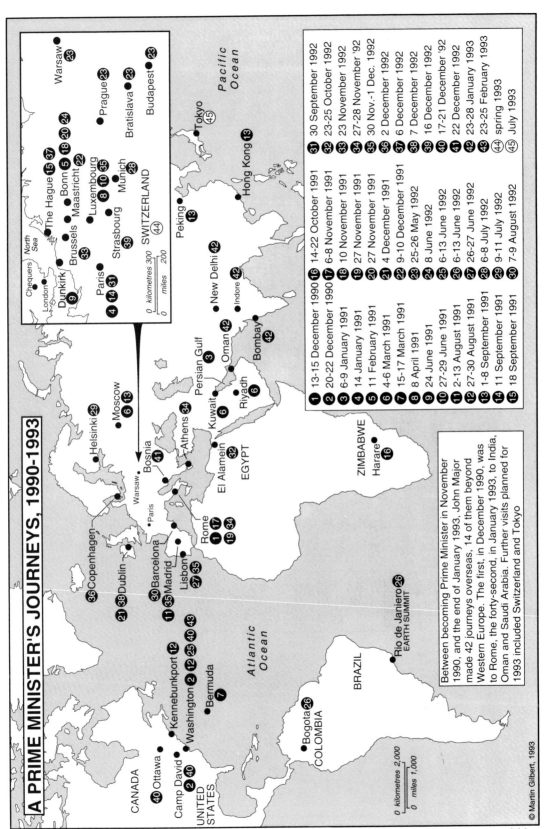

A PRIME MINISTER'S JOURNEYS, 1990-1993

Between becoming Prime Minister in November 1990, and the end of January 1993, John Major made 42 journeys overseas, 14 of them beyond Western Europe. The first, in December 1990, was to Rome, the forty-second, in January 1993, to India, Oman and Saudi Arabia. Further visits planned for 1993 included Switzerland and Tokyo

① 13-15 December 1990
② 20-22 December 1990
③ 6-9 January 1991
④ 14 January 1991
⑤ 11 February 1991
⑥ 4-6 March 1991
⑦ 15-17 March 1991
⑧ 8 April 1991
⑨ 24 June 1991
⑩ 27-29 June 1991
⑪ 2-13 August 1991
⑫ 27-30 August 1991
⑬ 1-8 September 1991
⑭ 11 September 1991
⑮ 18 September 1991

⑯ 14-22 October 1991
⑰ 6-8 November 1991
⑱ 10 November 1991
⑲ 27 November 1991
⑳ 27 November 1991
㉑ 4 December 1991
㉒ 9-10 December 1991
㉓ 25-26 May 1992
㉔ 8 June 1992
㉕ 6-13 June 1992
㉖ 6-13 June 1992
㉗ 26-27 June 1992
㉘ 6-8 July 1992
㉙ 9-11 July 1992
㉚ 7-9 August 1992

㉛ 30 September 1992
㉜ 23-25 October 1992
㉝ 23 November 1992
㉞ 27-28 November '92
㉟ 30 Nov.-1 Dec. 1992
㊱ 2 December 1992
㊲ 6 December 1992
㊳ 7 December 1992
㊴ 16 December 1992
㊵ 17-21 December '92
㊶ 22 December 1992
㊷ 23-28 January 1993
㊸ 23-25 February 1993
㊹ spring 1993
㊺ July 1993

© Martin Gilbert, 1993

141

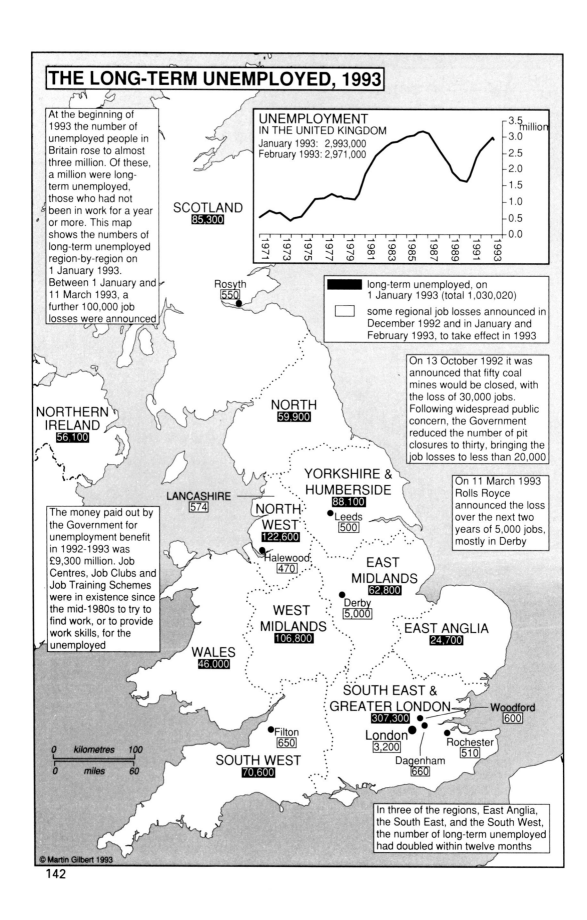

THE LONG-TERM UNEMPLOYED, 1993

At the beginning of 1993 the number of unemployed people in Britain rose to almost three million. Of these, a million were long-term unemployed, those who had not been in work for a year or more. This map shows the numbers of long-term unemployed region-by-region on 1 January 1993. Between 1 January and 11 March 1993, a further 100,000 job losses were announced

UNEMPLOYMENT
IN THE UNITED KINGDOM
January 1993: 2,993,000
February 1993: 2,971,000

SCOTLAND
85,300

Rosyth
550

long-term unemployed, on
1 January 1993 (total 1,030,020)

some regional job losses announced in
December 1992 and in January and
February 1993, to take effect in 1993

On 13 October 1992 it was announced that fifty coal mines would be closed, with the loss of 30,000 jobs. Following widespread public concern, the Government reduced the number of pit closures to thirty, bringing the job losses to less than 20,000

NORTHERN IRELAND
56,100

NORTH
59,900

YORKSHIRE & HUMBERSIDE
88,100

Leeds
500

On 11 March 1993 Rolls Royce announced the loss over the next two years of 5,000 jobs, mostly in Derby

LANCASHIRE
574

NORTH WEST
122,600

Halewood
470

EAST MIDLANDS
62,800

The money paid out by the Government for unemployment benefit in 1992-1993 was £9,300 million. Job Centres, Job Clubs and Job Training Schemes were in existence since the mid-1980s to try to find work, or to provide work skills, for the unemployed

WEST MIDLANDS
106,800

Derby
5,000

EAST ANGLIA
24,700

WALES
46,000

SOUTH EAST & GREATER LONDON
307,300

Woodford
600

Filton
650

London
3,200

Rochester
510

0   kilometres   100
0   miles   60

SOUTH WEST
70,600

Dagenham
660

In three of the regions, East Anglia, the South East, and the South West, the number of long-term unemployed had doubled within twelve months

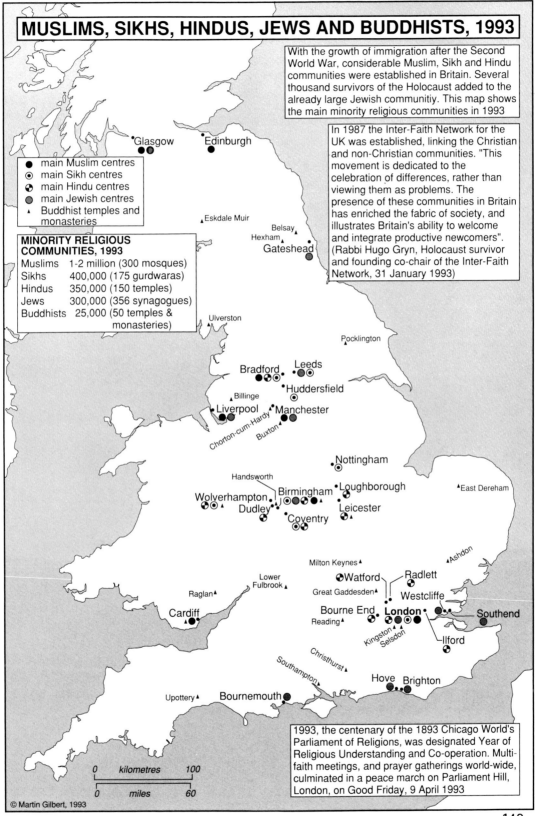

MUSLIMS, SIKHS, HINDUS, JEWS AND BUDDHISTS, 1993

With the growth of immigration after the Second World War, considerable Muslim, Sikh and Hindu communities were established in Britain. Several thousand survivors of the Holocaust added to the already large Jewish communitiy. This map shows the main minority religious communities in 1993

In 1987 the Inter-Faith Network for the UK was established, linking the Christian and non-Christian communities. "This movement is dedicated to the celebration of differences, rather than viewing them as problems. The presence of these communities in Britain has enriched the fabric of society, and illustrates Britain's ability to welcome and integrate productive newcomers". (Rabbi Hugo Gryn, Holocaust survivor and founding co-chair of the Inter-Faith Network, 31 January 1993)

- ● main Muslim centres
- ◉ main Sikh centres
- ◐ main Hindu centres
- ● main Jewish centres
- ▲ Buddhist temples and monasteries

MINORITY RELIGIOUS COMMUNITIES, 1993

Muslims	1-2 million (300 mosques)
Sikhs	400,000 (175 gurdwaras)
Hindus	350,000 (150 temples)
Jews	300,000 (356 synagogues)
Buddhists	25,000 (50 temples & monasteries)

Glasgow

Edinburgh

Eskdale Muir

Belsay

Hexham

Gateshead

Ulverston

Pocklington

Bradford   Leeds

Huddersfield

Billinge

Liverpool   Manchester

Chorton-cum-Hardy

Buxton

Nottingham

Handsworth

Wolverhampton   Birmingham   Loughborough

Dudley   Leicester

Coventry

East Dereham

Milton Keynes

Lower Fulbrook

Radlett

Watford

Raglan   Great Gaddesden   Westcliffe

Cardiff   Bourne End   London   Southend

Reading

Kingston   Selsdon   Ilford

Christhurst

Southampton

Upottery   Bournemouth   Hove   Brighton

Ashdon

1993, the centenary of the 1893 Chicago World's Parliament of Religions, was designated Year of Religious Understanding and Co-operation. Multi-faith meetings, and prayer gatherings world-wide, culminated in a peace march on Parliament Hill, London, on Good Friday, 9 April 1993

0   kilometres   100

0   miles   60

© Martin Gilbert, 1993

143

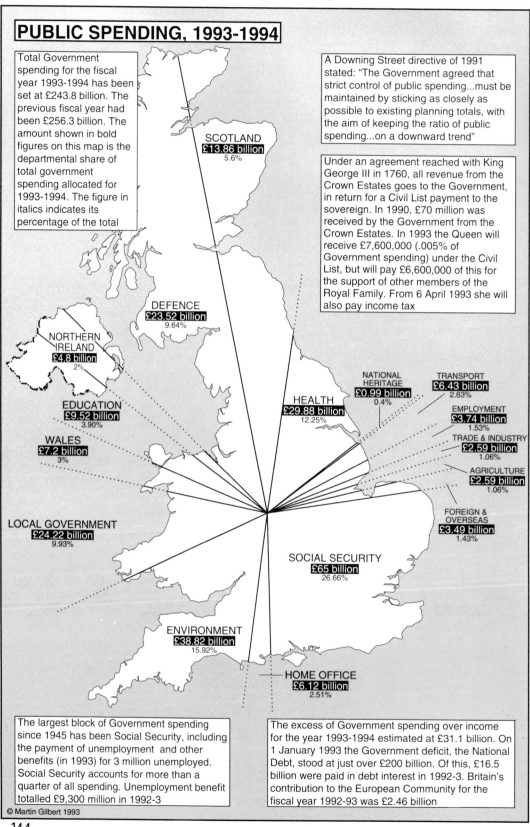

PUBLIC SPENDING, 1993-1994

Total Government spending for the fiscal year 1993-1994 has been set at £243.8 billion. The previous fiscal year had been £256.3 billion. The amount shown in bold figures on this map is the departmental share of total government spending allocated for 1993-1994. The figure in italics indicates its percentage of the total

A Downing Street directive of 1991 stated: "The Government agreed that strict control of public spending...must be maintained by sticking as closely as possible to existing planning totals, with the aim of keeping the ratio of public spending...on a downward trend"

Under an agreement reached with King George III in 1760, all revenue from the Crown Estates goes to the Government, in return for a Civil List payment to the sovereign. In 1990, £70 million was received by the Government from the Crown Estates. In 1993 the Queen will receive £7,600,000 (.005% of Government spending) under the Civil List, but will pay £6,600,000 of this for the support of other members of the Royal Family. From 6 April 1993 she will also pay income tax

SCOTLAND
£13.86 billion
5.6%

DEFENCE
£23.52 billion
9.64%

NORTHERN IRELAND
£4.8 billion
2%

EDUCATION
£9.52 billion
3.90%

WALES
£7.2 billion
3%

HEALTH
£29.88 billion
12.25%

NATIONAL HERITAGE
£0.99 billion
0.4%

TRANSPORT
£6.43 billion
2.63%

EMPLOYMENT
£3.74 billion
1.53%

TRADE & INDUSTRY
£2.59 billion
1.06%

AGRICULTURE
£2.59 billion
1.06%

LOCAL GOVERNMENT
£24.22 billion
9.93%

FOREIGN & OVERSEAS
£3.49 billion
1.43%

SOCIAL SECURITY
£65 billion
26.66%

ENVIRONMENT
£38.82 billion
15.92%

HOME OFFICE
£6.12 billion
2.51%

The largest block of Government spending since 1945 has been Social Security, including the payment of unemployment and other benefits (in 1993) for 3 million unemployed. Social Security accounts for more than a quarter of all spending. Unemployment benefit totalled £9,300 million in 1992-3

The excess of Government spending over income for the year 1993-1994 estimated at £31.1 billion. On 1 January 1993 the Government deficit, the National Debt, stood at just over £200 billion. Of this, £16.5 billion were paid in debt interest in 1992-3. Britain's contribution to the European Community for the fiscal year 1992-93 was £2.46 billion

© Martin Gilbert 1993

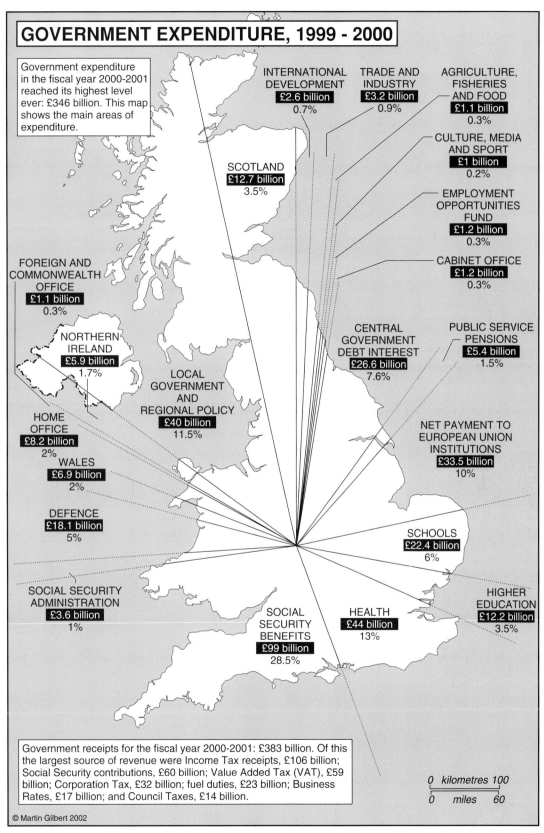

GOVERNMENT EXPENDITURE, 1999 - 2000

Government expenditure in the fiscal year 2000-2001 reached its highest level ever: £346 billion. This map shows the main areas of expenditure.

INTERNATIONAL DEVELOPMENT
£2.6 billion
0.7%

TRADE AND INDUSTRY
£3.2 billion
0.9%

AGRICULTURE, FISHERIES AND FOOD
£1.1 billion
0.3%

SCOTLAND
£12.7 billion
3.5%

CULTURE, MEDIA AND SPORT
£1 billion
0.2%

EMPLOYMENT OPPORTUNITIES FUND
£1.2 billion
0.3%

CABINET OFFICE
£1.2 billion
0.3%

FOREIGN AND COMMONWEALTH OFFICE
£1.1 billion
0.3%

NORTHERN IRELAND
£5.9 billion
1.7%

CENTRAL GOVERNMENT DEBT INTEREST
£26.6 billion
7.6%

PUBLIC SERVICE PENSIONS
£5.4 billion
1.5%

LOCAL GOVERNMENT AND REGIONAL POLICY
£40 billion
11.5%

HOME OFFICE
£8.2 billion
2%

NET PAYMENT TO EUROPEAN UNION INSTITUTIONS
£33.5 billion
10%

WALES
£6.9 billion
2%

DEFENCE
£18.1 billion
5%

SCHOOLS
£22.4 billion
6%

SOCIAL SECURITY ADMINISTRATION
£3.6 billion
1%

HIGHER EDUCATION
£12.2 billion
3.5%

SOCIAL SECURITY BENEFITS
£99 billion
28.5%

HEALTH
£44 billion
13%

Government receipts for the fiscal year 2000-2001: £383 billion. Of this the largest source of revenue were Income Tax receipts, £106 billion; Social Security contributions, £60 billion; Value Added Tax (VAT), £59 billion; Corporation Tax, £32 billion; fuel duties, £23 billion; Business Rates, £17 billion; and Council Taxes, £14 billion.

0   kilometres   100

0   miles   60

© Martin Gilbert 2002

145

The Twenty-First Century

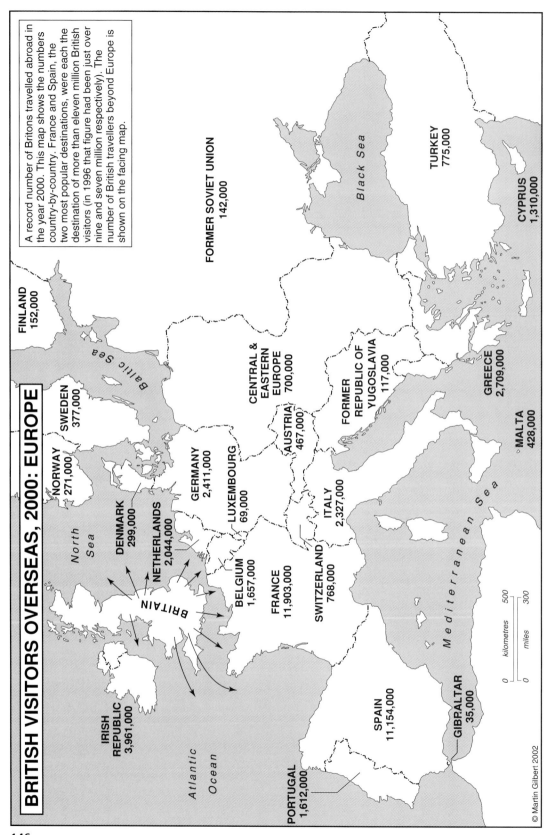

BRITISH VISITORS OVERSEAS, 2000: EUROPE

A record number of Britons travelled abroad in the year 2000. This map shows the numbers country-by-country. France and Spain, the two most popular destinations, were each the destination of more than eleven million British visitors (in 1996 that figure had been just over nine and seven million respectively). The number of British travellers beyond Europe is shown on the facing map.

FINLAND
152,000

FORMER SOVIET UNION
142,000

SWEDEN
377,000

NORWAY
271,000

Baltic Sea

North Sea

DENMARK
299,000

NETHERLANDS
2,044,000

GERMANY
2,411,000

LUXEMBOURG
69,000

AUSTRIA
467,000

CENTRAL & EASTERN EUROPE
700,000

BRITAIN

BELGIUM
1,657,000

FRANCE
11,903,000

SWITZERLAND
768,000

ITALY
2,327,000

FORMER REPUBLIC OF YUGOSLAVIA
117,000

Black Sea

TURKEY
775,000

IRISH REPUBLIC
3,961,000

Atlantic Ocean

GREECE
2,709,000

CYPRUS
1,310,000

MALTA
428,000

Mediterranean Sea

PORTUGAL
1,612,000

SPAIN
11,154,000

GIBRALTAR
35,000

0   kilometres   500
0   miles   300

© Martin Gilbert 2002

146

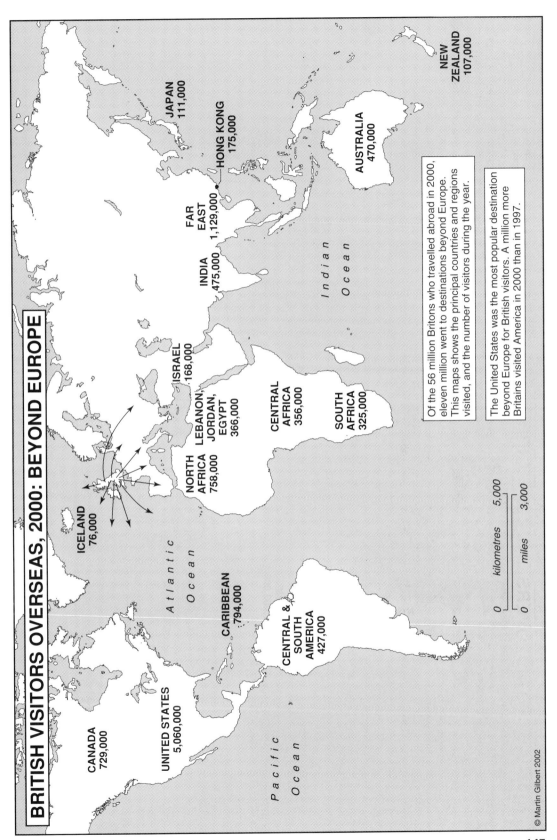

BRITISH VISITORS OVERSEAS, 2000: BEYOND EUROPE

JAPAN
111,000

NEW
ZEALAND
107,000

HONG KONG
175,000

FAR
EAST
1,129,000

AUSTRALIA
470,000

INDIA
475,000

Indian
Ocean

ISRAEL
168,000

LEBANON,
JORDAN,
EGYPT
366,000

CENTRAL
AFRICA
356,000

NORTH
AFRICA
758,000

SOUTH
AFRICA
325,000

ICELAND
76,000

Atlantic
Ocean

Of the 56 million Britons who travelled abroad in 2000,
eleven million went to destinations beyond Europe.
This maps shows the principal countries and regions
visited, and the number of visitors during the year.

The United States was the most popular destination
beyond Europe for British visitors. A million more
Britains visited America in 2000 than in 1997.

CANADA
729,000

UNITED STATES
5,060,000

CARIBBEAN
794,000

CENTRAL &
SOUTH
AMERICA
427,000

Pacific
Ocean

0   kilometres   5,000

0   miles   3,000

© Martin Gilbert 2002

147

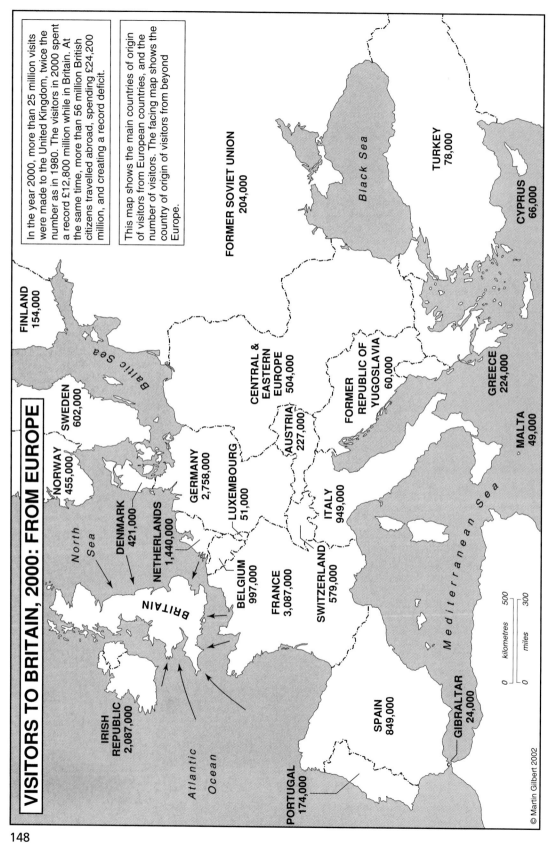

VISITORS TO BRITAIN, 2000: FROM EUROPE

In the year 2000, more than 25 million visits were made to the United Kingdom, twice the number as in 1980. The visitors in 2000 spent a record £12,800 million while in Britain. At the same time, more than 56 million British citizens travelled abroad, spending £24,200 million, and creating a record deficit.

This map shows the main countries of origin of visitors from European countries, and the number of visitors. The facing map shows the country of origin of visitors from beyond Europe.

FINLAND
154,000

SWEDEN
602,000

NORWAY
455,000

Baltic Sea

FORMER SOVIET UNION
204,000

DENMARK
421,000

NETHERLANDS
1,440,000

GERMANY
2,758,000

LUXEMBOURG
51,000

North Sea

BRITAIN

BELGIUM
997,000

FRANCE
3,087,000

SWITZERLAND
579,000

AUSTRIA
227,000

CENTRAL & EASTERN EUROPE
504,000

FORMER REPUBLIC OF YUGOSLAVIA
60,000

ITALY
949,000

IRISH REPUBLIC
2,087,000

Atlantic Ocean

PORTUGAL
174,000

SPAIN
849,000

GIBRALTAR
24,000

Mediterranean Sea

MALTA
49,000

GREECE
224,000

Black Sea

TURKEY
78,000

CYPRUS
66,000

0   500 kilometres

0   300 miles

© Martin Gilbert 2002

148

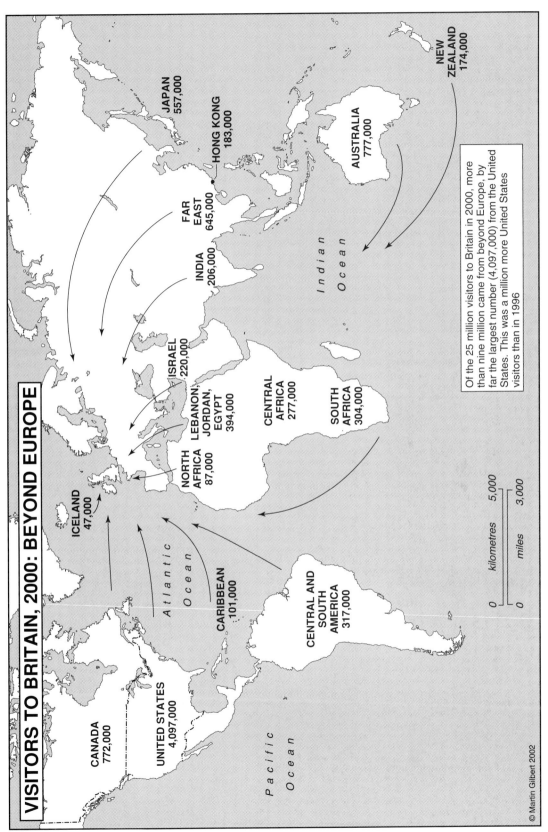

VISITORS TO BRITAIN, 2000: BEYOND EUROPE

CANADA
772,000

UNITED STATES
4,097,000

ICELAND
47,000

CARIBBEAN
101,000

CENTRAL AND
SOUTH
AMERICA
317,000

*Atlantic
Ocean*

*Pacific
Ocean*

NORTH
AFRICA
87,000

LEBANON,
JORDAN,
EGYPT
394,000

ISRAEL
220,000

CENTRAL
AFRICA
277,000

SOUTH
AFRICA
304,000

INDIA
206,000

FAR
EAST
645,000

HONG KONG
183,000

JAPAN
557,000

*Indian
Ocean*

AUSTRALIA
777,000

NEW
ZEALAND
174,000

Of the 25 million visitors to Britain in 2000, more
than nine million came from beyond Europe, by
far the largest number (4,097,000) from the United
States. This was a million more United States
visitors than in 1996

0   kilometres   5,000

0   miles   3,000

© Martin Gilbert 2002

149

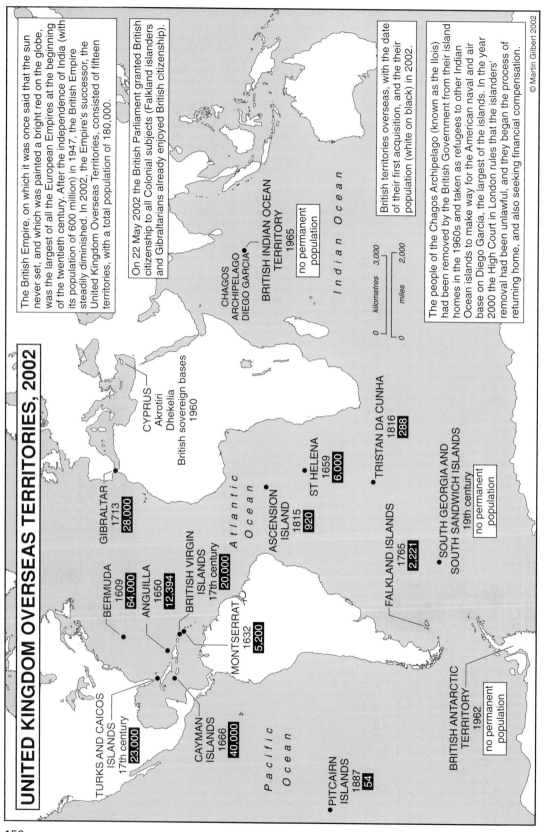

UNITED KINGDOM OVERSEAS TERRITORIES, 2002

The British Empire, on which it was once said that the sun never set, and which was painted a bright red on the globe, was the largest of all the European Empires at the beginning of the twentieth century. After the independence of India (with its population of 600 million) in 1947, the British Empire steadily diminished. In 2002, the Empire's successor, the United Kingdom Overseas Territories, consisted of fifteen territories, with a total population of 180,000.

On 22 May 2002 the British Parliament granted British citizenship to all Colonial subjects (Falkland islanders and Gibraltarians already enjoyed British citizenship).

British territories overseas, with the date of their first acquisition, and the their population (white on black) in 2002.

The people of the Chagos Archipelago (known as the Ilois) had been removed by the British Government from their island homes in the 1960s and taken as refugees to other Indian Ocean islands to make way for the American naval and air base on Diego Garcia, the largest of the islands. In the year 2000 the High Court in London rules that the islanders' removal had been unlawful, and they began the process of returning home, and also seeking financial compensation.

CHAGOS
ARCHIPELAGO
DIEGO GARCIA●

BRITISH INDIAN OCEAN
TERRITORY
1965

no permanent population

Indian Ocean

CYPRUS
Akrotiri
Dhekelia
British sovereign bases
1960

GIBRALTAR
1713
28,000

Atlantic Ocean

BERMUDA
1609
64,000

ANGUILLA
1650
12,394

BRITISH VIRGIN
ISLANDS
17th century
20,000

MONTSERRAT
1632
5,200

TURKS AND CAICOS
ISLANDS
17th century
23,000

CAYMAN
ISLANDS
1666
40,000

ASCENSION
ISLAND
1815
920

ST HELENA
1659
6,000

TRISTAN DA CUNHA
1816
288

FALKLAND ISLANDS
1765
2,221

SOUTH GEORGIA AND
SOUTH SANDWICH ISLANDS
19th century

no permanent population

BRITISH ANTARCTIC
TERRITORY
1962

no permanent population

Pacific Ocean

PITCAIRN
ISLANDS
1887
54

0 — kilometres — 3,000
0 — miles — 2,000

© Martin Gilbert 2002

150

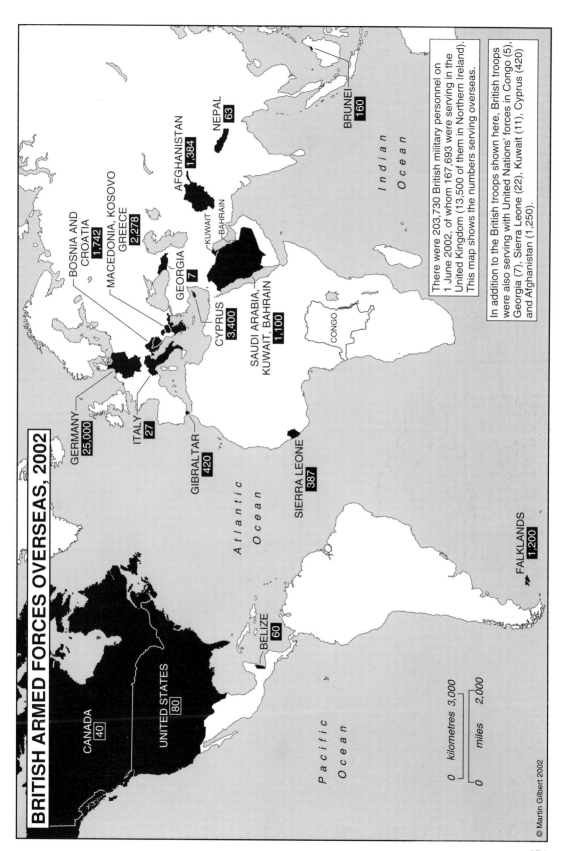

BRITISH ARMED FORCES OVERSEAS, 2002

CANADA 40

UNITED STATES 80

BELIZE 60

GIBRALTAR 420

SIERRA LEONE 387

FALKLANDS 1,200

GERMANY 25,000

ITALY 27

BOSNIA AND CROATIA 1,742

MACEDONIA, KOSOVO 2,278

GREECE

GEORGIA 7

KUWAIT

BAHRAIN

CYPRUS 3,400

SAUDI ARABIA, KUWAIT, BAHRAIN 1,100

AFGHANISTAN 1,384

NEPAL 63

BRUNEI 160

CONGO

Atlantic Ocean

Pacific Ocean

Indian Ocean

There were 203,730 British military personnel on 1 June 2002, of whom 167,693 were serving in the United Kingdom (13,500 of them in Northern Ireland). This map shows the numbers serving overseas.

In addition to the British troops shown here, British troops were also serving with United Nations' forces in Congo (5), Georgia (7), Sierra Leone (22), Kuwait (11), Cyprus (420) and Afghanistan (1,250).

0 kilometres 3,000
0 miles 2,000

© Martin Gilbert 2002

151

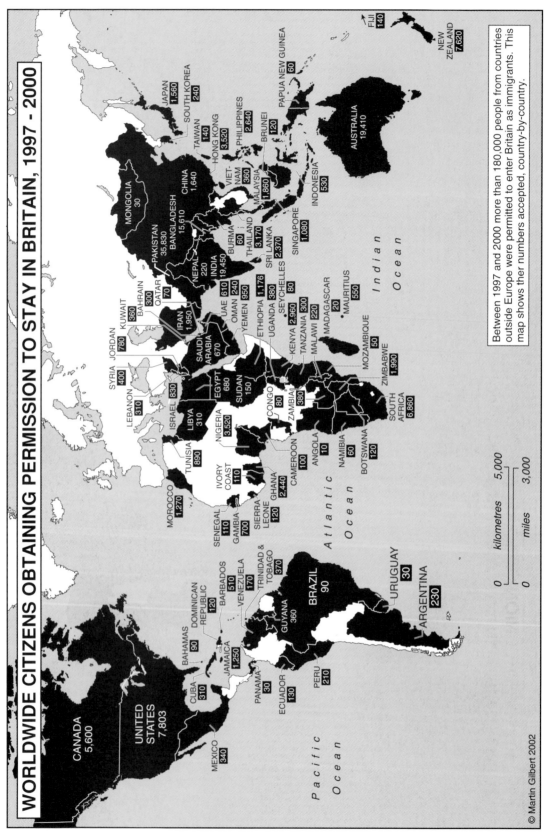

WORLDWIDE CITIZENS OBTAINING PERMISSION TO STAY IN BRITAIN, 1997 - 2000

FIJI 140

NEW ZEALAND 7,620

JAPAN 1,560

SOUTH KOREA 240

TAIWAN 140

HONG KONG 3,520

PHILIPPINES 2,640

BRUNEI 120

PAPUA NEW GUINEA 60

AUSTRALIA 19,410

MONGOLIA 30

CHINA 1,640

VIET-NAM 360

MALAYSIA 1,860

INDONESIA 530

BANGLADESH 15,610

BURMA 60

THAILAND 3,170

SINGAPORE 1,080

PAKISTAN 35,830

NEPAL 220

INDIA 19,450

SRI LANKA 2,370

Indian Ocean

BAHRAIN 300

QATAR 70

UAE 610

OMAN 240

YEMEN 950

ETHIOPIA 1,176

SEYCHELLES 80

MADAGASCAR 20

MAURITIUS 550

KUWAIT 360

IRAN 1,950

SAUDI ARABIA 670

UGANDA 380

KENYA 2,960

TANZANIA 300

MALAWI 220

MOZAMBIQUE 50

SYRIA 400

JORDAN 780

LEBANON 310

ISRAEL 830

EGYPT 680

SUDAN 150

CONGO 80

ZAMBIA 380

ZIMBABWE 1,990

LIBYA 310

NIGERIA 3,520

CAMEROON 100

ANGOLA 10

NAMIBIA 60

BOTSWANA 120

SOUTH AFRICA 6,860

TUNISIA 890

IVORY COAST 110

GHANA 2,440

MOROCCO 1,270

SENEGAL 110

GAMBIA 700

SIERRA LEONE 120

Atlantic Ocean

BAHAMAS 90

DOMINICAN REPUBLIC 120

BARBADOS 510

VENEZUELA 170

TRINIDAD & TOBAGO 370

GUYANA 360

BRAZIL 90

URUGUAY 30

ARGENTINA 230

JAMAICA 1,250

PANAMA 30

ECUADOR 130

PERU 210

CUBA 310

MEXICO 340

CANADA 5,600

UNITED STATES 7,803

Pacific Ocean

Between 1997 and 2000 more than 180,000 people from countries outside Europe were permitted to enter Britain as immigrants. This map shows ther numbers accepted, country-by-country.

0   kilometres   5,000

0   miles   3,000

© Martin Gilbert 2002

152

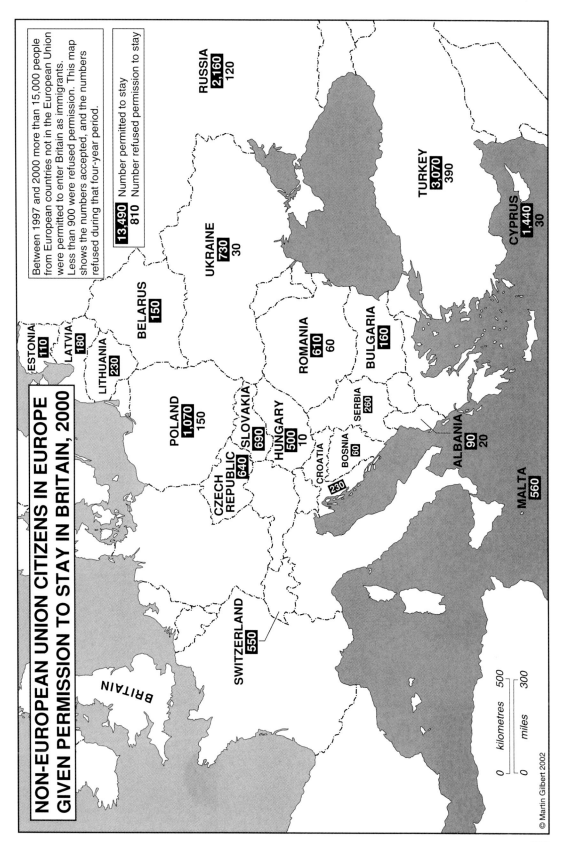

NON-EUROPEAN UNION CITIZENS IN EUROPE GIVEN PERMISSION TO STAY IN BRITAIN, 2000

Between 1997 and 2000 more than 15,000 people from European countries not in the European Union were permitted to enter Britain as immigrants. Less than 900 were refused permission. This map shows the numbers accepted, and the numbers refused during that four-year period.

13,490 Number permitted to stay
810 Number refused permission to stay

BRITAIN

SWITZERLAND **550**

ESTONIA **110**
LATVIA **180**
LITHUANIA **230**
BELARUS **150**
RUSSIA **2,160** 120
UKRAINE **730** 30
POLAND **1,070** 150
CZECH REPUBLIC **640**
SLOVAKIA **690**
HUNGARY **500** 10
CROATIA **230**
BOSNIA **60**
SERBIA **260**
ROMANIA **610** 60
BULGARIA **160**
ALBANIA **90** 20
TURKEY **3,070** 390
CYPRUS **1,440** 30
MALTA **560**

0 — 500 kilometres
0 — 300 miles

© Martin Gilbert 2002

BRITISH HUMANITARIAN AID OVERSEAS, 2000-2001

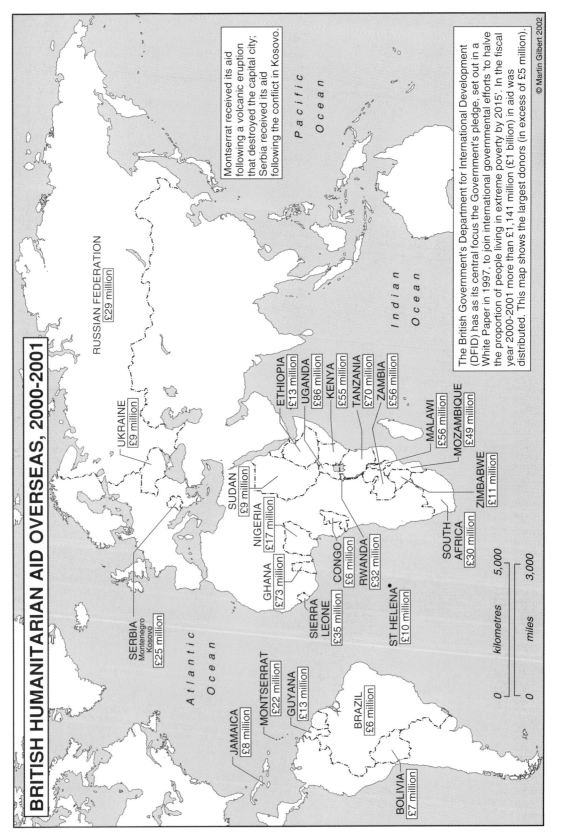

RUSSIAN FEDERATION
£29 million

Montserrat received its aid following a volcanic eruption that destroyed the capital city; Serbia received its aid following the conflict in Kosovo.

UKRAINE
£9 million

ETHIOPIA
£13 million

UGANDA
£86 million

KENYA
£55 million

TANZANIA
£70 million

ZAMBIA
£56 million

SUDAN
£9 million

NIGERIA
£17 million

GHANA
£73 million

SIERRA LEONE
£35 million

CONGO
£6 million

RWANDA
£32 million

ST HELENA
£10 million

MALAWI
£56 million

MOZAMBIQUE
£49 million

ZIMBABWE
£11 million

SOUTH AFRICA
£30 million

SERBIA
Montenegro
Kosovo
£25 million

MONTSERRAT
£22 million

GUYANA
£13 million

JAMAICA
£8 million

BRAZIL
£6 million

BOLIVIA
£7 million

Pacific Ocean

Indian Ocean

Atlantic Ocean

The British Government's Department for International Development (DFID) has as its central focus the Government's pledge, set out in a White Paper in 1997, to join international governmental efforts 'to halve the proportion of people living in extreme poverty by 2015'. In the fiscal year 2000-2001 more than £1,141 million (£1 billion) in aid was distributed. This map shows the largest donors (in excess of £5 million).

0   5,000   kilometres
0   3,000   miles

© Martin Gilbert 2002

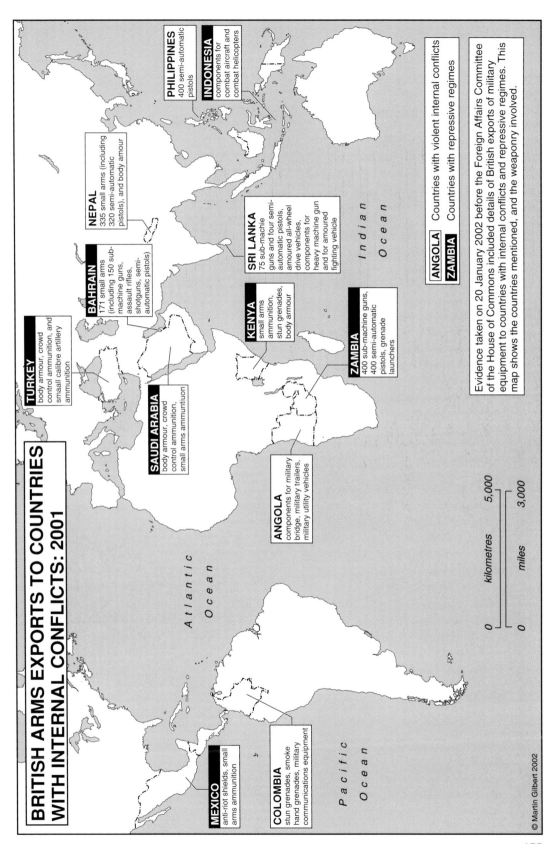

BRITISH ARMS EXPORTS TO COUNTRIES WITH INTERNAL CONFLICTS: 2001

PHILIPPINES
400 semi-automatic pistols

INDONESIA
components for combat aircraft and combat helicopters

NEPAL
335 small arms (including 320 semi-automatic pistols), and body armour

BAHRAIN
171 small arms (including 150 sub-machine guns, assault rifles, shotguns, semi-automatic pistols)

SRI LANKA
75 sub-machie guns and four semi-automatic pistols, amoured all-wheel drive vehicles, components for heavy machine gun and for armoured fighting vehicle

TURKEY
body armour, crowd control ammunition, and smaall calibre artillery ammunition

KENYA
small arms ammunition, stun grenades, body armour

ZAMBIA
400 sub-machine guns, 400 semi-automatic pistols, grenade launchers

SAUDI ARABIA
body armour, crowd control ammunition, small arms ammuntiuon

ANGOLA
components for military bridge, military trailers, military utility vehicles

MEXICO
anti-riot shields, small arms ammunition

COLOMBIA
stun grenades, smoke hand grenades, military communications equipment

Atlantic Ocean

Pacific Ocean

Indian Ocean

ANGOLA   Countries with violent internal conflicts
ZAMBIA   Countries with repressive regimes

Evidence taken on 20 January 2002 before the Foreign Affairs Committee of the House of Commons included details of British exports of military equipment to countries with internal conflicts and repressive regimes. This map shows the countries mentioned, and the weaponry involved.

0   kilometres   5,000

0   miles   3,000

© Martin Gilbert 2002

155

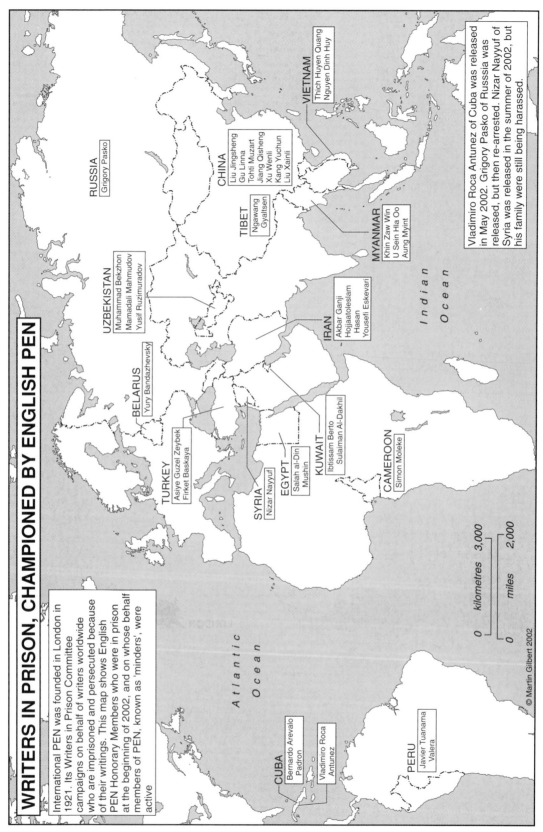

WRITERS IN PRISON, CHAMPIONED BY ENGLISH PEN

International PEN was founded in London in 1921. Its Writers in Prison Committee campaigns on behalf of writers worldwide who are imprisoned and persecuted because of their writings. This map shows English PEN Honorary Members who were in prison at the beginning of 2002, and on whose behalf members of PEN, known as 'minders', were active

Vladimiro Roca Antunez of Cuba was released in May 2002. Grigory Pasko of Russsia was released, but then re-arrested. Nizar Nayyuf of Syria was released in the summer of 2002, but his family were still being harassed.

RUSSIA
Grigory Pasko

CHINA
Liu Jingsheng
Gu Linna
Tohti Muzart
Jiang Qisheng
Xu Wenli
Kang Yuchun
Liu Xainli

TIBET
Ngawang Gyaltsen

VIETNAM
Thich Huyen Quang
Nguyen Dinh Huy

MYANMAR
Khin Zaw Win
U Sein Hla Oo
Aung Myint

UZBEKISTAN
Muhammad Bekzhon
Mamadali Mahmudov
Yusif Ruzimuradov

IRAN
Akbar Ganji
Hojjatoleslam
Hasan
Yousefi Eskevari

BELARUS
Yury Bandazhevsky

TURKEY
Asiye Guzel Zeybek
Firket Baskaya

SYRIA
Nizar Nayyuf

EGYPT
Salah al-Din
Mushin

KUWAIT
Ibtissam Berto
Sulaiman Al-Dakhil

CAMEROON
Simon Moleke

CUBA
Bernardo Arevalo
Padron

Vladimiro Roca
Antunez

PERU
Javier Tuanama
Valera

Atlantic Ocean

Indian Ocean

0   kilometres   3,000

0   miles   2,000

© Martin Gilbert 2002

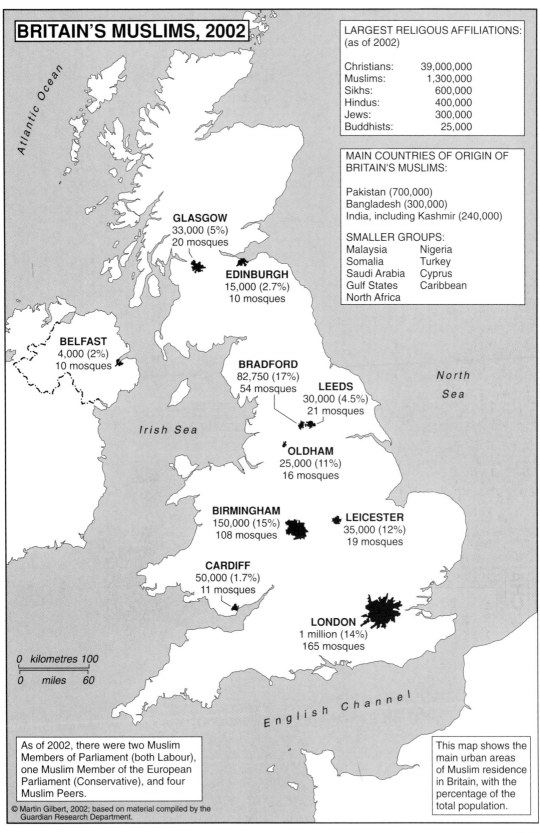

BRITAIN'S MUSLIMS, 2002

LARGEST RELIGOUS AFFILIATIONS:
(as of 2002)

Christians:	39,000,000
Muslims:	1,300,000
Sikhs:	600,000
Hindus:	400,000
Jews:	300,000
Buddhists:	25,000

MAIN COUNTRIES OF ORIGIN OF BRITAIN'S MUSLIMS:

Pakistan (700,000)
Bangladesh (300,000)
India, including Kashmir (240,000)

SMALLER GROUPS:
Malaysia   Nigeria
Somalia   Turkey
Saudi Arabia   Cyprus
Gulf States   Caribbean
North Africa

Atlantic Ocean

GLASGOW
33,000 (5%)
20 mosques

EDINBURGH
15,000 (2.7%)
10 mosques

BELFAST
4,000 (2%)
10 mosques

BRADFORD
82,750 (17%)
54 mosques

LEEDS
30,000 (4.5%)
21 mosques

Irish Sea

OLDHAM
25,000 (11%)
16 mosques

North Sea

BIRMINGHAM
150,000 (15%)
108 mosques

LEICESTER
35,000 (12%)
19 mosques

CARDIFF
50,000 (1.7%)
11 mosques

LONDON
1 million (14%)
165 mosques

0 kilometres 100
0 miles   60

English Channel

As of 2002, there were two Muslim Members of Parliament (both Labour), one Muslim Member of the European Parliament (Conservative), and four Muslim Peers.

© Martin Gilbert, 2002; based on material compiled by the Guardian Research Department.

This map shows the main urban areas of Muslim residence in Britain, with the percentage of the total population.

157